A TASTY SAMPLING OF THE BEST OF
AMERICAN COOKING:

From Shaker Village, Canterbury,
New Hampshire . . .
Shaker Vegetable Batter Soup

From Lincoln's New Salem, Illinois . . .
Mary Todd Lincoln's
White Almond Cake

From Indian City, U.S.A.,
Anadarko, Oklahoma . . .
Dried Corn Soup

From Historic St. Augustine, Florida . . .
Arroz Amarillo con Chorizos
(Yellow Rice with Sausages)

From Old Bethpage Village Restoration,
Long Island, New York . . .
Powell House Apple-Smothered
Pork Chops

From Tressl's Frontier Town,
Blackfoot, Idaho . . .
Frontier Lamb (or Beef) and Dumplings

RECIPES
~FROM~
AMERICA'S
RESTORED
VILLAGES

Jean Anderson

BALLANTINE BOOKS • NEW YORK

Library of Congress Catalog Card Number: 74-33629

ISBN 0-345-34708-0

This edition published by arrangement with Doubleday & Company, Inc.

Manufactured in the United States of America

First Ballantine Books Edition: November 1987

Grateful acknowledgment is made to The South Carolina Historical Society for permission to reprint the following material from The Collections of The South Carolina Historical Society: Biographical sketch of Harriott Horry, To Pickle Shrimps, To Wash Silk Stockings, To Make Castor Oil Pleasant, published in SCHM, Vol. 60 (1959).

The author also wishes to thank the following authors and publishers for permission to use and/or adapt the material listed below:
Fresh Corn and Mushrooms in Cream, Creamy Baked Shredded Cabbage, 1820s Water Ice Lemon, and Some Old Allaire Home Remedies from *The Calico Cooks, A Collection of Recipes by The Allaire Village Auxiliary*, published by North American Press, Kansas City, Missouri, for The Allaire Village Auxiliary, Copyright © 1969.
A White Fancy of Veall and Too Make a Fregasy of Chicken from *Penn Family Recipes, Cooking Recipes of William Penn's Wife Gulielma*, edited by Evelyn Abraham Benson, Copyright © Evelyn Abraham Benson 1966; printed by Trimmer Printing, Inc., York, Pennsylvania; George Shumway, Publisher, York, Pennsylvania.
Country Meat Loaf, Pork Loin and Cream Gravy, Shakertown Coleslaw, Country Dressing and Pleasant Hill Pecan Pie from *We Make You Kindly Welcome, Recipes from the Trustees' House Daily Fare, Pleasant Hill, Kentucky*, by Elizabeth C. Kremer, Copyright © 1970 Pleasant Hill Press, Harrodsburg, Kentucky; printed by The Keystone Printery, Lexington, Kentucky.
Abe's Butter-Browned Steak with Coffee-Mustard Sauce, Mary Todd Lincoln's White Almond Cake and Meringue-Topped Tart

For Ruth,
who proofed both the cooking
and the copy

Acknowledgments

I should like to thank, first of all, the staff members of each of the restored or re-created villages represented in this book, for without their research and valuable assistance the book could not have been written. And I should also like to thank individually the following persons who gave unselfishly of their time and talents, who shared their resources and historic recipes: Ann Bartkiewicz, Salem Public Library, Salem, Mass.; Inez S. Carr, the Pioneer Kitchen and Dining Rooms, Washington, Ark.; Louise Dill, Newagen, Me.; Melvin L. Houghton, the State Historical Society of Wisconsin, Madison, Wisc.; Winnifred C. Jardine, *Deseret News*, Salt Lake City, Utah; Chef Lindner, the Mills Hyatt House, Charleston, S.C.; Jean May, the Mills Hyatt House, Charleston, S.C.; Mrs. Lawrence K. Miller, Shaker Community, Inc., Hancock, Mass.; Julia S. Nason, Boothbay Harbor Region Chamber of Commerce, Boothbay Harbor, Me.; Claire Nelson, Historic Fallsington, Inc., Fallsington, Pa.; Rita H. O'Brien, Department of State, St. Augustine, Florida; Margaret Perry, *Early American Life*, Harrisburg, Pa.; Mrs. Granville T. Prior, the South Carolina Historical Society, Charleston, S.C.; Mary Regan, New Castle, N.H.; Don Richardson, Sr., Chamber of Commerce, Silver Dollar City, Mo.; Mrs. Melvin Sanderson, Murdo, S.D.; Alton H. Slagle, the New York *Daily News*, New York, N.Y.; John W. Snyder, CBS-TV, New York, N.Y.; Charles L. Tamminga, Division of Parks and Memorials, Springfield, Ill.; Roger L. Welsch, the University of Nebraska, Lincoln, Neb.; Charlene Whiteley, Moscow, Idaho; Lynne Whiteley, *ASTA Travel News*, New York, N.Y.; and a special thanks to Pamela V. Kobbé for helping to research, type, and proof the manuscript.

Contents

A Village-by-Village List of Recipes

The Midwest

The Southwest and West

Introduction

A merica's past, dramatic and colorful as it is, was until recently something to be learned by poring over history books. And many of us, alas, found the subject impersonal, even dull.

Today, however, American history is being *humanized* at dozens of restored and re-created villages scattered across the face of America and across more than two centuries of time. Here we cannot only learn about America's infancy and adolescence, we can *relive* it. We can squeeze into the smoky, cramped cabins at Plimoth Plantation in Massachusetts and see at first hand what life was really like for the Pilgrims, and in November we can see women preparing Thanksgiving dinner, not as it has been romanticized, but as it actually was.

At Colonial Williamsburg, we can dine at George Washington's favorite tavern, and we can eat what he ate. At Old Bethpage on Long Island we can learn the art of brick-oven cookery and we can sample crisp ginger cookies, fresh from that oven. At Old Salem in North Carolina we can tour a Moravian bakery (circa 1800) and we can buy yeasty loaves of bread and sacks of cookies to take home with us. At the Pennyslvania Farm Museum of Landis Valley we can watch how the early Pennsylvania Dutch dried herbs and apples and corn to carry them through the winter months. And in summer at Hancock Shaker Village in Massachusetts, we can take part in an old-time kitchen festival.

At a time when many Americans are feeling put upon by too many pressures and too many people, the restored and re-created villages, providing as they do glimpses of an earlier, simpler life, have become top tourist attractions. They are not, as you might suspect, confined to New England and the South. There are well over one hundred of them and you will find them throughout the Midwest, the Plains and Central States, the West and Southwest, the Middle Atlantic States as well as in New England and the South.

These are no mere museum pieces (at least those villages included here are not). They are "living," working villages where the homely arts are practiced. There are fishing villages where the catch is brought in and served forth as it was a hundred years ago; farm villages where wheat is sown, harvested, milled, and baked into crisp-crusted pies and buttery-crumbed cakes; dreamy Old South plantations where the kitchens, out back as in days gone by, produce mountains of flaky biscuits; mining camps and cattle towns where caldrons of stew bubble over open fires.

Featured in the pages that follow are forty-four of America's restored and re-created villages where food, cooking, and antique cooking equipment play more or less important roles. There may be daily cooking demonstrations, seasonal fairs and festivals; there may be village inns and taverns serving food characteristic of the area and era, and, failing those, nearby restaurants that do; there may be replicas of old-time kitchens, village museum cookbooks or other historic local cookbooks for sale at the village gift shops, and there may be village bakeries or sweetshops or pantries selling arrays of homemade breads, cakes, cookies, candies, pickles, jams, and preserves. With two exceptions (Shelburne Museum in Vermont and Greenfield Village in Michigan, neither of which is involved with food), the most celebrated villages are here: Colonial Williamsburg, Old Sturbridge Village, Mystic Seaport, Historic St. Augustine. But you will also find some equally fascinating villages little known outside of their immediate areas: Au Glaize Village and the Hale Farm and Western Reserve Village (both in Ohio); three early Shaker communes (at Hancock, Massachusetts; Canterbury, New Hampshire; and Pleasant Hill, Kentucky); Historic Fallsington, Pennsylvania; Stonefield Village in Wisconsin; the Amana Colonies in Iowa; the Ancient Cherokee Village at Tsa-La-Gi in Oklahoma; the Arkansas Territorial Restoration and Old Town San Diego, to list only a few.

The more than one hundred and fifty historic recipes included in this book have been provided by the various villages. And they are not what most of us have come to think of as "Early American." You will not find, for example, a single Indian pudding in the collection. Or Boston baked beans, although you will find dried beans (garbanzos, kidney, pinto, and pea beans) prepared in an array of frugal soups and stews, particularly among the pioneer recipes of the Midwest and Plains. For good reason. Dried beans (peas and lentils, too) kept well and traveled well. They were available, they were economical, they were nourishing, providing plenty of protein and calories. Finally, they were versatile, partnering well with whatever vegetables or meat the pioneer woman had on hand, and when no meat or vegetables were available, the dried beans could be boiled up with water and wild onions to make a satisfying meal. Apples were also good keepers, as were such root vegetables as potatoes, turnips, and parsnips. And so, for that matter, was cabbage, which accounts for the variety of unique cabbage dishes among these ancestral recipes (several unusual slaws, a baked shredded cabbage, a beef and cabbage oven dish).

You will find this a surprisingly ethnic repertoire, proving once again what a melting pot America is: Sopa de Cebolla (Spanish onion soup as prepared in early San Diego) . . . Abraham Lincoln's recipe for Butter-Browned

Steak with Coffee-Mustard Sauce...Hootsla (Egg Skillet Bread) as prepared by the Germans and Scandinavians in Nebraska...Pult (Ham-Stuffed Grated Potato Dumplings popular among the Norwegian immigrants in the Northwest)...Roast Venison with Juniper-Red Currant Sauce as it is served at the elegantly rebuilt grand old Mills House hotel in Charleston, South Carolina... William Penn's wife's recipe for a White Fancy of Veal ...Plimoth Roast Goose with Corn Bread and Currant Stuffing, which is thought to have been served at the first Pilgrim Thanksgiving...Line Camp Skillet Supper, the original Western Omelet created by early Chuck Wagon cooks of Kansas...Rose Water Ice Cream made by the Hancock Shakers...Brigham Young's Buttermilk Doughnuts...Piñon-Pumpkin Bread from the Rio Grande Indian Pueblos...and Hoosier Biscuit, which so impressed Henry Ward Beecher that he set the recipe down in his notebook, commenting that "no directions will be needed for eating."

The same might be said of the other old-time recipes included here, which cover, quite literally, everything from soup to nuts.

These recipes, together with the capsule profiles of the restored or re-created villages from which they come, are intended as a pleasant journey into nostalgia. A return to the uncommercial, more flavorful days of kitchen gardens and root cellars and keeping rooms. The recipes are as true to the originals as it was possible to make them, given supermarket groceries and modern kitchens. And wherever possible, the original versions have been included, quaint phrasing, misspellings and all. Early seasonings were, for the most part, simple, sometimes nothing more than salt and freshly ground pepper or nutmeg, sometimes such forgotten (though still readily available) flavorings as rose water and orange flower water. The shortenings used in these recipes are suet and lard, there being no vegetable shortenings in our great-great-grandmothers' day (even today pastry cooks prefer lard to vegetable shortening because of its superior flavor and greater shortening power).

Hopefully, you will rediscover through these recipes the honest flavor of fresh food prepared the old-fashioned way (no instant soups or sauces, no boxed cakes or puddings, and yet the recipes are neither difficult nor tiresome to prepare). They prove what inventive cooks women have been throughout the course of American history, whether they cooked on the hearth, in a brick oven, on a wood stove, or over a campfire. And finally, they prove that, no matter how frugal the meal, Americans have fared surprisingly well.

New England

Plimoth Plantation
Plymouth, Massachusetts

*T*he Mayflower...Plymouth Rock...the Pilgrims. They have all been so romanticized down the years that our images of them and the truth are, well, centuries apart.

Plimoth Plantation exists today primarily to dispel the myths, to separate fact from fantasy, to give us some clear notion of what life was actually like at Plimoth, what its people were like. Let's begin with the name Plymouth. It was spelled Plimoth (or Plimmoth) in the 1620s, so Plimoth is the way it is spelled at the re-created village.

As for the "Pilgrims," even the most pious of them did not, as we have come to believe, parade about in somber grays and blacks, heads bowed, hands in the prayer position. Moreover, they were a mixed group, those one hundred *Mayflower* passengers. Among them was the Leyden congregation, which came to the New World after a twelve-year exile in Holland. But these defectors from the Church of England were joined by a quite different group—homespun farm families mainly from the southeast of England. Religion motivated some of the colonists, it is true, but many others emigrated for economic reasons and were, for the most part, a rather roistering group given to greed and lust, as court records of early offenses make quite clear. The colonists' clothes were not drab grays and browns and blacks. They were scarlet and blue, pink and purple with now and then a quiet gray, brown, or black. These were a people closer in time to Columbus (1492) than to American Independence (1776), although that fact is difficult to grasp. They were a medieval people and they came woefully ill-prepared to carve a colony out of the New World wilderness.

Plimoth Plantation dates not to 1620, the year of the *Mayflower*'s arrival, but to 1627, the last year Plimoth remained within its original wooden enclosure (afterward, colonists moved into the surrounding countryside to work for themselves instead of for the good of the group).

The clearest picture we have of Plimoth in 1627 is that set down by a Dutch trader named Isaac de Rasieres, who described it as lying

> on the slope of a hill stretching east towards the sea coast, with a broad street about a cannon shot of 800 feet long leading down the hill; with a street crossing in the middle, northwards toward the rivulet and southwards toward the land. The houses are constructed of clapboards, with gardens also enclosed behind and at the sides with clapboards, so that their houses and courtyards are arranged in very good order, with a stockade against sudden attack; and at the ends of the streets there are three wooden gates. In the center, on the cross street, stands the governor's house, before which is a square stockade upon which four patereros are mounted, so as to enfilade the streets. Upon the hill they have a large square house, with a flat roof, built of thick sawn planks stayed with oak beams, upon the top of which they have six cannons, which shoot iron balls . . .

This early description, together with years of research by the Plimoth staff and visiting scholars, is the foundation of the re-created Plimoth Plantation, which stands not on the original site but two miles to the south of it.

To visit Plimoth Plantation today is to be jolted—and there is no more appropriate word—backward in time three and a half centuries.

This is not a prim, pin-neat village—all lace curtains. Chickens cackle and scratch about the gardens, pigs run loose in the streets, sheep graze the scruffy grass, children in period dress run barefoot. Wood fires burn in each cabin—even on hottest summer days—because these fires were the sole way in which food was cooked, cabins were heated and, often, illuminated as well.

The cabins were not—and are not—made of logs as one might expect. They are, instead, typical English thatched cottages of the early seventeenth century, framed with heavy square timbers. The walls are panels of wattle and daub, sheathed with short hand-riven cedar clapboards. The cottages are unpainted and weathering, in the Massachusetts salt air, to a deep silvery gray. The windows are tiny, mere portholes, but square rather than round. And the panes are paper, not glass. You won't find signs here: "Please Do Not Touch," "Please Keep Off the Grass." The Plimoth colonists had no such signs, and, indeed, visitors are encouraged to immerse themselves in the total Plimoth experience.

The houses are dim, smoke-filled, and sparsely furnished (few colonists had beds and slept, instead, on pallets on the floor). The yards are littered with bones, parings, and other fallout of cooking (which goes on daily at Plimoth today just as it did in 1627). Pumpkins run amok in the fields, as do Indian corn and squash— all foods the Indians taught the colonists to cultivate, all foods that helped save Plimoth from extinction.

Life was basic, life was grim—only half of the one hundred colonists survived the first winter. There were no luxuries at Plimoth—not even forks, a frivolity introduced by the Italians and an affectation taken up by English dandies. There were no dandies at Plimoth and the colonists ate, for the most part, with their hands, using knives only to cut up unmanageable pieces of meat and spoons to dip up broths and gravies.

Food was rustic, heavy, and high-calorie, an odd mixture of English and Indian. The principal meats were chicken, game birds, and pork (the few cows, first introduced in 1624, were valued as milk producers). Although the colonists proved to be clumsy fishermen, they did manage to keep fish or shellfish on the table most of the time. They had no sugar or molasses and used dark beers and ales as sweeteners. And their flour, for the most part, was corn flour.

No, it was not a romantic life the Plimoth colonists led. It was a grim struggle for survival against overwhelming odds. To wipe away the myths, you have only to prowl about Plimoth Plantation today, to crowd into the dim one- and two-room cabins, to talk with the costumed guide-hosts and hostesses who are busy performing the daily chores. Here you see Plimoth as it was—cluttered, smelly, noisy, cramped, and crowded. This was no New World dreamland. Nightmare is nearer the truth, especially if you should visit Plimoth on a blustering November day when the streets run knee deep in mud and the fires crackling on the stone hearths fill the cabins with smoke but do little to warm the bones. It's not the way we visualize life at Plimoth. But it's the way life was in 1627.

Plimoth Plantation features an active foodways program with hostesses in Pilgrim dress demonstrating early cooking techniques and preparing meals that are typical of seventeenth-century English yeoman fare. Authenticity, of course, is the aim of Plimoth Plantation, and to that end its historians, together with Dr. Jay Anderson, an ethnogastronomist at Pennsylvania State University, are preparing a Plimoth Plantation cookbook. That book may prove something of a myth-breaker. Our traditional Thanksgiving, Dr. Anderson points out, is in fact more Victorian than Pilgrim. The first Thanksgiving, moreover, was not, as we have been taught, a solemn giving of thanks to God. It was a roistering, *secular* Harvest Home, much like those celebrated in England after the ingathering of crops. We do know that that first feast was a long one, that, to prepare for it, Governor William Bradford sent four of Plimoth's best hunters into the woods, and that they returned home with wild ducks and geese, which the women stuffed and roasted. According to Dr. Anderson, Pilgrims fancied spicy, sweet stuffings instead of the heavily saged stuffings we prefer today. Here, then, based upon Dr. Anderson's research, is a recipe for roast goose very much like that the Pilgrims prepared. *One word of caution:* Today's farm-raised geese, unlike wild geese, are exceedingly fat. And in order for most of that fat to cook out of the bird as it roasts, you must prick the skin frequently—about every thirty minutes. And you must also pour off the drippings as they accumulate in the roasting pan (they may amount to as much as three cups!)

Plimoth Roast Goose with Corn Bread and Currant Stuffing

MAKES 8 SERVINGS

1 ready-to-cook goose, weighing 10 to 12 pounds
Salt
Goose neck and giblets
6 cups water

Corn Bread and Currant Stuffing:
6 cups coarse corn bread crumbs
¾ cup dried currants
1¼ teaspoons salt
½ teaspoon ground cinnamon
¼ teaspoon ground nutmeg (preferably freshly ground)
⅛ teaspoon ground mace

1 cup heavy cream, beaten with 1 egg until frothy
⅔ cup stout, dark ale, or beer

Tart Giblet Gravy:
3 tablespoons roast goose drippings
5 tablespoons flour
3 cups goose giblet broth
The chopped, cooked giblets and neck meat
1 cup stout, dark ale, or beer
¼ cup cider vinegar
1 teaspoon salt
⅛ teaspoon ground nutmeg (preferably freshly ground)
¼ teaspoon freshly ground pepper (optional)

Rub the goose inside and out with salt; set aside. Place goose neck, giblets, and water in a large, heavy saucepan, bring to a simmer, cover, and simmer 20 minutes. Remove the goose liver and refrigerate to use later. Continue simmering the neck and remaining giblets, covered, for 2 to 2½ hours until tender. Remove giblets from broth and chop; also chop the liver and combine with other giblets. Cut meat from neck in small pieces and add to giblets, then refrigerate. Measure out 3 cups of giblet broth and refrigerate also (any leftover broth may be saved for soup). Meanwhile, prepare the stuffing and begin roasting the goose.

To make the stuffing, simply mix all ingredients together—the mixture will be quite moist and pudding-like, but this is as it should be. Stuff lightly into the neck and body cavities of the goose—do not pack the stuffing in, as it will expand considerably as the goose roasts. Skewer neck skin of goose flat to the back, skewer and lace the body cavity shut, then truss the bird so that it will be compact and roast more evenly. Place goose breast side up on a rack in a very large roasting pan, and prick the skin very well all over with a sharp-pronged fork. Place goose, uncovered, in a very hot oven (425°) and sear for 20 minutes. Lower oven temperature to moderately slow (325°), remove as many accumulated drippings from the roasting pan as possible with a bulb baster, then again prick the goose all over with the sharp-pronged fork. Continue roasting the goose, uncovered, allowing about 20 minutes cooking time per pound of goose. You must prick the goose well about every half hour and ladle off the accumulated pan drippings so that neither the bird nor the stuffing will be greasy. When the goose is a rich caramel brown and when you can move the legs easily in their hip sockets, the bird is done. Remove from the oven and let stand at room temperature for 20 minutes—this resting period helps the juices to settle and facilitates carving.

It also gives you time to make the gravy: Blend the goose drippings and flour together in a large, heavy saucepan; set over moderate heat. Add the giblet broth and whisk until slightly thickened, then boil, uncovered, about 10 minutes, stirring occasionally, until quantity reduces slightly. Lower heat so that liquid just ripples on the surface, stir in chopped giblets and neck meat, stout, vinegar, salt, nutmeg, and, if you like, the pepper. Turn heat to low and let mellow while arranging the goose on the platter. Remove skewers and lacings from goose, center on a heated large platter, and garnish, if you like, with clusters of red and green grapes. Pour gravy into a heated gravy boat.

Cinnamon and nutmeg, mace and cloves were all spices known to the Pilgrims at Plimoth. Sugar and honey, however, were scarce, so a heavy dark beer or porter was used to sweeten both desserts and vegetables. The recipe here is prepared much as it would have been in the early days of Plimoth, and surprisingly good it is, too. Other long-cooking vegetables may be prepared the same way—winter squash, pumpkin, turnips, provided they are cut in small (1½- to 2-inch) chunks.

Parsnips Stewed in Dark Beer or Stout

MAKES 4 SERVINGS

1 pound parsnips, peeled and cut in 2-inch chunks (halve
the thick chunks from the top of the parsnips length-
wise so that they will cook tender in about the same
amount of time as the thinner root ends)
1 cup dark beer or stout
A 1-inch piece of stick cinnamon
2 large blades of mace
3 whole cloves
Pinch of salt
Pinch of pepper

Place all ingredients in a heavy, medium-size saucepan
and simmer, covered, 30 to 35 minutes until you can
pierce parsnips easily with a fork. Turn heat to low and
simmer, uncovered, 10 to 15 minutes longer until the
beer or stout has thickened into a glaze. Remove cinnamon, mace, and cloves and serve parsnips hot as an accompaniment to roast fowl, ham, or pork.

The Pioneers' Village and Salem
Massachusetts

*N*o New World town, perhaps, exerted as great an impact on the industrial, social, religious, and cultural life of America as Salem. And nowhere else in America is it possible to walk chronologically through so many centuries of history.

The place to begin is the Pioneers' Village at Forest River park, a reproduction of the settlement in the wilderness that *was* Salem in 1630. The Pioneers' Village is, in fact, one of America's first recreated villages, having been built in 1930 to commemorate the three hundredth anniversary of the founding of Massachusetts. Calvin Coolidge strolled through the village streets in 1931, toured the brush wigwams like those occupied by the first Puritans, the later clapboard, thatch-roofed homes, the "Governor's fayre house," the village square with its pillories and stocks, the saltworks, the log-sawing pit, the forge, the fish drying racks, the brick kiln. He was impressed. "It would be wholesome," he said at the time, "to think more of these things. It would reduce complaint and increase contentment." It does, certainly, for to visit the Pioneers' Village is to learn something of the hardship and discomfort endured by the Puritans.

Salem, unlike the colony at Plimoth, flourished almost from the beginning. The Puritans, backed by a going

English company, set straightaway about building a town. They brought proper tools, craftsmen to operate them, and within a few years after their arrival had hammered the rough edges off the New England wilderness, founded a town, and established themselves in a variety of businesses—the making of salt, bricks, lumber, and metalwork, the business, too, of trading with Indians and other settlers. The Puritans, by and large, were a better educated people than the colonists at Plimoth, and they were a higher class of Englishmen (many brought with them bond servants). The Puritans were hard working, they were pious, but they were not as prim and unyielding as textbooks and historical novels would lead us to believe. They, like the Plimoth settlers, did not dress in drab colors, for, as the Reverend Francis Higginson, leader of a group of two hundred settlers that arrived in 1629, wrote, the "sad colors" of their dress included purple and green and orange. Black, it appears, was for civil dignity, scarlet for the military, russets and browns for the rank and file. These were close to Elizabethan times and both the men and women of Salem still dressed in the Elizabethan fashion. Men wore doublets and full breeches, women tight bodices and full skirts ballooned about the hips by farthingales.

Life was rigorous at the start, and the winter of 1630 was particularly desperate, there being little food and only earthen dugouts and wigwams for shelter. The Puritans persisted, however, quickly cleared their lands, and set about growing crops—but only those that could be used for food or medicine. As the Reverend Higginson noted: "Little children here by the setting of corn, may earn much more than their own maintenance." He added that he "saw great stores of whales and grampuses and such abundance of mackerels that it would astonish one to behold; likewise codfish, abundant on the coast, and in their season are plentifully taken . . . and abundance of lobsters, and the least boy in the plantation may both catch and eat what he will of them . . ."

Cooking, in those wigwams and early clapboard

cabins, indeed at the "Governor's fayre house," a tall, straight, two-story structure with a massive central chimney, was done over open fires. Skillets and kettles were three-legged, so that hearth coals could be raked underneath them. Baking was done in an early version of the reflector oven, which also stood on the hearth.

In addition to the New World fish, fowl, wild berries, Indian corn, squash, beans, and pumpkins, the Puritans brought with them to Salem a variety of English staples. An inventory of the ship *Arbella* (named for the Lady Arbella, who was aboard) lists: "42 tuns of beer (10,000 gallons); 14 tuns of drinking water; 2 hogsheads Syder [cider]; 1 hogshead Vinegar; 16 hogsheads meat, beef, pork and beef tongues; 600 lbs. haberdyne [salt cod]; 1 bbl. salt; 100 lbs. suet; 20,000 biscuits—15,000 brown, 5,000 white; 1 bbl. flour; 30 bu. oatmeal; 11 firkins butter; 40 bu. dried pease; 1½ bu. mustard seed."

Recipes, in the beginning, were rustic—simple soups or stews or fish hashes that could be cooked easily over open fires, and, as for sweets, suet puddings that could be steamed in kettles on the hearths.

But Salem quickly prospered, and to move from the Pioneers' Village, where it all began, to the House of Seven Gables (1668) on Turner Street is to appreciate the industry and determination of the Puritans. That tall, imposing structure, immortalized by Nathaniel Hawthorne, was built just thirty-eight years after the Puritans set ax to the wilderness. And on the grounds of this historic house can be seen a group of other Puritan homes, now restored and open to the public; the Retire Beckett House (1655), Hathaway's House (1682), and Hawthorne's birthplace (1740).

These homes, compared to the crude dwellings at the Pioneers' Village, seem almost grand, particularly when you consider that most of them are well over three hundred years old. But grander still are the mansions lined up along Essex Street, homes built by wealthy shippers and importers during the eighteenth and nineteenth centuries, when Salem reigned as the capital of the great clipper fleets and when Derby Wharf (1760—1860) was piled high with the world's riches. (The Peabody Museum, housed in the old East India Maritime Hall, circa 1799, is filled with relics and mementos of seafaring Salem.)

Salem is better known, perhaps, as the capital of witchcraft, and everywhere about town stand macabre reminders of those days when the "possessed" were hung or burned at the stake: Gallows Hill, the Essex County Courthouse, where transcripts of the early witchhunt hearings are displayed, the Salem Witch Museum, where thirteen sound-and-light dioramas re-enact those awesome days of the occult.

Nowhere in America will you find a greater chronology or concentration of early American history than at Salem, spanning as it does nearly two hundred and fifty years of progress—from Massachusetts' earliest beginnings to New England's age of affluence.

&

In 1910 the Esther C. Mack Industrial School of Salem, Massachusetts, published a small collection of recipes called *What Salem Dames Cooked*. It included recipes from seventeenth- and eighteenth-century Salem cookery books, and among the early recipes was this unusual chicken pie. Here is the original version, as it appeared in *The Compleat Cook's Guide*, 1683, followed by an up-to-date version as true to the original as possible.

To Make a CHICKEN-PYE

After you have truft your chickens, then break their Legs and Breaft-bones, and raife your cruft of the beft Pafte, lay them in a Coffin clofe together, with their bodies full of butter, then lay upon and underneath them, Currans, great Raifins, Pruans, Cinnamon, Sugar, whole Mace and Sugar, whole Mace and Salt; then cover all with a good ftore of butter, and fo bake it; then pour into it white wine,

rofe-water, fugar, cinnamon, and vinegar mixt together, with Yolks of two or three Eggs beaten
amongft it, and fo serve it.

Rose water may seem an odd flavoring for chicken,
but, when combined with wine, prunes, raisins, and currants, it is mellowing rather than flowery. To simplify
serving of the chicken pie, we have called for stripping
the meat from the roasted chicken, mixing it with the
rose water sauce, then baking it underneath a flaky
pastry rather than on top of it, because a bottom crust
does, in today's ovens, become soggy.

Chicken Pie with Rose Water, Currants, Prunes, and Raisins

MAKES 6 TO 8 SERVINGS

½ cup (1 stick) unsalted butter
1 roasting chicken (about 4 pounds), trussed and ready to
    roast
The chicken liver and heart
1½ teaspoons salt (about)
¼ teaspoon freshly ground pepper (about)
3 tablespoons dried currants
3 tablespoons golden seedless raisins
6 prunes, pitted and coarsely chopped
A ½-inch piece of stick cinnamon
1 large blade of mace
2 tablespoons raw sugar or light brown sugar
1¼ cups dry white wine
1 tablespoon cider vinegar
2 tablespoons rose water (obtainable in specialty food shops)
1½ cups light cream (about)
3 egg yolks, lightly beaten

Pastry:
1¼ cups sifted all-purpose flour
½ teaspoon salt
5 tablespoons lard
¼ cup cold water (about)

Tuck ¼ cup (½ stick) of the butter into the body cavity of the chicken; place the chicken liver and heart in a small bowl, cover loosely, and refrigerate until time to prepare the sauce. (The neck and gizzard may be saved to use in making stock or soup if you like; you won't need them for this recipe.) Rub the chicken all over with the salt and pepper, using about 1 teaspoon salt and all but a pinch of the ¼ teaspoon pepper. Place chicken in a shallow roasting pan and scatter the currants, raisins, and chopped prunes into pan around chicken; add stick cinnamon and blade of mace. Dot remaining ¼ cup butter over chicken and fruits in pan. Sprinkle 1 tablespoon of the raw sugar over the chicken and pour ¾ cup of the dry white wine into the pan. Roast chicken, uncovered, in a moderate oven (350°), basting frequently with pan drippings, about 2 hours or until chicken is very brown and leg moves easily in the hip socket. Remove chicken from oven and cool until easy to handle. Remove stick cinnamon and blade of mace from roasting pan and discard.

While chicken cools, prepare the sauce: Skim 2 tablespoons of fat from the top of the pan drippings and heat until bubbly in a medium-size saucepan. Mince reserved chicken liver and heart, add to saucepan, and stir-fry 2 to 3 minutes until lightly browned. Add remaining salt and pepper to saucepan, also remaining 1 tablespoon of raw sugar, remaining ½ cup dry white wine, the vinegar and rose water. Simmer, uncovered, about 10 minutes until reduced in volume by about one half. Meanwhile, lift chicken from roasting pan to a wire rack to finish cooling. With a slotted spoon, scoop currants, raisins, and prunes from pan drippings and reserve. Pour drippings into a 1-quart measure, then add light cream until drippings and cream total 2½ cups; blend in beaten egg yolks. Pour a little of the hot saucepan mixture into cream mixture, stirring briskly, then mix all back into saucepan and heat and stir over lowest heat 1 minute. Remove sauce from heat and stir in reserved currants, raisins, and prunes. Cool sauce while you cut meat from the chicken.

With a sharp small knife, cut meat from chicken, slicing the breast into nice thick slices. Layer chicken meat into a shallow 6-cup baking dish (about 9 to 10 inches in diameter), pour sauce over all, and toss lightly to mix. Let stand while preparing the pastry.

To make the pastry: Place flour and salt in a small mixing bowl, cut in lard with a pastry blender until the texture of uncooked oatmeal, then add water, a little at a time, tossing mixture briskly with a fork just until pastry clings together in a ball. Roll out on a lightly floured pastry cloth to a circle about 1½ inches larger in diameter than the baking dish you are using. Moisten rim of baking dish, ease pastry circle into place on top, roll pastry edges underneath even with rim of dish and crimp to seal, making a high fluted edge. Cut decorative steam vents over surface of pastry.

Bake the chicken pie in a moderate oven (350°) for 45 to 50 minutes until filling is bubbly and pastry golden brown. To serve, cut pie-shaped wedges of pastry, place one on each dinner plate, and top with a hearty portion of chicken filling.

Here's another early Salem recipe, this one from *The Frugal Housewife*, 1730. It calls for breast of mutton, perhaps more readily available then than lamb, and directs the cook to prepare it thus:

TO CARBONNADE A BREAST OF MUTTON

Take a breast of mutton, half bone it, knick it across. Season it with pepper and salt, then broil it before the fire whilst it be enough, sprinkling it over with bread crumbs; let the same be a little Gravy and butter and a few shred capers; put it upon the dish with the mutton. Garnish it with horse-radish and pickles. This is a proper side-dish at noon or a bottom dish at night.

The following version calls for lamb (mutton being more difficult to obtain) and has been adapted for today's ovens. It's delicious, nonetheless, with the same tart caper gravy.

Breast of Lamb Carbonnade with Caper, Bread Crumb, and Butter Gravy

MAKES 4 SERVINGS

2 breasts of lamb (about 1½ pounds each)
1 teaspoon salt
¼ teaspoon freshly ground pepper
2 tablespoons soft fine bread crumbs

Caper, Bread Crumb, and Butter Gravy:
½ cup melted unsalted butter
3 tablespoons finely minced capers
1 tablespoon caper juice
2 tablespoons cider vinegar
¼ cup soft fine bread crumbs

Have the butcher trim as much fat as possible from the lamb breasts, then ask him to crack the ribs at the base so that the breasts will be easier to carve. Rub the breasts well on all sides with salt and pepper, lay them flat on a rack in a large roasting pan, and roast, uncovered, in a moderate oven (350°) about 1 hour or until the lamb, when cut between the ribs, shows the merest tinge of pink. Scatter the 2 tablespoons bread crumbs over the breasts, return to oven, and roast about 5 minutes longer until crumbs are nicely toasted.

To prepare the gravy: Stir together the butter, capers, caper juice, vinegar, and bread crumbs, pour into a saucepan and keep warm. To serve lamb, carve into sections 2 to 3 ribs wide and top each portion with some of the gravy. Pass remaining gravy.

In this day of instants and mixes, steamed puddings have become a part of America's vanishing culinary arts. They do require long, slow cooking, it's true, but they are not difficult to prepare. This old-fashioned suet pudding, sweetened with molasses and raisins—no sugar— is dark and fine-textured. Moreover, it's economical if you have a friendly butcher who will give you the suet. Serve the pudding hot, just as it comes from the mold, or serve at room temperature. You may want to add a sauce, a hard sauce for example, or simply top the portions with whipped, lightly sweetened cream.

Salem Suet Pudding

MAKES 6 TO 8 SERVINGS

3 cups sifted all-purpose flour
1 cup finely minced or ground suet (you'll need about ⅓ pound of suet)
1 cup finely minced seedless raisins
1 cup molasses mixed with 1 teaspoon baking soda
1 cup milk

Place flour in a large mixing bowl, then with your hands or with a pastry blender, work in the suet until the mixture is about the texture of uncooked oatmeal. Add raisins and work in the same way, using your hands (the raisins tend to stick together, so rub them slowly into the flour until they are evenly distributed). Combine the molasses-soda mixture and milk, pour all at once into the bowl, and stir just until no patches of dry ingredients show. Spoon batter into a well-buttered 1-quart steamed pudding mold, filling no more than ⅔ full (this amount of batter should be exactly right). Snap on the pudding mold cover. Lower the mold onto a rack in a very large deep kettle containing about 1 inch of boiling water—the bottom of the pudding mold must not touch the water. Cover the kettle and keep the water at a slow boil so that sufficient steam will build up to cook the pudding. Steam for 4 hours exactly, checking the water level in the kettle about every hour or so and adding more boiling water if the kettle threatens to boil dry. Just remember that the pudding mold must not touch the water. When pudding is done, lift mold gently from the kettle and set upright, still with the lid on, on a wire cake rack and cool for 15 minutes. Open mold, loosen pudding around edges with a thin-blade spatula, then invert onto a serving plate. You may have to let the pudding firm up for another 10 to 15 minutes before cutting, or, if you prefer, cool to room temperature before serving. Serve as is or top with sweetened whipped cream (1 cup heavy cream whipped until stiff with 2 tablespoons confectioners' sugar).

Old Sturbridge Village
Sturbridge, Massachusetts

❧❧❧

"We're 150 years out of date," proclaims *The Village Patriot*, the newspaper-guide of Old Sturbridge Village. "Our buildings are antiques. Our floors, steps and stairs are old and worn...our roads and paths are unpaved ways of the early 1800s."

As a village, however, Old Sturbridge is new. It opened officially in 1946, and since then more than seven million Americans and foreigners have wandered through its streets to learn what New England village life was like during America's first fifty years as a republic (1790–1840). What they see is no dream village but a painstaking re-creation that began in 1936 and continues yet.

Village roots date even further back, to the 1920s, when industrialist Albert B. Wells of nearby Southbridge began collecting early New England furniture, farm tools, and implements. As so often happens with collections, Well's rapidly outgrew his home and a succession of outbuildings and barns. Clearly more space was needed. Wells toyed with the idea of a museum, but his son George came up with a better idea.

Why not build a museum village where the antiques could be displayed in a more natural setting? Wells's brother, Joel Cheney Wells, himself a collector of New

England clocks and paperweights, endorsed the plan and within a few weeks a site was found—a 167-acre farm on the banks of the Quinebaug River, fifty-eight miles southwest of Boston. There were rolling woodlands and meadows, an eighteenth-century farmhouse, an early woodworking shop, and a carriage house.

Old Sturbridge was on its way to becoming a dot on the map. A typical village plan was laid out, its focal point the common, and then year after year, as historic buildings became available, they were acquired. Today there are forty major historic buildings at Old Sturbridge —homes, shops (including a bakeshop), a Friends' meeting house, a one-room schoolhouse, a bank, a blacksmith shop, a carding mill, a covered bridge. Most existed elsewhere in New England—in Vermont, New Hampshire, Connecticut, and Maine as well as in Massachusetts—and were moved overland to Old Sturbridge, restored, renovated, and furnished with antiques of the era and area.

This, however, is no mere collection of buildings cluttered with antiques. Old Sturbridge bustles with activity. Artisans in period dress demonstrate early Yankee crafts: potting, spinning, and weaving, candle dipping and cabinetmaking, pickling, preserving, and fireplace cooking. There is a village blacksmith, a tinsmith, a pewterer, a printer, a miller, a cooper, a wood turner, a broommaker, even an herbalist who mixes up teas, tisanes, and early remedies out of "simples" (medicinal herbs) grown in the village herb garden. There is also the Village Tavern on the Green, where you can sit down to an old-fashioned meal.

Sheep graze the common in summer because, Old Sturbridge historians point out, these public grassy plots were used more for pasturage than for pleasure. At the Pliny Freeman farm, crops are planted and gathered in just as they were a hundred and fifty years ago. And the sheep, oxen, cows, pigs, and poultry you see there have been imported from around the world because these are the species early New England farmers kept.

Yes, Old Sturbridge is a busy village, especially in late winter during the maple sugaring, in May when there are sheep to shear, in October during the Antique Collector's Weekend, and in November, at Thanksgiving, when for days ahead, kitchens in the Village homes are filled with the rich aromas of baking.

To stroll the woodland trail at Old Sturbridge Village, to pause by the millpond, to meander along the unpaved streets, to tour the houses and watch the demonstrations is to sample, for a day or half day, life as our ancestors lived it. And to realize that their rugged life, rooted in the soil, was perhaps more rewarding than automated life of today.

Wild turkey was the bird of Thanksgivings past, a scrawnier, tougher bird than the plump, farm-raised turkey we enjoy. The recipe below, nearly a hundred and fifty years old, is used today at Old Sturbridge Village. The stuffing is made with ground suet instead of butter, and flavored with lemon and sweet marjoram. Ham was an optional addition in olden days, depending upon whether or not there were any tag ends of smoked ham on hand. The best ham to use is a salty, heavily smoked one—Smithfield or Virginia ham, for example. Our great-great-great-grandmothers were more inventive about using up surplus stuffing than we are today: instead of plunking it into a casserole to roast alongside the turkey, they shaped it into small balls, browned them in butter, then used them to garnish the turkey platter.

Roast Turkey with Lemon and Ham Stuffing Balls

MAKES 6 TO 8 SERVINGS

1 (10-pound) fresh or thawed frozen turkey
¾ teaspoon salt
¼ teaspoon freshly ground pepper

¼ cup unsifted all-purpose flour
½ pound unsalted butter, melted (for basting)

Lemon and Ham Stuffing Balls:
6 cups soft fine bread crumbs
1 cup firmly packed ground suet
1¼ cups minced Smithfield or Virginia ham
2½ teaspoons leaf marjoram, crumbled
Finely grated rind of 1 large lemon
Juice of 1 large lemon
1½ teaspoons salt
⅛ teaspoon freshly ground pepper
⅛ teaspoon freshly grated nutmeg
2 egg yolks
¼ cup melted unsalted butter (for browning stuffing balls)

Giblet Gravy:
The turkey neck and giblets
6 cups water
7 tablespoons fat from turkey pan drippings
6 tablespoons flour
½ teaspoon salt
⅛ teaspoon pepper

Rub the turkey inside and out with salt and pepper, then rub the skin of the turkey well all over with flour to coat evenly and lightly. Prepare the stuffing by mixing together with your hands the bread crumbs, suet, ham, marjoram, lemon rind and juice, salt, pepper, nutmeg, and egg yolks. Fork up mixture so that it is fluffy and drop lightly into both neck and body cavities of the turkey. Refrigerate remaining stuffing until about an hour before serving. Skewer neck skin of turkey flat to the back, enclosing stuffing in neck cavity, then using poultry pins and twine, lace the body cavity shut. Truss the turkey so that it is as compact as possible. Place breast side up on a rack in a large, shallow roasting pan and roast, uncovered, in a moderately slow oven (325°) for 1 hour. Baste lavishly with melted butter and roast about 2 hours longer, basting often with remaining butter and pan drippings, until turkey is richly browned and the leg joint moves easily.

While turkey roasts, prepare the stock for the gravy. Place turkey neck and giblets in a large, heavy saucepan, add the water, and simmer, uncovered, for 20 minutes; remove liver and heart and refrigerate. Continue simmering neck and gizzard as long as turkey roasts; discard the neck and mince the gizzard, liver, and heart. Strain the turkey stock, measure out 2½ cups, and add the minced gizzard, liver, and heart (save any remaining stock to use in soups or sauces later).

About 1 hour before the turkey has finished roasting, shape the remaining stuffing into balls about the size of crab apples (1½ to 2 inches in diameter) and brown lightly in a skillet in the ¼ cup melted butter. Transfer balls to a small baking pan, arranging one layer deep. Pour any skillet drippings over balls, cover snugly with foil, and set in oven with turkey to bake for 1 hour. When turkey is done (it will take about 3 hours for a 10-pound bird), remove from oven and let rest 20 minutes on the kitchen counter so that juices will settle and carving will be easier. Turn oven off but leave stuffing balls in oven to keep warm.

To make the gravy: Quickly skim 7 tablespoons of fat from the drippings into a medium-size saucepan and blend in the flour. Heat and stir until mixture begins to turn a pale brown. Add the 2½ cups giblet stock and the minced giblets and heat and stir until mixture thickens, about 2 to 3 minutes. Turn heat to lowest point, add salt and pepper, and let gravy mellow until you are ready to serve the turkey.

Remove twine and poultry pins from turkey, arrange on a heated large platter. Surround with stuffing balls, ruffs of watercress, and, for added color, clusters of whole raw cranberries. Pour gravy into a gravy boat and pass.

A simple way to prepare onions and a delicious one, too, because the onions remain fresh and sweet. Simmering the onions in a combination of milk and water is said to minimize the cooking odor and, indeed, it does seem to.

Sturbridge-Style Creamed Hashed Onions

MAKES 4 SERVINGS

3 very large sweet onions (Spanish or Bermuda)
½ cup milk
1½ cups water
2 tablespoons unsalted butter
½ teaspoon salt
Pinch of freshly ground pepper
Pinch of freshly grated nutmeg
¼ cup light cream

Peel the onions and slice each in half crosswise. Place onions in a large, heavy saucepan, add milk and water, cover, and simmer 12 to 15 minutes until onions are tender but still a bit crisp. Drain onions in a colander, then chop coarsely. Return onions to pan, add butter, salt, pepper, nutmeg, and cream, and cook, uncovered, stirring now and then, over lowest heat for 10 minutes. Serve piping hot. Delicious with roast turkey or chicken.

Such a basic recipe—three ingredients only—and yet this cranberry sauce, prepared at Old Sturbridge Village, is one of the best you will ever eat. The brown sugar gives a caramel richness to the cranberries. The sauce is delicious with roast turkey, of course, but also with roast chicken and baked ham.

Brown Sugar Cranberry Sauce

MAKES ABOUT 3 CUPS

1 quart fresh or frozen cranberries
½ cup water
1 pound dark brown sugar

Wash and sort the cranberries carefully, discarding any thin wiry stems and blemished berries. Place cranberries in a medium-size heavy saucepan, add water and bring to a boil. Adjust heat so that liquid ripples gently and cook, uncovered, 35 to 40 minutes until cranberries burst and cook down to a marmalade thickness. You'll have to watch them closely and stir occasionally lest they boil dry and scorch. Stir in the brown sugar and when it dissolves remove sauce from heat and cool to room temperature.

Marlborough Pudding is one of those honest, old-fashioned desserts few cooks bother to prepare anymore, perhaps because it *is* bothersome to make—apples to cook and sieve, cake or bread to grate into fine crumbs, pastry to mix and roll. The most authentic version—served at Old Sturbridge Village at Thanksgiving—calls for a border of puff paste, which requires a crisp cold day and plenty of patience if the pastry is to be flaky and light. We suggest substituting the frozen patty shells or a simple pastry (your favorite piecrust recipe) or, to make things easier still, eliminating the pastry altogether and topping the baked pudding with a border of sweetened whipped cream ruffs. Marlborough Pudding is such a moist, velvet-crumbed dessert, delicately perfumed with rose water and lemon rind, that you will find your efforts well rewarded.

Marlborough Pudding

MAKES 6 SERVINGS

6 large tart green apples, peeled, cored, and quartered
½ cup water
⅔ cup sugar
½ cup butter
Finely grated rind of 1 large lemon
Juice of 1 large lemon

6 eggs, beaten till light and frothy

¼ cup rose water (obtainable in specialty food shops and also in some pharmacies)

¼ teaspoon ground nutmeg (preferably freshly ground)

1½ cups soft fine bread or spongecake crumbs

1 tablespoon coarse granulated or regular granulated sugar

Whipped Cream Border (optional):

1 cup heavy cream, beaten to stiff peaks with 2 tablespoons confectioners' sugar

Pastry Border (optional):

3 thawed, frozen patty shells (from a 10-ounce package)
   OR
½ the recipe of your favorite single-crust piecrust recipe

Place apples in a large, heavy saucepan, add water and bring to a slow boil. Cover and simmer 12 to 15 minutes until apples are quite tender but still hold their shape. Press apples and their juices through a fine sieve into a mixing bowl; add sugar and butter and stir until butter melts. Cool to room temperature. Stir in the lemon rind and juice, then fold in the beaten eggs. Mix in the rose water and nutmeg, then fold in the bread or cake crumbs. Pour into a well-buttered 2-quart soufflé dish or straight-sided baking dish and, if you do not want to add the pastry border, sprinkle the coarse or regular granulated sugar evenly on top and bake straightaway in a moderate oven (350°) for about 1 hour until puffed, lightly browned, and the mixture quivers gently in the center when the dish is nudged. Remove pudding from oven and cool to room temperature. Top with a border of whipped cream ruffs, piped through a pastry bag fitted with a decorative tip and serve.

To Make the Pastry Border:

With Frozen Patty Shells: Stack the 3 thawed patty shells on top of one another on a lightly floured pastry cloth, then, using a floured, stockinette-covered rolling pin, roll out into a circle about ⅛-inch thick and 8 to 10 inches in diameter. Cut out 8 to 10 rounds, using a floured 2-inch biscuit cutter, place rounds on a baking sheet, and bake in a hot oven (400°) 10 to 12 minutes until puffed and lightly golden *before baking the pudding*. Lower oven heat to 350° for baking the pudding, and let the pastry circles stand at room temperature while pudding bakes. Sprinkle the pudding with sugar and bake as directed for 35 minutes. Gently arrange pastry rounds around the edge of the pudding, pressing down gently to anchor them, then bake pudding at 350° for 25 minutes more until puffed and golden. Cool to room temperature before serving.

With Piecrust: Make up ½ recipe of your favorite single-crust piecrust recipe, then roll out as you would for pie on a lightly floured pastry cloth. Using fancy heart- or crescent-shaped cookie cutters (they should measure about 2 inches across at the widest point), cut out 6 to 8 hearts or crescents. Arrange on top of unbaked pudding, sprinkle the 1 tablespoon of coarse or regular granulated sugar over the top (including the pastry cutouts), then bake the pudding for 1 hour at 350° as directed.

Optional Topping: To dress up the pastry-bordered pudding, top each portion with sweetened whipped cream (simply whip as directed for the whipped cream border).

Hancock Shaker Village
Hancock, Massachusetts

*J*ust six years after Mother Ann Lee, the daughter of an English blacksmith and the founder of the Shaker sect, arrived in New York Harbor, a band of Shakers began building a community, apart from the world, in the furrowed green hills of the Berkshires in western Massachusetts. The year was 1780 and Hancock Shaker Village was the third of nineteen Shaker communes to be established in America. It lasted for one hundred and eighty years, but finally in 1960, it closed, its few remaining members being too old or too feeble to keep the commune going.

Shakerism, which reached its height just before the Civil War and then numbered some six thousand Brethren and Sisters, has virtually no followers today. Its rules are too strict: total celibacy, a sharing of all property, a shunning of artifice and embellishment, a shutting out of the world. So the Shaker communes have died one by one, and of the original nineteen only two remain active today: Canterbury, New Hampshire (described later), and Sabbathday Lake in Maine.

Hancock Shaker Village was one of the last to close, but the demise of its active life did not mean the death of the village. A history-minded group of citizens immediately set about turning the old commune into a museum village, where the artistry and ingenuity of the Hancock Shakers could be preserved.

In many ways, the Shakers were a people ahead of their time. They espoused celibacy, it is true, but they also advocated equal rights for women. Thus at Hancock, each of the six "Families" was presided over by elders and eldresses, Families that contained about one hundred Brethren and Sisters each during the commune's most flourishing years in the 1830s.

Hancock Shaker Village was primarily an agricultural commune, although the Brethren and Sisters here were also busy manufacturing and selling tools, implements, and furniture to the "world" (their ladder-back chairs are collectors' items today). The Hancock Shakers packaged their seeds, dried and bundled up their herbs, and conserved thousands of jars of pickles and sweetmeats. Efficiency was their motto, and as they set about their daily tasks, they devised dozens of ingenious laborsaving devices.

The buildings at Hancock Shaker Village are models of architectural purity, designed to fulfill the community's needs, nothing more. They were models, too, of neatness and practicality.

But purity, neatness, and practicality are not to be interpreted as drab and unimaginative. Hancock Shaker Village is anything but, as a stroll through the orchards and herb garden, a tour of the eleven restored buildings easily prove (there are nineteen buildings in all, and the remaining eight are presently being restored). The most architecturally outstanding building is perhaps the round stone barn, built in 1826, which consists of two doughnut-shaped galleries enclosing an open central well. A far-out design for that period, true, but a functional one as well. Hayracks, for example, could be driven up through the two-lane-wide barn door, onto a circular gallery. Then, as the wagon drove around the gallery, the Brethren atop the hayrack pitched hay into the central well. By the time the wagon had gone full circle, the hay had all been pitched, and the wagon rumbled back out the door for another load.

If the Hancock Shaker Brethren were skilled agriculturalists and craftsmen, the Sisters were equally skilled cooks. In the spacious cookrooms in the basement of the Brick Dwelling, they not only prepared meals for the Shaker Families, but also put up vast quantities of vegetables and fruits from their own gardens and orchards. Each summer these restored cookrooms again buzz with activity and send forth tantalizing aromas during the week-long Shaker Kitchen Festival. Its purpose is to pay tribute to the culinary artistry and expertise of the Shaker Kitchen Sisters, and to give visitors a taste of the recipes that made them famous. Shelves of the adjoining Good Room are lined with fresh-baked breads, cakes, and cookies, with pickles, jams, and preserves (all of them for sale).

Hancock Shaker Village is not so large or impressive as Shakertown at Pleasant Hill, Kentucky (described later on in this book, but its trim picket fences, its proud wooden homes painted cheerful reds, ochers, and warm beiges, its backdrop of meadowlands, orchards, and comfortably worn foothills, provide a clear and uncontrived view of what life in this Shaker commune was all about one hundred and fifty years ago.

The Shakers at Hancock kept a herd of dairy cows, which provided plentiful supplies of milk and cream, both of which were used fresh and made into cheese. They also grew their own herbs to use in cooking as well as in the preparation of medicines. The following bread, flavored with both cheese and dill, was a particular favorite.

Brethren Cheddar Bread

MAKES 4 LOAVES (EACH 7⅜ x 3⅝ x 2¼ INCHES)

4 cups sifted all-purpose flour
2 tablespoons sugar
3 teaspoons baking powder
1¼ teaspoons salt
½ cup unsalted butter
4 cups coarsely shredded sharp Cheddar cheese
1 tablespoon minced fresh dill or 1 teaspoon dill weed
2 eggs, lightly beaten
2 cups milk

Sift together into a large mixing bowl the flour, sugar, baking powder, and salt. Using a pastry blender or two knives, cut the butter into the dry ingredients until crumbly—about the texture of uncooked oatmeal. Stir in the shredded cheese and the dill. Combine the eggs and milk, then add all at once, stirring just enough to moisten the dry ingredients uniformly. Divide batter among 4 very well-greased 7⅜ x 3⅝ x 2¼-inch loaf pans and bake in a hot oven (400°) for 35 to 40 minutes or until loaves are nicely browned and sound hollow when thumped. Cool loaves upright in their pans on wire racks for 10 minutes, then invert and remove from pans. Slice fairly thick (about ½-inch thick) and serve. (*Note:* These loaves freeze well. Simply wrap snugly in aluminum foil or plastic food wrap and place in the freezer. Bring to room temperature before slicing.)

There grows at Hancock Shaker Village an ancient apothecary rose—*Rosa gallica*—its stem and branches trained along a fence. The Shakers grew it not for its beauty (they never grew flowers as decoration), they used it to make rose water, an ingredient in many of their medicines and recipes. Today rose water has lost favor as a flavoring (we seem to prefer vanilla and almond), and yet if you can find rose water at your local specialty food shop or pharmacy, by all means buy it and try it in this old Shaker recipe for ice cream. It imparts a lovely, elusive bouquet.

Rose Water Ice Cream

MAKES 6 TO 8 SERVINGS

2 cups light cream
4 egg yolks
1 cup sugar
Pinch of salt
1 tablespoon rose water
2 cups heavy cream, whipped

Heat the light cream in a heavy, medium-size saucepan over moderate heat just until bubbles begin to appear around the edges of the pan. Meanwhile, beat the egg yolks with the sugar and salt just until well blended. Mix a little of the scalded cream into the egg yolk mixture, then stir all back into saucepan. Reduce heat to low and cook, stirring constantly, until slightly thickened—3 to 5 minutes. Remove from heat and stir in rose water. Cool slightly, then fold in the whipped cream. Pour into a 2-quart soufflé dish or straight-sided bowl and freeze until firm. (*Note:* You can freeze the ice cream in a hand-cranked freezer—and this would have been the Shaker way. But if you do, do not whip the heavy cream—it may turn to butter as the ice cream is churned—simply stir it into the egg yolk mixture, pour into the freezing can, add the dasher, and freeze as the manufacturer of your particular freezer recommends.)

The Hancock Shaker Sisters were famous for their pickles and preserves, and this old recipe is still being sold at the Good Room in the basement of the Brick Dwelling. This building, constructed in 1830, contained the communal dining room and meeting room, the Ministry Dining Room, and, in the basement beside the Good Room, the Great Cook Room, now restored and furnished with antique Shaker cooking equipment and implements so that it looks today just as it did more than a hundred years ago.

Good Room Zucchini Pickles

MAKES 3 PINTS

2 pounds small, tender zucchini
2 medium-size yellow onions, peeled and sliced very thin
2 quarts cold water (about)
¼ cup pickling salt
1 pint white vinegar
1 cup sugar
1 teaspoon celery seeds
1 teaspoon mustard seeds

Wash the zucchini well but do not peel, then slice very thin and place in a large crock or bowl along with the onion slices. Pour in the water, adding more if needed to cover the zucchini and onions, then sprinkle in the salt. Let stand 1 hour, drain well, and place in a medium-size enamel kettle. Mix the vinegar, sugar, celery and mustard seeds in a saucepan and bring to a full rolling boil. Pour over the zucchini and onions and let stand 1 hour. Set kettle over moderate heat and bring all to a boil. Pack zucchini and onions boiling hot in 3 hot, sterilized pint-size preserving jars, filling to within ¼ inch of the tops with the pickling liquid. Screw lids down tightly, then process 10 minutes in a boiling water bath. Cool jars to room temperature, then store in a cool, dark, dry place.

Mystic Seaport
Mystic, Connecticut

G*ulls* ride the wind overhead, salt water laps at the wharf pilings, ships tug at their mooring lines. This is Mystic Seaport and the ships you see berthed alongside the serpentine waterfront are tall, proud sailing ships, nineteenth-century ships (for the most part New England built and New England based) that sailed the seven seas. The pride of the fleet is the 133-foot-long *Charles W. Morgan*, built in 1841 at the yard of Jethro and Zachariah Hillman in New Bedford, Massachusetts. She is the last of America's great wooden whaleships and, as such, was designated a National Historic Landmark in 1967.

But this is no ghost fleet you see at Mystic Seaport, for one of this outdoor museum's functions is to assemble, restore, and preserve the schooners and sloops, packets and small craft that plied inshore and offshore waters in America's great age of sail together with the industries and crafts that supported these ships.

Mystic Seaport, a re-created nineteenth-century New England port, sprawls for forty acres along the banks of the Mystic River on what had originally been the shipyard of George, Clark, and Thomas Greenman. This yard alone, between 1838 and 1878, launched nearly a hundred vessels, small and large, including the famous clipper *David Crockett*, which rounded Cape Horn twenty-five times on its runs between New England and San Francisco. Cape Horn *was* the sea lane West during the nineteenth century, there being no Panama Canal, and it was an often stormy passage that tested the ships and the men who sailed them.

The shipyards at Mystic are not idle today, for Mystic Seaport is busily restoring and maintaining the ships in port. What you see here, as you stroll the waterfront, is what you might have seen a hundred years ago in any one of New England's lively seaports. There is the ship-yard office, the ropewalk where ropes are made, the sail loft, rigging loft, chandlery (ship's store), shipsmith shop, where bands for masts, hoops for casks, and chain cable links are forged, the cooperage, where barrels are made. There are, in addition, a lifesaving station which stood, originally, on nearby Block Island, a lighthouse (replica of the one at Brant Point in Nantucket), a hand pumper fire engine (also from Block Island), a planetar-ium where the mysteries of celestial navigation are ex-plained, a clock shop, a tavern, an apothecary, a chapel, a school.

With demonstrations in the art of figurehead carving, in weaving, printing, coopering, and cooking, ship rig-ging and smithing, with more than forty buildings (some of them restored, some of them replicas) lined up along the cobblestone streets, with a fleet of nearly two hundred historic vessels (from kayaks and dories to schooners and the majestic *Charles W. Morgan*), Mystic Seaport, founded in 1929, is without question one of America's most impressive outdoor museum villages.

It is, as its guide map says, "a bright chapter in Amer-ica's history—a chapter devoted to those self-reliant men and women of the New England seacoast whose fortitude, devotion and hardy industry developed our country's great seafaring tradition."

"If there is any mission a museum, or even a cooking demonstration like ours has," says Sandy Oliver, interpreter/researcher at Mystic Seaport, "it is to convey to our visitors the idea that people a hundred and fifty or two hundred years ago were as creative, innovative, and intelligent as we are today; that technological advance is not necessarily the result of a more intelligent race, but rather the result of years of collective knowledge, each generation building on the last." The two recipes that follow prove her point. We print them first in their original style because, as Ms. Oliver says, reading these instructions is "like meeting with the women who wrote them long ago."

This recipe for Clam Pie comes from a manuscript recipe book, dated 1829, inscribed "Charlotte T.W. Gilbert from her friend C.D. Waters." The manuscript belongs to the Old Sturbridge Village Library Collection but is representative of the seafood dishes demonstrated in the homes at Mystic Seaport.

CLAM PIE

After the clams are boiled & well washed, Shake some pepper & beaten cloves over them, a lump of butter & a little flour. Paste at the bottom and top of the dish & fill it up with the liquor of the clams.

Here, then, is a twentieth-century adaptation, based upon the old recipe but more specific as to times, temperatures, and techniques. The recipe, you'll note, calls for no salt because fresh clams themselves are salty.

Clam Pie

MAKES AN 8-INCH PIE, ABOUT 6 SERVINGS

2 dozen shucked, fresh littleneck or cherrystone clams
4 tablespoons unsalted butter
6 tablespoons flour
2 cups liquor drained from clams (if there is not sufficient

clam liquor, add enough bottled clam juice to round the
measure out at 2 cups)
⅛ teaspoon freshly ground pepper
⅛ teaspoon ground cloves
Pastry (your favorite recipe) for an 8-inch 2-crust pie

Pour the clams and their liquor into a small saucepan and
simmer gently, uncovered, 5 to 8 minutes, just until the
clams' skirts ruffle. Place a fine-mesh sieve over a 1-
quart measuring cup and drain clams, saving the liquor,
which will be used for the sauce. Rinse the clams, still in
the sieve, well under cool running water; set clams aside.
Rinse and dry the saucepan, then add the butter, set over
moderate heat and melt. Off heat, blend in the flour, then
return pan to heat and "work" butter-flour paste several
minutes with a wooden spoon until smooth. Off heat
once again, add the 2 cups clam liquor, pepper, and
cloves. Whisk briskly to mix, return to heat, and continue whisking until thickened and smooth. Turn heat to
lowest point and let sauce mellow about 5 minutes until
all raw floury taste is gone. Meanwhile, roll out half the
pastry and fit into an 8-inch piepan, leaving about a 1-
inch overhang all around. Roll out the remaining pastry
into a circle about the same size as the first. Stir reserved clams into sauce, then pour into pastry-lined piepan. Ease top crust into place, roll top and bottom crust
overhangs up together even with rim of piepan and
crimp, making a high fluted edge. With a sharp knife, cut
decorative steam vents in the top crust. Bake pie in a hot
oven (400°) 25 to 30 minutes until pastry is nicely
browned and filling is bubbly. Remove pie from oven and
let stand at room temperature about 5 minutes before
serving. Cut into 6 wedges and serve.

From *The Frugal Housewefe or Complete Woman
Cook*, by Sussannah Carter, published by G. & R. Waite,
New York, 1803, comes this early recipe for preparing
cod. Its straightforward title does little to suggest the
elegance of the dish.

TO STEW A COD

Cut your cod in slices an inch thick, lay them in the bottom of a large stew-pan, season them with nutmeg, beaten pepper, and salt, a bundle of sweet herbs, and an onion, half a pint of white wine, and a quarter of a pint of water; cover it close and let it simmer softly for five or six minutes; then squeeze in the juice of a lemon; put in a few oysters and the liquor, strained, a piece of butter as big as an egg rolled in flour, and a blade or two of mace; cover it close and let it stew softly, shaking the pan often. When it is enough, take out the sweet herbs and onion, and dish it up; pour the sauce over it. Garnish with lemon.

For the modern version, we have taken the liberty of changing the title so that the modern cook will have more of an idea as to the character of the recipe. It is a subtly seasoned dish, with both the cod and the oysters no more than heated through so that they are supremely moist and tender.

Cod Steaks and Oysters in Lemon Sauce

MAKES 4 SERVINGS

4 fresh cod steaks cut 1 inch thick (each should measure
    about 4 inches across)
Pinch of ground nutmeg (preferably freshly ground)
⅛ teaspoon freshly ground pepper
¼ teaspoon salt (about)
1 medium-size yellow onion, peeled but left whole
1 sprig of fresh parsley
1 bay leaf
1 large sprig of fresh thyme (or ¼ teaspoon dried whole
    thyme)
1 large sprig of fresh marjoram (or ½ teaspoon dried leaf
    marjoram)
1 large sprig of fresh summer savory (or ¼ teaspoon dried leaf
    summer savory)

1 cup dry white wine
½ cup water
3 tablespoons butter kneaded until smooth with 5 tablespoons
    flour
12 shucked fresh oysters
½ cup strained oyster liquor
2 tablespoons lemon juice
1 blade of mace
Lemon slices or wedges to garnish

Lay the cod steaks in the bottom of a large, shallow, heavy kettle so that they do not overlap. Sprinkle each lightly with nutmeg, pepper, and salt. Add onion to the kettle, also the parsley, bay leaf, thyme, marjoram, summer savory, wine, and water; bring to a simmer over moderately low heat, cover, and cook 4 minutes. With a broad spatula or pancake turner, very carefully lift two of the cod steaks, one at a time, and stack on top of the other two cod steaks so that there will be room in the kettle to stir the sauce as it thickens. Add the butter-flour paste and heat, stirring constantly, 1 to 2 minutes until thickened and smooth. Again using the spatula or pancake turner, carefully return the two cod steaks to their original position in the kettle. You must handle them very gently lest they break apart. Add the oysters, oyster liquor, lemon juice, and blade of mace, cover and simmer 4 to 5 minutes longer, just until oysters ruffle about the edges. Taste for salt and add a pinch more if needed. With the spatula or pancake turner, lift cod steaks to a heated platter. Remove onion from the kettle and discard, also the blade of mace, parsley sprig, bay leaf, and fresh herb sprigs if used (the dried herbs, obviously, will have cooked into the sauce and cannot be removed). Ladle oysters and sauce over cod steaks, garnish with lemon slices or wedges and, if you like, ruffs of parsley.

Haddock and cod are both fine for fish chowders, but modern traditionalists in New England insist on haddock, according to historians at Mystic Seaport. You can use frozen haddock fillets, but fresh fish gives the chowder a flavor of the sea.

Haddock Chowder

MAKES 8 SERVINGS

⅛ pound salt pork, cut in ¼-inch cubes
2 large yellow onions, peeled and coarsely chopped
2¼ cups water
3 large potatoes, peeled and cut in ½-inch cubes
2 teaspoons salt
2 pounds fresh haddock fillets
2 cups milk
2 cups light cream
3 tablespoons butter
⅛ teaspoon pepper

Brown salt pork cubes slowly in a large, heavy kettle over moderate heat until all the fat melts out and the cubes are crisp and brown. At the same time, boil the onions in the water in a covered saucepan 10 minutes; add potatoes and salt, re-cover, and simmer 15 minutes. Pour potatoes, onions, and cooking water into kettle with salt pork. Add haddock, cover, and simmer 10 to 15 minutes until haddock is tender—it will break apart as it cooks. Add milk, cream, butter, and pepper and heat, uncovered, just to serving temperature. This will take about 5 miutes over a low heat. Do not allow mixture to boil or it may curdle. Ladle into large soup plates and serve with pilot biscuits or oyster crackers.

Shaker Village
Canterbury, New Hampshire

*T*he Shaker sect, two years older than America itself, is virtually extinct. It was founded by Mother Ann Lee, an English immigrant regarded by her thousands of disciples as the female reincarnation of Christ. Today all the Brethren have died, less than a dozen primbonneted Sisters linger. As they pass on, so too will the religious movement.

Shaker Village at Canterbury, a cluster of white frame buildings standing foursquare upon a green hilltop, is one of the two remaining active Shaker communities in America (the other is Sabbathday Lake in Maine). But only a few elderly Sisters remain at Canterbury, and since 1959 they have been phasing their once busy agricultural commune into a village museum so that the Shaker heritage will not be lost.

And what happens when these Sisters die? According to Eldress Bertha Lindsay, the village has been incorporated and some thirty of its friends—antiquarians and concerned public citizens—will take over the task of completing the restoration, refurnishing the buildings in the straightforward, functional furniture for which the Shakers are famous, resowing the gardens, replanting the orchards, and maintaining what the Sisters call their "restoration of an eighteenth-century Utopian community."

Meanwhile, the Sisters carry on, tending their kitchen gardens, preparing the old Shaker recipes that they have gathered together in a slim pamphlet (two of those recipes are included here), welcoming the visitors who come to tour the commune, its barns and outbuildings, its proud cupola-crowned Meeting House (built in 1782), and its unoccupied two- and three-story white clapboard homes.

The two other restored Shaker Villages described in separate sections—Hancock Shaker Village in Massachusetts and Shakertown at Pleasant Hill in Kentucky—are more sprucely restored, more geared to tourism (in these two sections you will find fuller descriptions of the Shakers and their contributions to American arts and architecture, agriculture and engineering, crafts and cuisine). These two are villages reborn, revitalized, their gates thrown open to the world. But only at Canterbury, New Hampshire, will you see an actual Shaker commune simultaneously living out its last days and slipping into history as a restored village.

Here is an unusual soup—a delicate vegetable broth into which batter is poured just before serving. The broth thickens considerably, so that in the end the mixture is more like creamed vegetables than soup. It's a bland but filling soup, a meal in itself.

Shaker Vegetable Batter Soup

MAKES 6 TO 8 SERVINGS

2 quarts water
2 tablespoons medium pearl barley
2 medium-size potatoes, peeled and cut in ¼-inch cubes
1 large carrot, peeled and cut in small dice

1 large white turnip, peeled and cut in small dice
1 large stalk celery, cut in small dice (include some leaves)
¾ cup light cream
2 tablespoons butter
2 teaspoons salt
⅛ teaspoon freshly ground pepper

Batter:
1 cup milk
1 egg
1 cup sifted all-purpose flour
½ teaspoon salt

Bring the water, barley, potatoes, carrot, turnip, and celery to a boil in a large, heavy kettle over moderate heat. Cover, reduce heat slightly, and simmer 1 hour. Uncover and simmer ½ hour longer. Stir in cream, butter, salt, and pepper and let bubble gently.

To make the batter: Combine the milk and the egg in a small mixing bowl, then stir in the flour and salt—the batter will be about the consistency of a pancake batter. Pour the batter slowly on top of the gently bubbling soup, distributing as evenly as possible, then cook, uncovered, for 10 minutes. The batter will thicken the soup considerably, some of it will clump like small dumplings. Ladle soup into large bowls and serve, accompanied if you like, by a sharp chunk of Cheddar cheese.

This golden, sweet, yeast-raised biscuit owes both its color and flavor to puréed, cooked winter squash—acorn and butternut are perhaps the easiest varieties to use. To make the purée, simply cut the squash in good-sized chunks (about 2 inches long and 1 inch wide), peel, then boil in unsalted water until tender; drain very well, then put through a food mill. For this recipe you will need 1½ cups purée, which one large acorn squash or one small butternut squash should provide. Or, if you prefer, you can use one package (12 ounces) frozen, cooked winter squash. It turns out to be precisely the right amount. But you must thaw the squash completely before you use it.

Shaker Raised Squash Biscuits

MAKES 3 TO 3½ DOZEN

1 envelope active dry yeast
½ cup lukewarm water
6 to 6½ cups sifted all-purpose flour
¾ cup sugar
½ teaspoon salt
4 tablespoons melted butter
2 eggs
1½ cups puréed, cooked winter squash
1 cup scalded milk, cooled to lukewarm

Dissolve the yeast in the lukewarm water, stir in about ¼ cup of the flour and 1 tablespoon of the sugar to make a sponge, cover, and set in a warm, dry place to proof for ¾ hour. Mix in about 1 more cup of the flour, all the remaining sugar, the salt, melted butter, eggs, and squash. Then add the remaining flour (4¾ to 5¼ cups) alternately with the scalded milk, beginning and ending with the flour. You will need only enough flour to make a soft but kneadable dough. Cover bowl of dough with cloth, set in a warm, dry spot, and allow to rise until double in bulk, about 1½ hours. Stir dough down, turn onto a well-floured board or pastry cloth, and sprinkle top of dough with flour (at this point dough will seem quite sticky, so you will have to keep flouring your hands and sprinkling the dough with flour as you work with it). Shape into a ball and knead lightly 3 to 5 minutes. Divide dough in half, and roll out, half at a time, to a thickness of ½ inch. Using a floured 2½-inch biscuit cutter, cut dough into rounds. Reroll and cut scraps. Place biscuits about ½ inch apart on ungreased baking sheets, cover with cloth, and set in a warm, dry place to rise for ½ hour. Bake biscuits in a very hot oven (425°) about 15 minutes until nicely browned on top. For a nice glossy finish, brush the tops of the biscuits with a little melted butter as soon as they come from the oven. Serve oven hot with plenty of butter.

Strawbery Banke
Portsmouth, New Hampshire

George Washington...Lafayette...Paul Revere ...John Paul Jones...Daniel Webster. These are the most famous figures to stride through the pages of Portsmouth's history. But there are others, less renowned perhaps, but no less important to this early New England seaport.

Situated by the Piscataqua River on that sliver of New Hampshire that fronts the Atlantic, Portsmouth was until recently a town that Maine-bound tourists dashed through as quickly as possible. It had little of interest to offer, a seafaring town all but killed by the railroad. Its harbor, once filled with barks and brigs and schooners bound for foreign ports, stood derelict for years and eventually deteriorated into a dumping ground.

There was talk in the 1930s of rescuing and restoring the two-hundred-year-old buildings in the Puddle Dock area. Buried underneath the trash, conservation-minded citizens pointed out, was considerable historic treasure. Some of it, in fact, dated back to New Hampshire's original settlement of Strawbery Banke, the small waterfront town built in 1630 on a bank of wild strawberries by eighty English settlers from Portsmouth and London.

Preservation fever hadn't yet struck Portsmouth, so the plans were shelved until the 1960s, when a new project was set before the Urban Renewal Agency: raze the eyesore waterfront and build there a modern apartment city.

Portsmouth conservationists were horrified. Preservation fever began to spread, and when it was discovered that the high-rise apartment complex had proved too expensive, history-minded citizens proposed that the Urban Renewal funds be used to restore the centuries-old waterfront.

In a precedent-setting decision, the agency agreed to provide $600,000 for the restoration. The people of Portsmouth raised another $200,000 and the rehabilitation of the ten-acre waterfront site began.

In 1964, Strawbery Banke, Inc., the organization formed to oversee the restoration, bought the restored site and its twenty-seven buildings from Urban Renewal. Today, there are more than thirty historic buildings at Strawbery Banke, some of them moved there from elsewhere in Portsmouth, about a third of them now fully restored and fitted out with furnishings of the area: a rustic general store; the old meeting house; the Governor Goodwin Mansion; the Sherburne, Clark, Chase, and Walsh Houses, straight and proud homes dating from the seventeenth and eighteenth centuries. There is a boatshop where straight-sided Banks dories are crafted the old Portsmouth way out of wood. There are weavers at work, spinsters, and blacksmiths. There are not at present, however, any cooking demonstrations, but the recipes that follow are all early Portsmouth favorites, taken from ancestral receipt books.

Restoration continues at Strawbery Banke, and those buildings not yet open to the public can be inspected close at hand from the outside on walking tours, as can four other historic Portsmouth houses near the restoration site (the oldest of these is Jackson House, circa 1664).

Visitors have come to Strawbery Banke by the thousands, among them Mrs. Lyndon B. Johnson during a 1967 beautification tour of New England.

"What a wonderful vignette of life you are re-creating here for visitors throughout the world," she said.

Her visit helped to put Strawbery Banke on the map. And Portsmouth, New Hampshire, is today a destination, not simply a city to hurry through. Its waterfront, no longer an eyesore, is the city's pride. A place to pause, to poke about, to sniff the salt air and imagine what a rollicking port this was two hundred years ago.

For more than two centuries, Portsmouth, New Hampshire, lived by the sea. And grew rich from the sea. It is not surprising, thus, that seafood figured prominently in the local diet. There were fat sweet oysters, for example, prepared as quickly and simply as possible so that none of the delicate sea-fresh flavor was lost. One of the best oyster recipes to come out of Portsmouth is this one for oyster stew. It is the fisherman's way, utterly straightforward, with nothing more to season than salt and pepper. And it is delicious.

Sailor Ben's Oyster Stew

MAKES 6 SOUP-COURSE SERVINGS, 4 MAIN-COURSE SERVINGS

1 pint fresh, shucked oysters and their liquor
Water
1 quart cold milk
¼ cup unsalted butter
¼ teaspoon salt (about)
Pinch of white pepper
1 cup coarse cracker crumbs (pilot, oyster, or soda crackers)

Drain off and measure the oyster liquor, then add enough cold water to total 1 cup. Place the oysters and the 1 cup oyster liquor in a large, heavy saucepan and heat over moderately low heat 2 to 3 minutes—just until the oysters' skirts begin to crinkle. Pour in the cold milk, add the butter, and bring slowly to a simmer without stirring. "Do not allow the oysters to boil," cautions Sailor Ben. "Boiling toughens oysters." Season with salt and pepper, add the cracker crumbs, but again do not stir. Set the stew on the back of the stove for 20 minutes, where it will keep hot but not boil. Taste for salt and pepper and add more if needed. Ladle into bowls and serve.

In Portsmouth, as in Boston, cod is a beloved fish. Particularly fresh cod, right off the boat. Here is one of those simple, old-fashioned recipes too few people make any more—Cod Fish Hash. It is nothing more than one part minced fresh cod to two parts diced boiled potatoes, hashed with butter and cream and seasoned with salt and pepper. It is subtle in flavor. And it is superb.

Cod Fish Hash

MAKES 4 TO 6 SERVINGS

1 pound boned and skinned fresh cod
4 medium-size potatoes, boiled until tender and cooled
¾ cup light cream
¼ cup unsalted butter
1 teaspoon salt
⅛ teaspoon pepper

Mince the cod fine and set aside. Peel the potatoes and dice—they should be coarser in texture than the cod. Heat the cream and butter in a large, heavy skillet over moderate heat until the butter melts; add the cod and cook 2 to 3 minutes, just until the cod turns opaque—do not allow mixture to boil. Add the pototoes, salt, and pepper and continue to cook and stir 3 to 4 minutes longer, just until piping hot (you don't want the mixture to brown). Serve at once—for breakfast, lunch, or supper.

Gooseberries, so popular in Colonial New England, have fallen from favor. And so, too, has that lovely old-fashioned dessert, Gooseberry Fool. Fools—nothing more than thick purées mixed with stirred custard and topped with sweetened whipped cream—were made with all kinds of berries. But the tart, green gooseberry makes a particularly fine and refreshing fool as this old Portsmouth, New Hampshire, recipe proves. Fresh gooseberries come to market in late June and early July, and if you are able to obtain them, by all means try this exquisite old recipe. The gooseberries, admittedly, are pesky to top and stem, tedious to purée, but the results are *so* worth the effort.

Gooseberry Fool

MAKES 6 SERVINGS

Gooseberry Purée:
1 quart fresh gooseberries, washed
2 tablespoons water (about)
2 cups sugar

Stirred Custard:
1 cup milk
2 tablespoons sugar
2 eggs, lightly beaten
⅛ teaspoon freshly grated or ground nutmeg

Whipped Cream Topping:
1 cup heavy cream
3 tablespoons confectioners' sugar
Freshly grated or ground nutmeg

Pick over the gooseberries carefully, discarding any that are soft or badly blemished; remove stems and blossom ends from remaining gooseberries. Place berries in a large, heavy saucepan, crush slightly, then stir in water and sugar. Set over low heat and simmer, uncovered, 10 to 15 minutes until skins pop and berries are mushy.

Watch carefully and, if berries threaten to scorch, add another tablespoon or so of water. Set a large, fine-mesh strainer over a large mixing bowl and press the berries through the strainer, using a wooden spoon. Have patience—this is a slow job because you must extract as much of the berry pulp as possible. Keep mashing and pressing the berries until only the seeds and skins remain in the strainer—this will take about half an hour. Set the purée aside while you prepare the stirred custard. In the top of a double boiler, combine milk, sugar, and beaten eggs. Set *over*—not *in*—simmering water and cook and stir until mixture is about the consistency of thick gravy —about 5 minutes. Mix in nutmeg. Set double boiler top in a bowl of cold water to quick-cool the custard. When custard is cool, combine with the gooseberry purée and pour into a pretty glass dessert dish. Whip the cream with the confectioners' sugar until stiff peaks form, then spoon and spread over the top of the purée. Sprinkle nutmeg on top. Set the fool, uncovered, in the refrigerator and chill several hours before serving. The whipped cream will thicken up still further so that when the fool is served, it becomes the "base" for the gooseberry-custard sauce.

☙

"Bake," read the instructions for this old-fashioned recipe "until the cake begins to smell good." "Good" is an understatement. The cake, loaded as it is with fresh blueberries, smells "ambrosial." It is, as one taster commented, "A huge batch of blueberries held together with a little batter." The cake is, in fact, so chock-full of berries that it softens on standing to an almost pudding-like consistency. Which makes it even *better*. The recipe comes from the Nutter family, grandparents of Portsmouth-born author Thomas Bailey Aldrich, who wrote *Peck's Bad Boy*.

New Hampshire Blueberry Cake

MAKES A 9 x 9 x 2-INCH LOAF CAKE

⅓ cup butter (or as the original recipe reads "butter the size
    of an egg")
1 cup sugar
1 large egg
2 cups sifted all-purpose flour
1 teaspoon baking soda
½ cup sour milk or buttermilk ("If no sour milk," the original
    recipe directs, "use sweet milk with 1 teaspoonful of
    cream of tartar")
3 cups fresh blueberries, washed and stemmed

Cream the butter until light, then add sugar and continue
creaming until fluffy. Beat in egg. Mix flour and soda and
add alternately with the sour milk, beginning and ending
with the dry ingredients. The batter will be very stiff, but
it *must* be to support the load of blueberries now to be
added. Pat blueberries dry on paper toweling and stir
into the batter. Spread batter in a well-greased 9 x 9 x
2-inch baking pan. Bake in a moderately slow oven (325°)
45 to 50 minutes until cake is nicely browned on top and
has pulled from sides of pan. Or until, as the old recipe
says, "The cake begins to smell good." Cool cake upright
in its pan on a wire rack to room temperature before
cutting.

Boothbay Railway Museum and Old Boothbay Junction
Boothbay, Maine

*I*t may seem odd that a seafaring, pleasure-boating community has built itself a replica whistle-stop village and a railroad museum. And yet railroads were as integral to the development of Maine as they were to the rest of America. Indeed, the rise of the steam engine signaled the decline of shipping along Maine's boulder-strewn coast.

Today, it is the railroads that are in decline, thanks to jets that can whisk passengers from Portland to New York in less time than it took the old Maine Central to chug from Skowhegan to Wiscasset. Thanks, too, to superhighways and modern trucking, which are supplanting the freight train. So to preserve one moment in Maine's history—the heyday of railroading—the Boothbay Railway Museum and Old Boothbay Junction have been built.

This is a replica village rather than a restoration, although there are two early restored depots here, both moved to the museum site from elsewhere in Maine as they became defunct—one from the town of Freeport, the other from Thorndike. Both are filled with souvenirs and mementos of the Age of Steam.

There is an old steam engine here, too, Maine's only steam-operated, two-foot gauge train, which makes runs in summer around the village (the village and museum are open only in summer). There is also an old wooden standard-gauge caboose, once used on the Maine Central Railroad (the caboose was where the crew slept and ate). Although there are no cooking demonstrations aboard, indeed no active foods program at the village, touring the caboose and the depots and riding the old narrow-gauge train show clearly what life was like for both passengers and crew. Food for the crew was prepared aboard—filling, simple fare. But travelers were more apt to eat at a whistle-stop Depot Lunch (sampling local home cooking) or to pack their own lunches, tucking into their hampers foods that both traveled and "ate" well (a steamed pudding for dessert, perhaps, like those included among the old Maine recipes that follow).

The replica village shows the sights an early rail traveler might have seen, either through the train window or at first hand on a village stroll (in the old days, steam engines paused frequently to take on water, coal, and mail, and during such stops passengers often detrained to stretch their legs). There's a General Store at Boothbay Junction, a Depot Lunch, a Carriage Shed, a Cooper Shop, a Village Blacksmith, a Little Red Schoolhouse, a Post Office, a Barber Shop, a Bank, and, although they do not relate directly to railroading, three antique museums (one devoted to dolls and doll houses, one to toys, and the third to antique automobiles).

On the whole, however, the Railway Museum, the Old Junction Depot, and the stretch of narrow gauge track punctuated by coal pits, water towers, and flag stops, preserve for today and tomorrow the great railroad years of yesterday.

If this century-old Maine recipe is to taste as it did in days past, it must be made with home-grown—or at least vine-ripened—tomatoes. The pithy, flavorless, plastic wrapped tomatoes of today are not worth the time it takes to peel and slice them.

Scalloped Tomatoes the Maine Way

MAKES 6 SERVINGS

8 juicily-ripe, medium-size tomatoes, peeled, cored, and
    sliced ¼ inch thick
2 cups fine soft bread crumbs
2 tablespoons melted butter
1 teaspoon salt
1 teaspoon dry mustard
1 teaspoon sugar
¼ teaspoon freshly ground pepper
1 tablespoon finely grated onion
2 tablespoons butter
2 slices of bread, buttered and cut in ¼-inch cubes

Place the sliced tomatoes in a large mixing bowl. In a
second bowl, toss the bread crumbs with the melted butter until well mixed. Blend together the salt, mustard,
sugar, and pepper, sprinkle over crumbs, and toss to
mix. Add grated onion and toss once again. Pour crumb
mixture over tomatoes and, using your hands, mix well
—never mind if the tomatoes break apart. Spoon into a
buttered 9 x 9 x 2-inch baking dish, dot with the 2 tablespoons butter, and scatter buttered cubes evenly on top.
Bake, uncovered, in a moderate oven (350°) for 1 hour or
until bubbly and bread cubes are touched with brown.
Remove from oven and let stand at room temperature 15
minutes before serving so that mixture has time to
thicken up slightly. Serve in small bowls.

&

Steamed puddings were popular in Maine in its
growing-up years as they were elsewhere about New
England. This particular recipe from the Boothbay Harbor region is spicy, sweet, and exceedingly moist. It
makes a small pudding, but a pudding rich enough to
serve six persons. Serve it for dessert, warm or cold,
plain or topped with whipped cream.

Steamed Carrot and Potato Pudding

MAKES 6 SERVINGS

1 cup sifted all-purpose flour
1 teaspoon baking soda
1 teaspoon ground cinnamon
1 teaspoon ground nutmeg
1 teaspoon salt
½ teaspoon ground cloves
1 cup sugar
1 cup seedless raisins, finely chopped
1 cup coarsely grated raw carrot (about 1 large carrot)
1 cup coarsely grated raw Irish potato (about 1 medium-size
    potato)
¼ cup melted butter

Place flour, soda, cinnamon, nutmeg, salt, cloves, and
sugar in a large mixing bowl and stir well to mix. Add
raisins and, using your hands, toss in the dry mixture
until evenly coated (the raisins tend to stick together, so
keep working them into the dry ingredients until all
clumps are broken up). Add grated carrot and potato and
mix in evenly with your hands. Add melted butter and
work in with your hands until as evenly distributed as
possible. (The mixture will be dry and crumbly, but add
no liquid. The potatoes and carrots will both release considerable moisture during the steaming, and the pudding
will hold together beautifully in the end.) Spoon mixture
into a very well-buttered 1-quart steamed pudding mold
and snap on the cover. Lower onto a rack in a deep
kettle containing about 1 inch of boiling water. Check to
make sure that the bottom of the pudding mold does not
actually touch the water. Cover the kettle and steam the
pudding for 3 hours—the water in the bottom of the kettle should boil slowly throughout. Check occasionally
and add more boiling water if kettle threatens to boil dry,
but do make certain that you do not add so much water
that it touches the pudding mold. When pudding has

steamed 3 hours, lift gently to a cake rack and let cool upright for 10 minutes with the lid still on the pudding mold. Uncover mold, loosen edges of pudding with a thin-blade knife or spatula, then invert on a small serving plate. The pudding, when steamed, will fill the mold only half to two-thirds, and that is as it should be. This is a pudding heavy with raisins, potato, and carrot, moist, dense of texture, and rich. Cut into slim wedges and serve, accompanied, if you like, with freshly whipped cream.

🍮

Another old-fashioned Maine steamed pudding, this one buttery and firm, textured with chocolate-caramel flavor. It's easy to make and, unlike other steamed puddings, cooks for one hour only. Serve with sweetened whipped cream, with hard sauce, or with the Foamy Egg Sauce given below.

Steamed Brown Sugar Chocolate Pudding with Foamy Egg Sauce

MAKES 6 SERVINGS

2 cups sifted all-purpose flour
1 cup firmly packed dark brown sugar
2 tablespoons cocoa
1 teaspoon baking soda
1 cup buttermilk or sour milk
¼ cup melted butter

Foamy Egg Sauce (Makes about 1½ cups):
2 eggs
¾ cup sifted confectioners' sugar
½ teaspoon vanilla

In a medium-size mixing bowl, stir together the flour and brown sugar, then with your hands, work together until all brown sugar lumps are gone. Stir in cocoa and baking soda. Combine buttermilk or sour milk and melted butter and add all at once. Stir just enough to mix. Pour batter into a well-buttered 1-quart steamed pudding mold, snap on cover, and lower onto a rack in a deep kettle containing about 1 inch of boiling water. Cover kettle and steam the pudding for 1 hour—the water in the kettle should boil gently and should not at any time touch the bottom of the pudding mold. Remove pudding mold from kettle and let cool upright on a wire cake rack, with the cover still on the mold, for 10 minutes. Uncover mold, loosen pudding around edges of mold with a thin-blade spatula or knife, and invert onto a small serving plate. Cut into wedges and serve topped with Foamy Egg Sauce or with another topping of your choice.

To make the foamy egg sauce: Beat the eggs in a small bowl until very thick and fluffy—almost the consistency of mayonnaise. Add the confectioners' sugar gradually, beating all the while, until thick and creamy. Beat in the vanilla. Pour into a small sauceboat and serve over the Steamed Brown Sugar Chocolate Pudding. (*Note:* This sauce will separate on standing, so prepare it just before serving. If there is leftover sauce, refrigerate, then beat hard again before serving until uniformly creamy and thick.)

"This mincemeat will keep well in a covered stone jar," read the directions of this early Down East recipe. Maine, of course, is bitter cold in winter so that spoilage there is perhaps not the problem it is apt to be elsewhere in America. To be on the safe side, since this mincemeat contains suet, pressure-process the jars as directed in the modern adaptation below. Green tomato mincemeat is delicious served as a relish with roast fowl, game, pork, or baked ham.

Green Tomato Mincemeat

MAKES ABOUT 6 PINTS

3 pounds small, hard green tomatoes, washed, cored, and
    chopped but not peeled
3 pounds tart green apples, peeled, cored, and chopped
2 pounds seedless raisins
1 cup coarsely ground suet
1 cup cider vinegar
4 pounds dark brown sugar
2 tablespoons salt
2 tablespoons ground cloves
1 tablespoon ground nutmeg (preferably freshly ground)
The grated rind of 1 orange (optional)

Drain the chopped tomatoes well in a colander set over a
large mixing bowl; measure the tomato juice and discard.
Place tomatoes in a large enamel or stainless steel kettle,
add to them a volume of water equal to the amount of
tomato juice you discarded. Bring mixture to a boil,
drain through a colander, again measuring the juice and
discarding. Return to kettle, once again adding a volume
of water equal to the amount of juices drained off, and
bring to a boil. Repeat once more the draining and scalding process—this will make 3 times in all. Drain tomatoes once again, return to kettle, and add all remaining
ingredients, including the grated orange rind if you like.
Bring slowly to the boil. Adjust heat so that mixture bubbles very gently and cook about 10 minutes, stirring only
if needed to keep mixture from sticking, until clear and
marmalade-like in appearance. Ladle boiling hot mincemeat into hot sterilized pint-size preserving jars, leaving
1 inch of headroom at the top. Screw lids down tightly,
then process jars in a pressure canner at 10 pounds pressure for 25 minutes, following the manufacturer's instructions for your particular pressure canner. After
processing, cool jars to room temperature, then store on
a cool, dry shelf away from light.

Middle Atlantic States

The Farmers' Museum and Village Crossroads
Cooperstown, New York

In 1786, a wealthy lawyer and land speculator named William Cooper obtained a vast green tract of Catskill wilderness. He founded a town there on the shores of Lake Otsego, the better to lure farmers, tradesmen, and craftsmen into the area. And he packed up his own family and moved them from New Jersey to his new village of Cooperstown, the better to keep watch on his holdings.

Few Americans have heard of William Cooper, but his son they know well. He was James Fenimore Cooper.

Young Cooper spent his childhood in manorial splendor at Otsego Hall in Cooperstown and at Fenimore Farm, directly north. He loved the Catskill country, returned to it in 1814 (after sojourns at Yale and at sea), bringing with him his young bride. He retreated to Fenimore Farm for a few years, left, then returned some years later to Cooperstown, and it was here that he began to write the famous *Leatherstocking Tales*, which portray life on the American frontier (two of these books—*The Deerslayer* and *The Pioneers*—are nostalgic journeys to the Cooperstown of his youth).

Cooper deplored the "laceration," as he called it, of the green wilderness by encroaching civilization. So it is ironic, perhaps, that what had once been the Cooper farmstead is today headquarters of the New York State Historical Association, which is re-creating a frontier community reminiscent of Fenimore Cooper's boyhood.

The Catskills, in Cooper's day, were the frontier, and it was to these mountains and lake-dappled valleys that pioneers made their way from New England, carrying on their backs the few crude implements with which they would clear the land and build their homes. It is the story of these rugged pioneers that unfolds at the Farmers' Museum and Village Crossroads, frontier life as it existed between the Revolutionary War and the Civil War. But it is not strictly a man's world that the visitor sees, it is a woman's world, too, for without the frontiersman's wife, the frontier would never have been tamed.

"Man works from sun to sun," the old saying goes, "but woman's work is never done." And never was that fact made more clear than at the Farmers' Museum, where exhibits and demonstrations show how women spun the yarn and wove the cloth, dipped the candles and made the soap, preserved in salt the meat of the animals their husbands had slaughtered, made the sausage and smoked the hams, extracted glue from the animal by-products, dried the fruits and vegetables, and cooked the meals.

The Farmers' Museum provides a glimpse of family life on the frontier, and the Village Crossroads portrays the somewhat more civilized life of the village artisans, tradesmen, and professional men who accompanied the farmers into the wilderness to minister to their needs. It is not a restored village, but an outdoor folk museum. The buildings lined up along the rutted village streets, however, are all genuinely old (as are their furnishings), and all have been moved to Village Crossroads from historic communities within a hundred-mile radius of Cooperstown: the old fieldstone Schoolhouse (1828), the fully stocked Country Store (1820), the two-story stone Blacksmith Shop (1827), still bearing the scars of an early accident (the blacksmith unwittingly dropped a hot iron into a keg of gunpowder), the Druggist's Shop (1832), the Printing Office (1828), the Doctor's Office (1830s), the Lawyer's Office (1829), the Bump Tavern (1796), which is used today for social gatherings just as it was a century and a half ago, the white frame Methodist church (1791), and the red salt box of the Lippitt Homestead (1793). Today, as in the days of Joseph Lippitt, the homestead is a working farm. Cows are fed and milked, chickens and geese and ducks run loose in the barnyard, as does a sentry peacock (the raucous squawk of these birds alerted the pioneer to the presence of interlopers and possible danger). The old Lippitt Homestead kitchen is busy once again as women in period dress prepare hefty farm fare in the old stone fireplace and demonstrate the arts of butter churning and cheese making.

James Fenimore Cooper's presence hovers about Village Crossroads, but nowhere is it more strongly felt than at Fenimore House across the way, where his personal belongings, mementos, and manuscripts are displayed. This is not the original house of Fenimore Farm but a mansion built in the early 1930s by Edward Severin Clark, whose brother, Stephen C. Clark, conceived the idea of the Farmers' Museum and whose art collection forms the basis of that displayed at Fenimore House. Clark maintained that there were only "good art and bad art." He clearly had an eye for "good art," but the collection contains as much folk art as fine art, including as it does everything from toys to trinkets, wood carvings to canvases (two of which are by the late Grandma Moses, who lived near Cooperstown).

The Farmers' Museum and Village Crossroads are no mere showcase of the Catskill frontier. They are, in a way, a time capsule; the Leatherstocking days of Cooper come to life.

The Old Bump Tavern at Cooperstown, with its four columns across the front and its first- and second-story piazzas, looks rather like an antebellum Southern mansion. Something transplanted from the red clay hills of Georgia. But it was built near Ashland, New York, in 1796 to serve travelers making their way along a busy early trail (now Route 23)—ladies, gentlemen, teamsters, drovers, and pioneer families headed west (there were separate public rooms for men and women, as was the custom in those days). Moved piece by piece to Cooperstown in 1952, reassembled and furnished with period antiques, the tavern represents an important phase of early-nineteenth-century American life. Sheep graze on the front lawns as they did a century and a half ago, and on occasion, whenever the Farmers' Museum staff re-creates period dinners, it becomes once again a cheerful, bustling place with candles glowing, fires crackling on the hearths, and delicious aromas issuing from the kitchen. The recipes used for those dinners, three of which are included here, are taken from manuscripts and mid-nineteenth-century cookbooks that exist in the museum collection.

Fried Grated Potatoes

MAKES 4 TO 6 SERVINGS

4 medium-size potatoes, boiled until firm-tender, cooled to
     room temperature, and peeled
1 egg
1 teaspoon salt
⅛ teaspoon freshly ground pepper
6 tablespoons unsalted butter (about)

Grate the potatoes, using the second-coarsest side of a four-sided grater, into a large mixing bowl. In a second, smaller bowl, beat the egg with the salt and pepper until frothy; pour over the potatoes and mix thoroughly. Let stand 10 minutes, then mix well again until mixture clings together (it should not resemble mashed potatoes but rather grated potatoes held together by a thin batter). Heat 4 tablespoons of the butter in a very large, heavy skillet over moderate heat until it froths and bubbles. Drop the potato mixture into the skillet by heaping tablespoonfuls, making 6 large mounds with plenty of space between them. Flatten mounds into cakes with a pancake turner and brown 10 to 12 minutes on each side. Don't turn the cakes until they are quite crispy and brown on the bottom. And turn only once during cooking. The potatoes will absorb the butter as they cook, and after you turn the cakes, you will probably have to add the additional 2 tablespoons of butter. Serve skillet hot as a vegetable or in place of cereal for breakfast, accompanied by fried ham or sausage.

This pudding, made with mashed Irish potatoes, is a dessert—supremely buttery and spicy, and aromatic of brandy, rose water, and lemon. Its texture is moist and velvety, halfway between a soufflé and a steamed pudding. And, like a soufflé, it collapses soon after being taken from the oven. Time the baking carefully so that you can serve the pudding straightaway. It is delicious as is and even better topped with a drizzling of light cream.

Potato Pudding

MAKES 6 TO 8 SERVINGS

3 cups unseasoned mashed potatoes (do not pack into the measure)
1¼ cups unsalted butter, at room temperature
1½ cups sugar
¼ cup rose water (obtainable at food specialty shops and pharmacies)
¼ cup brandy
Finely grated rind of 1 large lemon
Juice of 1 large lemon
1 teaspoon ground cinnamon
½ teaspoon ground mace
¼ teaspoon ground nutmeg
6 large eggs

Place the mashed potatoes in a large, fine-mesh sieve and rub through the sieve, pressing with a wooden spatula or spoon. Let the sieved potatoes fall lightly into a large mixing bowl—do not press or pack them down. When all have been sieved, set aside for the time being. Cream the butter until very light and silvery, then add the sugar gradually, creaming all the while until fluffy. Beat in the rose water, brandy, lemon rind, lemon juice, cinnamon, mace, and nutmeg. Beat the eggs at high speed with an electric mixer until very thick and light— about the consistency of mayonnaise. This will take about 10 minutes of continuous, hard beating. Add the beaten eggs to the creamed butter mixture alternately with the sieved potatoes, beginning and ending with the potatoes and folding in lightly each time with a rubber spatula. Pour pudding into a lightly buttered 2½-quart soufflé dish or straight-sided baking dish and bake, uncovered, in a moderate oven (350°) for 1 to 1½ hours— just until pudding is puffed and brown. When properly done, the pudding should quiver lightly as the baking dish is nudged; it should be neither soupy nor firm. Spoon at once into dessert dishes and top, if you like, with a trickle of light cream. Or pass the cream separately so that everyone can help himself.

A dense, buttery-crumbed cake much like a pound cake. What makes it different are its flavorings: dry white wine, brandy, cinnamon, and nutmeg. In the old days this was known as a "keeping cake," because, snugly wrapped, it kept moist and tender (in cool weather) for about two weeks. It's unlikely, however, that there will be any left to keep at the end of a week, because one helping invites another and another and another.

Washington Cake

MAKES A 10-INCH TUBE CAKE

4 cups sifted all-purpose flour
1 teaspoon baking powder
2 teaspoons ground cinnamon
1 teaspoon ground nutmeg
¼ teaspoon salt
1 pound unsalted butter, at room temperature
3 cups sugar
2 tablespoons dry white wine
2 tablespoons brandy
6 large eggs, at room temperature
1 cup milk, at room temperature

Sift the flour with the baking powder, cinnamon, nutmeg, and salt onto a piece of wax paper and set aside. Cream the butter until very light and silvery, then add the sugar gradually, creaming all the while until fluffy. Stir in the wine and brandy. Beat in the eggs, one at a time, mixing only enough to incorporate. Add the sifted dry ingredients alternately with the milk, beginning and ending with the dry ingredients (it's best to make about four additions of each). Do not beat hard at this point, simply mix as lightly as possible, making sure that no streaks of dry ingredients remain in the batter. Spoon the batter (it will be quite thick) into a well-buttered and floured 10-inch tube pan. Bake in a moderately slow oven (325°) for about 1 hour and 25 to 30 minutes or until cake begins to pull from sides of pan, is lightly browned on top, and a finger, pressed lightly into the cake, leaves an imprint that vanishes slowly. Remove cake from oven and cool upright in its pan on a wire cake rack for 10 minutes (it will fall slightly, but that is what accounts for the fine, dense texture). With a thin-blade spatula, loosen cake around edges of pan and around the central tube. Place a large cake plate on top of pan, invert and turn cake out. Let cool to room temperature before serving. And cut the slices thin—the cake is unusually rich.

Old Bethpage Village Restoration
Old Bethpage, Long Island

*I*n the middle of Long Island, surrounded by a tangle
of expressways and acres of tract houses, stands Old
Bethpage, an eighteenth- and nineteenth-century country
village. Except for a distant radar tower and an occasional jet whizzing by, Old Bethpage is so removed from
the twentieth century that to stroll through it is to forget
smog and horns honking and endless asphalt shopping
centers. It is to forget, too, that Manhattan lies just
thirty-seven miles away.

Sturdy wood-shingled and clapboard houses square
up along old plank roads; a blacksmith shop; a simple
white house in the Greek Revival style where Walt
Whitman is said to have lived; a general store piled high
with tin horns, china dolls, and penny candies; a seed
and feed store where Theodore Roosevelt traded; a tai-
lor's shop, a cobbler's, and a carpenter's; a farm where
horses, cows, and sheep graze peacefully around a duck
pond; an inn where two cents of Old Bethpage currency
will buy a fizzing glass of birch beer and a pretzel.

There was no Old Bethpage on Old Long Island. It is
a re-created village—but its buildings are all genuinely
old, rescued from the path of oncoming bulldozers by
history-minded citizens. The purpose of Old Bethpage is
to preserve not only Long Island's early Dutch and Eng-

lish heritage but also a swatch of the pastoral Long Island that was, to interest today's city-bred generation in yesterday's country-bred.

Old Bethpage is no stage-set village. It is a working farm community comprised of some 224 acres and twenty eighteenth- and nineteenth-century buildings, all meticulously renovated and furnished with museum-piece furniture. There are cows, not for local color, but for milk, cream, butter, and cheese; there are hogs (for ham, bacon, and sausage), laying hens, vegetable gardens, and orchards. There are sausage-making demonstrations, lessons in butter churning, ham curing, preserving, and pickling. And there are artisans at work, dipping candles, embroidering, and tailoring.

Families arrive by the carload to watch farm hands at work, to sample ginger cookies from the old brick oven, to help, perhaps, with the jam or jelly making, to hitch a ride atop a hayrack or, if there is new-fallen snow, in a horse-drawn sleigh. They come, in short, to discover the old-fashioned joys of a day in the country.

The Conklin House, built in 1820 and restored in 1850, was moved overland to Old Bethpage from the Village of the Branch in Smithtown. It had been the home of Long Island's stagecoach drivers and is thought to have been where Walt Whitman lived while a teacher at Smithtown. This scallop chowder, named for the Conklin House, is an old Long Island favorite. To make it, you need tiny, sweet fresh bay scallops. Take care that the chowder *never* boils, only ripples gently so that the scallops will be meltingly tender.

Conklin House Scallop Chowder

MAKES 6 TO 8 SERVINGS

2 cups water
1½ teaspoons salt

¼ cup butter
2 small yellow onions, peeled and sliced paper thin
1 pound small fresh bay scallops
1 cup finely diced potatoes
1 quart milk
⅛ teaspoon white pepper

Bring the water and salt to a boil in a large saucepan, turn heat down so that the water simmers, and let stand while you sauté the onions. Melt butter in a large, heavy skillet, add onions and sauté just 5 minutes. Transfer with a slotted spoon to a plate and reserve. Add scallops to skillet and sauté, stirring gently, just 5 minutes, until the juices run out. Add scallops, onions, and potatoes to the simmering water, cover, and simmer very gently 30 minutes. Add the milk and pepper and heat, uncovered, just to serving temperature—do not let the chowder boil or the scallops will toughen. Ladle into heated soup bowls and serve with plenty of crisp, salty crackers.

Old Bethpage Village Restoration sprawls over much of what had been the Powell Farm in the rolling midlands of Long Island. The weathered, shake-covered Powell House, built in 1850, remains in its original site, and the farm, today as yesterday, is a general working farm where livestock, poultry, fruits, and vegetables are raised. The following recipe, an old favorite, uses apples and pork produced on the farm.

Powell House Apple-Smothered Pork Chops

MAKES 6 SERVINGS

6 loin pork chops, cut 1 inch thick
¾ teaspoon salt
1 teaspoon rubbed sage
3 tablespoons pork chop drippings (add bacon drippings, if needed, to total 3 tablespoons)

3 tablespoons flour
2 cups hot water
3 tablespoons molasses
1 tablespoon cider vinegar
½ cup seedless raisins
3 tart cooking apples, peeled, cored, and sliced into rings
    about ½ inch thick

Rub both sides of pork chops with salt (using about ¼ teaspoon) and with all of the sage. Brown chops on both sides in a large, heavy skillet over high heat, then remove from pan. Measure drippings and, if necessary, add enough bacon drippings to total 3 tablespoons. Return drippings to skillet, blend in flour, then add hot water and cook and stir over moderate heat until thickened and smooth. Stir in molasses, vinegar, raisins, and remaining 1/2 teaspoon of salt. Place the chops back in the skillet, pushing them down in the gravy and spooning some of the raisins up on top. Lay apple rings over the chops, cover skillet, and simmer slowly ¾ to 1 hour until chops are tender and cooked through (make a tiny slit near the bone of one chop, and if no pink shows in the meat, the chops are done). Serve the chops topped with apples and a generous ladling of the raisin gravy.

Cookbooks today tell you that duckling is very fat, that it doesn't need to be basted, that it is best stuffed with tart fruits, if at all, and that the duck drippings are fit only for greasing your boots. This Old Bethpage recipe for roast duckling seems to break all the rules, but the results prove that early Long Island cooks knew what they were about—the duckling skin is light and crisp, the meat juicy straight through to the bone, the bread stuffing fluffy and light, and the gravy, made of chopped giblets and pan drippings, not the least bit greasy.

Long Island Roast Duckling with Sage-Bread Stuffing and Giblet Gravy

MAKES 2 TO 3 SERVINGS

1 duckling (fresh or thawed frozen) weighing 4½ to 5 pounds
Salt
Pepper
1 cup water
2 tablespoons butter

Bread Stuffing:
4 cups fairly fine soft white bread crumbs
1½ teaspoons rubbed sage
¼ teaspoon salt
⅛ teaspoon pepper
⅔ cup cold water
⅓ cup melted butter

Giblet Gravy:
3 tablespoons duckling drippings
3 tablespoons flour
1⅓ cups water or milk
The cooked duckling giblets, chopped
Salt and pepper to season

Remove the giblets from the duckling and lay in the bottom of a large, shallow roasting pan. Sprinkle the cavity of the duckling lightly with salt and pepper.

Prepare the stuffing: Place the bread crumbs in a large bowl; add sage, salt, and pepper and toss to mix. Scatter the cold water over the top, a little at a time, tossing all the while with a fork. The point, simply, is to moisten the crumbs uniformly. Add the butter and toss again. Drop the stuffing loosely into the body cavity of the duckling, then skewer and lace the opening shut. Place duckling breast side up on a rack in the roasting pan, pour in the 1 cup water and add the 2 tablespoons of butter. Roast, uncovered, in a moderately hot oven (375°) 1 hour, basting frequently with pan juices. Remove the giblets from the pan, chop fairly fine, and set aside.

Continue roasting the duckling, basting often, about 1 to 1½ hours longer until crisp and brown and you can move the drumstick easily in its hip socket. Let duckling stand at room temperature 10 minutes.

Make the gravy: Spoon 3 tablespoons of the duckling drippings (including as many browned bits as possible) into a small saucepan and blend in the flour. Set over moderate heat, add the water or milk, and heat and stir until thickened and smooth and no raw taste of flour remains, about 5 minutes. Add chopped giblets, salt and pepper to taste, then heat and stir 1 to 2 minutes longer. Remove skewers and lacing from duckling, place on a heated platter, and serve. Pass the gravy separately.

Women wearing nineteenth-century calico farm dresses scurry about the big country kitchen of the Powell House every day, firing up the old brick oven and mixing together dough for the cookies they will pass out later in the day to school children touring Old Bethpage. These crispy ginger rounds never fail to make a hit.

Brick-Oven Ginger Cookies

MAKES ABOUT 3½ DOZEN COOKIES

¾ cup butter or shortening
1 cup sugar
¼ cup molasses
1 egg
2 cups sifted flour
2 teaspoons baking soda
1 teaspoon ground ginger
1 teaspoon ground cinnamon
½ teaspoon salt

Cream together well the butter or shortening, sugar, and molasses; beat in the egg. Sift the flour with the soda, spices, and salt and stir into the creamed mixture. Chill dough until firm enough to shape. With your hands, pinch off bits of dough and roll into small balls about the size of walnuts. Roll balls in granulated sugar, place about 2 inches apart on greased baking sheets and bake in a moderate oven (350°) 12 to 15 minutes until nicely browned around the edges (the balls will flatten out as they bake). With a spatula, lift cookies to wire racks to cool.

The Deserted Village at Allaire
New Jersey

"**D**eserted" is not quite the right word, for Allaire today, after years of neglect, is coming alive again, thanks to a new master plan to restore it to its mid-nineteenth-century heyday. This historic village, buried in the Pine Barrens of northeastern New Jersey, boomed and died with the bog iron industry. It was a mill town, an iron town, where at the Howell Works, tons of pig iron were produced between 1822 and 1846 for James P. Allaire's foundry in New York City, the foundry that cast the brass air chamber for Robert Fulton's famous steamboat *Clermont*, as well as the cylinder for the *Savannah*, the first American steamship to cross the Atlantic.

Like many isolated New Jersey towns, Allaire was largely self-sufficient. The Ironworks, of course, were the core of the town, but there were farms here, too, producing food for the community, there were the row houses where the married foundry workers lived with their families, the Foreman's Cottage, the village Church (its bell cast at the foundry with a few gold coins fused in so that the bell would always ring true), the village Bakery, a sawmill and gristmill, the Blacksmith Shop, the General Store (an early three-story shopping center where townspeople could buy everything from food to furnishings to fabrics), a carpenter's shop, an enameling furnace (where the iron cookware cast at Allaire was enameled), a carriage house, and the homestead where James Allaire stayed on his frequent visits to the village.

A *Gazetteer of the State of New Jersey*, published in 1834, provides a clear picture of what early Allaire was like, as well as the Pine Barrens in which it nestled:

> ... west of the marsh which girds the seashore, lies an immense sandy plain, scarce broken by any inequalities and originally covered by a pine and shrub-oak forest—a great portion of which has been once, and some of it twice, cut over. There are many square miles on which there is not a human inhabitant, and where the deer, foxes, and rabbits are abundant, and the wolf and bear find a lair to protect their race from expiration. But in many places the echo is awakened by the woodsman's axe, the louder din of the forge hammer, and the forest glares with the light of the furnace or glass house.

That was the way it was when Allaire, known then simply as the Howell Works, was flourishing. But within less than twenty years, the works had been shut down (America's westward push had unearthed richer stores of higher-grade iron ore, which destroyed the bog iron industry), and bit by bit, the town began to die. Allaire himself died in 1858, but his unmarried son lived on in seclusion in what was fast becoming a ghost town.

Gustav Kobbé portrays that ghost town in his book *Jersey Coast and Pines*, published in 1889:

> Except for the settlements along the railroad, the forest is broken only by a few lonely roads—almost abandoned old-time stage routes and lumber tracks; by narrow, swift, resinous-colored streams flowing silently through the colonnades of pines, or the gloomy labyrinths of cedar swamps,

toward the system of bays to the east or toward Delaware Bay; or by deserted, decaying shanties, grouped around the ruins of the forges which this region harbored in the days long since passed, when the manufacture of iron from bog ore was one of the most important industries in the country. The most extensive and picturesque ruins of this kind are at Allaire, where the only stack still standing among the Pines may be seen—a pathetic reminder of the spirit of enterprise which created the place and of the activity whose sounds once echoed through the now silent forests.

The forests are not so silent today. Nor is Allaire a forgotten town, moldering in the Pine Barrens. Two of the old row houses have been restored. So, too, have the Foreman's Cottage (it is today a Post Office), the village Church (where services are held in summer), the Bakery (where old-fashioned breads, cakes, and cookies are sold), the Farm House (with an herb garden at the kitchen door), the Blacksmith Shop (its iron lintels cast at the old foundry), the General Store (fully stocked with merchandise reminiscent of the 1830s), the Carpenter Shop (where a craftsman works today), the Enameling Furnace (now a museum), a barn, the Carriage House (which houses a collection of early wagons, traps, and sleighs).

Restoration continues, but enough of old Allaire has already been revitalized to provide an in-depth look at one of America's early industrial towns, which like so many others, felt a brief flush of prosperity, then perished.

In order to raise funds for the continuing restoration of the Deserted Village at Allaire, the Allaire Village Auxiliary has put together a small spiral-bound cookbook, *The Calico Cooks* (so named because Auxiliary women, like their Allaire antecedents, wear simple calico costumes as they go about re-creating dozens of fascinating and unusual recipes, among them receipts and home remedies for the homemaker of 1822. "Here," the Auxiliary women note in their Introduction, "you are on your own because the old receipts are untested." For this cookbook, however, they have been tested, updated, and, whenever necessary, adapted to today's terms and techniques. And very good they are, too. We make no such claims for the home remedies and offer them only because they, too, suggest what life was like in the Jersey Barrens a hundred and fifty years ago.

Fresh Corn and Mushrooms in Cream

MAKES 6 SERVINGS

6 large ears of sweet corn, husked
4 tablespoons butter
1 medium-size yellow onion, peeled and chopped fine
½ pound fresh mushrooms, wiped clean and coarsely chopped
1 cup light cream
1 teaspoon salt (about)
¼ teaspoon freshly ground pepper

Cut the kernels from the ears of corn and set aside (to do this, simply cut straight down along the cob with a sharp knife, freeing the kernels). Melt the butter in a large, heavy skillet over moderate heat, add the onion and sauté about 5 minutes until limp and pale golden but not brown. Add the mushrooms and continue sautéing for another 5 minutes, until mushrooms begin to give out their juices. Add the corn, cream, salt, and pepper, cover, turn heat to low, and simmer slowly 40 to 45 minutes until corn is tender and no longer has a raw taste. You'll have to check the skillet occasionally and stir the mixture now and then. If it seems to be cooking too dry (and it shouldn't if you keep the heat very low), add a little more cream. Just before serving, taste for salt and add a bit more if needed. Serve piping hot.

Somewhat like a baked coleslaw, but without the vinegary tartness.

1820s Water Ice Lemon

Creamy Baked Shredded Cabbage

MAKES 4 SERVINGS

4 cups moderately coarsely shredded cabbage (use the second
    coarsest side of a four-sided grater)
1 egg, lightly beaten
½ cup light cream or milk
1 tablespoon melted butter
2 teaspoons sugar
1 teaspoon salt
½ teaspoon celery seeds
¼ teaspoon ground nutmeg (preferably freshly ground)
⅛ teaspoon freshly ground pepper

Place the cabbage in a medium-size mixing bowl, add all remaining ingredients, and toss well to mix. Pour into a well-buttered 1-quart casserole, cover, and bake in a moderate oven (350°) 40 to 45 minutes or until bubbly and cream mixture seems to have set softly, rather like a stirred custard. Serve oven-hot.

Halve this recipe if your freezer space is limited. If not, make up the full amount and keep on hand to enjoy during a hot spell in summer.

1820s Water Ice Lemon

MAKES 12 TO 14 SERVINGS

3 cups boiling water
2½ cups sugar
Juice of 5 large lemons
Finely grated rind of 1 large lemon

6 cups ice water

½ teaspoon rose water (obtainable at specialty food shops and also at many pharmacies; if you are unable to find rose water, simply leave it out of the recipe)

¼ teaspoon vanilla

1 cup egg whites

Mix the boiling water and sugar in a large, heavy saucepan, set over high heat, and boil, uncovered, without stirring, 10 minutes. Meanwhile, combine the lemon juice, lemon rind, ice water, rose water, and vanilla in a very large heatproof mixing bowl. When the sugar syrup has boiled 10 minutes, stir into the lemon juice mixture. Beat the egg whites until they form soft peaks, then beat into the lemon mixture. It will be impossible to incorporate them completely because the beaten egg whites are so much lighter than the lemon mixture—no matter, they will be beaten in after the mixture has partially frozen. Pour into two large shallow pans (the 13 × 9 ×2-inch baking pan is a good size), set in freezer, and freeze until mushy—about 1½ to 2 hours. Empty contents of one pan into your largest electric mixer bowl, then beat with the mixer at high speed until uniformly light and fluffy. Pack into freezer cartons and return to freezer. Repeat with remaining pan of water ice lemon. Freeze until firm. When serving, scrape a tablespoon over surface of ice lemon, shaving it up in frothy crystals, rather than digging in with the spoon and scooping out big chunks. Mound up in dessert dishes and serve.

Some Old Allaire Home Remedies

TO PREVENT MORTIFICATION: Make a poultice of elder blows and biscuits.

CURE FOR THE LOVE OF LIQUOR: Take one orange a half hour before breakfast. Avoid places where spirits are sold.

SHRUB FOR THE SICK: One sour (lemon), two sweet (sugar), three strong (rum), four weak (water).

TO CURE A TOOTHACHE: Hops steeped in water or a bag of ashes applied to the cheek.

TO CURE NERVOUS HEADACHE: A ground mustard poultice applied to the back of the neck between the shoulders.

FOR A BEE STING: Hartshorn or salt moistened in water.

Historic Fallsington and Pennsbury Manor
Pennsylvania

"*T*he Green Towne," is what William Penn called Historic Fallsington in Bucks County, Pennsylvania. His own home, Pennsbury Manor, lay just four miles away on a knoll overlooking the Delaware River, and it was to Fallsington that Penn rode to attend Quaker meetings.

Today Historic Fallsington calls itself "the town that time forgot." It is an apt description, for if you should swerve off southbound U.S. 1 in the vicinity of Trenton, New Jersey, cross the Delaware, and pull into Meeting House Square at Fallsington, you sense that you are not merely a few miles off course but several hundred years as well. For here, within the shadow of that twentieth-century sprawl of tract houses called Levittown, stands this tiny historic village, looking very much as it did in William Penn's day. Here, under the giant sycamores and elms of Main Street and Yardley Avenue nestle some fifteen historic homes and buildings, a three-hundred-year short course in Pennsylvania arts and architecture.

Fallsington's most historic building is the Moon-Williamson House, a log cabin built in 1685 and one of the oldest homes in Pennsylvania still standing on its original site. It is the prototype of the log cabin that pioneers built on their treks west, the very symbol, in fact, of the American frontier. But the log cabin, historians tell us, was introduced to America by Swedes who had settled in the Delaware River valley in the mid-seventeenth century. The English colonists never built such cabins, as the crude wigwams and wooden structures at Pioneers' Village in Salem and Plimoth Plantation prove. The Swedish log cabins proved infinitely superior—sturdier, snugger in winter, more comfortable and spacious, which is why they were quickly adopted by the pioneers.

What is remarkable about Historic Fallsington—in addition to the fact that it lies hidden at the heart of a megalopolitan maze—is that it has been preserved and restored solely through the efforts of its history-minded citizens. There were no fat grants given to Fallsington—by the federal government or by philanthropic millionaires. It has all been salvaged by Fallsington residents, friends, and neighbors. It is the result of considerable labor and love.

The restoration began in 1953, when the Burges-Lippincott House (1780) was put up for sale. When it appeared that prospective buyers were more interested in destroying the house than in preserving it, a group of concerned citizens rallied. They formed Historic Fallsington, Inc., a nonprofit organization, bought the old two-story Pennsylvania fieldstone house, and set about the task of restoring it (its carved doorway is considered the most beautiful in Bucks County and its carved fireplace and stairway rare examples of eighteenth-century design and craftsmanship).

Today five other historic buildings have been acquired by Historic Fallsington, Inc., restored and opened to the public: the Moon-Williamson log cabin described earlier; the Gambrel Roof House, erected in 1728 as a meeting house when the earlier house where William Penn had worshiped became too small for its congregation; the Stage Coach Tavern (1798), once a busy way station for farmers on their way to the Delaware River wharves with wagonloads of produce; the Gillingham Store (early nineteenth century); and the Schoolmaster's House

(1758), where two hundred years ago Quaker children—girls as well as boys—were schooled.

In addition to these buildings owned and operated by Historic Fallsington, Inc., the town is filled with privately owned historic buildings, some of which are opened to the public during such special occasions as Fallsington Day, a colonial country fair held each autumn to raise funds for the continuing preservation. It's a merry time for all, but it's an educational time, too, for demonstrations are given in colonial cooking, arts, and crafts. Volunteers don period dress and Historic Fallsington slips nearly three hundred years back in time to 1683, when William Penn's followers and friends established their town "commencing at the meeting of the Falls."

The town so struck William Penn's fancy that he chose to build his own plantation nearby. Pennsbury Manor, he called it, and it has been reconstructed today on forty acres of the original estate that Penn bought from the Indians in 1682. It is a remarkable home for so early a period in American history, a stately mansion combining Georgian elegance with Quaker simplicity.

Like Historic Fallsington, Pennsbury Manor is open to the public, and the two, neighbors today as they were three hundred years ago, preserve for America the Pennsylvania of William Penn, "the ideal American state," according to the eminent nineteenth-century American historian, Henry Adams. "Easy, tolerant, and contented."

Through the painstaking research of Evelyn Abraham Benson, the "cooking recipes of William Penn's Wife Gulielma" have been assembled in a facsimile edition titled *Penn Family Recipes*, which is offered for sale at the restored family home, Pennsbury Manor on the Delaware River. A manuscript copy of the recipes, brought from England to America, was discovered recently among the Penn family papers, and it is these that are printed in Guli Penn's own quaint words and misspellings. Here, then, are two of the 144 collected recipes, set down first as Guli Penn wrote them, then in modern-day terms for modern-day cooks who may have difficulty following the seventeenth-century directions. Both recipes are surprisingly elegant and as sophisticated as any twentieth-century ways to prepare veal or chicken. Judging from the book, William Penn ate very well indeed.

A White Fancy of Veall (Guli Penn's Version)

Take youre velle and
Cutt it in Indiferent thin peces,
Chop it a Little
Dredge it well with flouer,
then fry it with butter brownish
then putt a Littell weke broath
which you may stew it in a prity while,
then beat the yeolks of 4 eggs
4 or 5 spunfulls of thick Creme
and a Littell nutmeg.
when it is well beaten putt it too the fregasy,
and shake it well over the fire with a bitt of butter
you may lard the velle if you plese—

A White Fancy of Veal (Modern Version)

MAKES 2 TO 4 SERVINGS

1 pound veal scallops, pounded thin as for scaloppine
½ teaspoon salt (about)
¼ teaspoon pepper (about)
¼ cup flour (about)
4 tablespoons unsalted butter
½ cup chicken broth
2 egg yolks
¾ cup light or heavy cream
⅛ teaspoon nutmeg

Sprinkle scallops lightly on both sides with salt and pepper, then rub both sides with flour. Cut the scallops into pieces 2 to 3 inches wide. Melt 3 tablespoons of the butter in a very large, heavy skillet, and when it begins to bubble and brown, add veal and brown quickly on both sides. Remove veal to a large plate, cover with foil, and set in a warm oven. Add broth to skillet and heat and stir, scraping up browned bits from bottom of skillet. Beat egg yolks with cream and nutmeg until frothy, then slowly pour in hot skillet mixture, stirring all the while. Return to skillet, add remaining tablespoon of butter, set over *lowest* heat, and cook and stir until thickened— about the consistency of thin gravy. Have patience, this will take 10 to 12 minutes. Don't rush the process and don't, at any time, let the sauce boil or it will curdle. Return veal to skillet and heat about 1 minute longer, basting with the sauce. Serve at once.

Too Make a Fregasy of Chicken
(Guli Penn's Version)

Take your chicken flea [flay] them and
Cutt them in peces
and boyle them gently in butter
with a bunch of sweet herbs,
after they have bin a prittey while in,
putt some good broth to them,
and when allmost enough, a gill of white wine
then take the yeolks of 4 or 5 eggs,
and sum shred parsley
½ a nutmeg grated
and sum juce of Lemon
and if you have not that 2 or 3 spunfulls of vinegar
beate them well together,
and when the other is enough, put this to it
sturing it up and downe together a Littell while
you may putt mushrons to it, and slised Lemon,
this is for 4 Littell biskets
putt a bitt or 2 of butter too the eggs and

other things
when you mix them together—

A Fricassee of Chicken (Modern Version)

MAKES 4 SERVINGS

1 broiler-fryer (about 3½ pounds), cut up for frying
4 tablespoons unsalted butter
½ pound mushrooms, wiped clean and sliced thin
½ teaspoon leaf marjoram, crumbled
¼ teaspoon leaf thyme, crumbled
¼ teaspoon ground nutmeg (preferably freshly ground)
Finely grated rind of ½ lemon
2 cups chicken broth
½ cup dry white wine
2 tablespoons minced parsley
Juice of ½ lemon
⅛ teaspoon freshly ground pepper
5 egg yolks, lightly beaten

Brown the pieces of chicken well on all sides in the butter in a large, heavy Dutch-oven type kettle. Push the chicken to one side, add the mushrooms and brown, about 10 minutes. Add the marjoram, thyme, nutmeg, grated lemon rind, chicken broth, and wine, cover, and simmer gently for 40 to 45 minutes or until you can pierce the chicken easily with a fork. Remove pieces of chicken to a warmed plate, cover loosely, and keep warm while preparing the sauce. Add parsley, lemon juice, and pepper to kettle liquid and boil, uncovered, 10 minutes to reduce slightly. Turn heat under kettle to lowest point. Briskly stir a little of the hot kettle liquid into the beaten egg yolks, then stir back into kettle and heat, whisking vigorously about 1 minute until thickened—sauce should be about the consistency of gravy. Do not at any time allow sauce to boil or it will curdle. Return pieces of chicken to kettle, spooning sauce over them, then dish up on a heated platter and garnish, if you like, with slices of lemon and ruffs of parsley.

Apples were the fruit early Pennsylvania colonists prized most, and they learned to prepare them in dozens of ways. Hot mulled cider was a great favorite at Historic Fallsington, as was this Apple Pandowdy.

Apple Pandowdy

MAKES 6 SERVINGS

5 cups peeled, cored, and sliced tart apples (about 5 medium-size apples)
½ cup firmly packed light brown sugar
¼ teaspoon ground cinnamon
¼ teaspoon ground nutmeg (preferably freshly ground)

Batter:
1¼ cups sifted all-purpose flour
1½ teaspoons baking powder
¼ teaspoon salt
⅛ teaspoon ground nutmeg
⅔ cup unsalted butter
⅓ cup sugar
1 egg
½ cup milk

Place the sliced apples in a well-buttered 2-quart baking dish. Mix brown sugar with cinnamon and nutmeg and sprinkle on top of the apples. Toss lightly. Bake, uncovered, in a moderate oven (350°) 30 to 35 minutes until apples are soft, stirring once or twice. For the batter (and begin this about 10 minutes before the apples are done), sift the flour with the baking powder, salt, and nutmeg onto a piece of wax paper and set aside. Cream the butter and sugar until fluffy, then beat in the egg. Add the sifted dry ingredients alternately with the milk, beginning and ending with the dry ingredients. Spread the batter evenly on top of the cooked apples, return to the oven (still at 350°), and bake, uncovered, 35 to 40 minutes longer until the cake topping is nicely browned and begins to pull from sides of baking dish. Let stand at room temperature about 5 minutes before serving. Spoon into dessert bowls and, if you like, pass rich, thick cream for those who would like it poured over their apple pandowdy.

Some Old Home Remedies from Historic Fallsington

FROSTED FEET: Scrape 1 turnip into a teacup of lard. Let it stew slowly on the back of the stove for 24 hours. Strain out the turnip, let the lard cool and apply at night before retiring.

LOCK JAW: Hold the wound in smoke from burning woollen rags.

INFLAMED EYES: Apply raw oyster, raw beef, or tea grounds.

CATARRH ON THE BREAST: Make a tar plaster—equal parts of tar, tallow and beeswax.

Pennsylvania Farm Museum of Landis Valley

Lancaster, Pennsylvania

It's a kindly, softly country there, back of Philadelphia among the German towns, Lancaster way. Little houses and bursting big farms, fat cattle, fat women, and all as peaceful as Heaven might be if they farmed there.

*T*hus wrote Rudyard Kipling of the Pennsylvania Dutch Country, which remains today one of the most colorful corners of America. The Amish do still bounce about the back roads in their gray buggies, the Mennonites in their black buggies. But progress threatens to crowd them out. Turnpikes and freeways have been hurled across their countryside, industries are churning fumes into the air, and the bucolic days of Lancaster, Berks, and Lebanon Counties may be numbered.

Except at the Pennsylvania Farm Museum of Landis Valley, where two centuries of Pennsylvania farm life and folk art have been compressed into one hundred acres and some two dozen re-created and restored buildings. Life moves at a leisurely pace here: bread is set to "proof" in the Tavern Kitchen, corn to parch in the Settler's Cabin. Spinning wheels whir in the Red Barn, looms thump. In the fields, a Conestoga lumbers along, drawn by six fine Belgian horses, their harnesses jingling with bells. This is the Pennsylvania of the early Pennsylvania Dutch and Scotch-Irish who molded the land and the life style.

This museum village, like others elsewhere in America, began with a collection. In this case, the collection of two bachelor brothers, George Diller Landis and Henry Kinzer Landis, who as boys in the 1880s began gathering birds' eggs, Indian relics, and minerals around the family farm. As the two grew older, their interest in collecting intensified and expanded to include guns, hand-crafted furniture of the Pennsylvania Dutch, hand-thrown pottery, toleware, (painted tin), pewter, china, coverlets, and quilts. By 1925 the Landis collection numbered some quarter million pieces representative of early Pennsylvania rural life, domestic arts and crafts. To house them, the Landis Valley Museum was set up, and later helped along by funds from the Oberlaender Trust. After the liquidation of that trust in the early 1950s, the Pennsylvania Historical and Museum Commission took over, establishing the Pennsylvania Farm Museum of Landis Valley, restoring more of the original buildings, and trucking others in from nearby towns.

To visit Landis Valley today is not to peer into an endless succession of museum cases. It is to slip into eighteenth- and nineteenth-century Pennsylvania. To sample a cookie or cake at the Tavern, to see herbs grown and dried, to see flax retted in the fields, to watch rugs grow inch by inch on the broadlooms, to poke about the country store and buy a sack of penny candy. But most important, perhaps, it is to tour the Landis Homestead (circa 1870) where two small boys, squirreling away the curiosities of childhood, began what is now considered the nation's finest collection of early Pennsylvania implements, arms, and artifacts.

The Tavern is what visitors are apt to remember about the Pennsylvania Farm Museum of Landis Valley, for it is here, in the brick-paved kitchen, that baking is done and here, too, that samples are laid out on an early stretcher-base pine tavern table set with pewter. It is brick-oven baking at its best (the oven is set inside a walk-in size fireplace of roughhewn stone). The recipes used are those of the early Pennsylvania Dutch (German) settlers: a dark, moist Shoo-Fly Cake made without eggs, Nothing Crumb Cake, Soft Sugar Cookies. Here, too, you might find a big kettle of Potpie (Chicken-Noodle Stew) bubbling away over a crackling fire or a black iron pot of corn meal mush. The Tavern Kitchen is not only a showcase for the art of Pennsylvania Dutch cooking, but also for such early implements of fireplace and brick-oven cookery as cranes and trammels, chestnut and coffee roasters, waffle irons and pierced ladles, redware (glazed earthenware baking molds) and tinware.

Potpie

MAKES 8 TO 10 SERVINGS

1 stewing hen (about 4 pounds), disjointed
10 cups water
2 teaspoons salt
⅛ teaspoon pepper
⅛ teaspoon saffron strands, crushed
5 small potatoes, peeled and halved

Potpie (Egg Noodle Squares):
2 eggs
2 tablespoons vegetable oil
2 cups sifted all-purpose flour
¼ teaspoon salt
2 tablespoons water (about)

Place chicken, neck, and giblets in a large, heavy kettle, add water, salt, pepper, and saffron, and bring to a rolling boil. Adjust heat so that liquid bubbles gently, cover, and cook 1 to 1½ hours until chicken is very tender. Remove chicken pieces from broth; discard neck. Add potatoes to kettle, cover, and simmer while preparing chicken. Remove skin from chicken and discard. Cut meat in bite-size chunks and return to kettle.

To make the potpie: Combine eggs and oil; place flour

and salt in a large bowl. Add egg mixture and work together with one hand (mixture is very sticky so keep one hand free). Then add water, a tablespoon at a time, to form a very stiff dough—about like piecrust. Roll out ⅛ inch thick on a lightly floured board or pastry cloth, then cut in 2-inch squares. Drop potpie, one at a time, into boiling chicken broth so that they do not stick together. When all have been added, cover kettle and boil gently 30 to 40 minutes until potpie and potatoes are tender. Ladle into large soup bowls and serve, garnishing, if you like, with fresh minced parsley.

Potato filling is a thrifty combination of potatoes and stale bread used by the Pennsylvania Dutch to stuff fowl. It is such a favorite that it is also simply baked in a casserole and served as an accompaniment to meat. This is the version prepared at the Pennsylvania Farm Museum.

Potato Filling

MAKES 6 TO 8 SERVINGS

2 quarts peeled, cubed raw potatoes (about 12 medium-size
    potatoes)
1 quart water
1½ teaspoons salt
¼ pound butter
½ cup finely chopped onion
1 cup finely diced celery
½ to 1 cup milk
6 slices stale bread, broken into small pieces
2 eggs
Pinch of powdered sage (or more if you like the flavor of sage)

Place potatoes, water, and 1 teaspoon of the salt in a large saucepan, bring to a boil, cover, and cook until potatoes are tender, 15 to 20 minutes. While potatoes cook, melt butter in a small skillet, add onion and celery and let sauté slowly, stirring now and then (they will be ready about the time the potatoes are done). Drain potatoes, then mash well with a potato masher, adding enough milk to make them creamy. Mix in onion, celery, and any butter in pan, the remaining ½ teaspoon salt and the bread. Stir in eggs, one at a time, then season to taste with sage. Spoon into a buttered 2-quart casserole and bake, uncovered, 35 to 40 minutes in a moderate oven (350°) until tipped with brown.

The Pennsylvania Dutch are as apt to make apple pies with *schnitz* (dried apples) as with fresh apples, and the pies have an altogether different flavor and texture. The filling is softer, somewhat like applesauce, tarter, and of a rich butterscotch color. At the Pennsylvania Farm Museum women demonstrate, on occasion, the schnitzing of apples, and for those who would like to try their own hands at it at home, they hand out these printed instructions to visitors.

HOW TO DRY APPLES

Select only good solid apples. We prefer a good hard winter apple such as a McIntosh. Pare quarters and slice about ⅛-inch thick. Lay on cookie sheets on which a clean towel has been placed. They may be dried in any clean airy room or close to heat. They need not be oven dried.

NOTE: Oven drying, however, is one of the quickest and easiest ways to schnitz apples, provided that you have an oven that will maintain a very low "keep-warm" temperature of about 175°F. Quarter the apples, pare and core each quarter, then slice ⅛ inch thick. Spread apple slices out in a single layer on cookie sheets lined with clean dish towels, place in a 175° oven, and let stand until apples are crisp and pale tan. The drying will take about 16 to 20 hours—easily done overnight and during the following morning. As for yield, 1 medium-size apple (McIntosh or Rhode Island Greening) will provide about ½ cup of schnitz, 1 large apple (Newton Pippin, Rome Beauty, or Red Delicious) about ¾ cup of schnitz. Once the apples are dried, bundle into plastic bags and store in a cool, dry place or, if you prefer, in the freezer.

Schnitz Pie (Dried Sour Apple Pie)

MAKES A DOUBLE-CRUST 9-INCH PIE

Schnitz Filling:
1 quart schnitz (dried, sliced sour apples)
1 quart water
Juice of ½ lemon
1 cup sugar
1 tablespoon cornstarch
1 tablespoon butter

Crust:
2¼ cups sifted all-purpose flour
¾ teaspoon salt
½ cup lard (not vegetable shortening)
⅓ cup cold water (about)

Prepare the filling first so that it will have time to cool and thicken up slightly before it is ladled into the piecrust. Simmer schnitz in the water in a covered saucepan 25 to 30 minutes until apple slices are tender but not mushy; add lemon juice. Blend about 2 tablespoons of the sugar with the cornstarch, then add to schnitz along with remaining sugar; heat and stir until mixture thickens and turns clear, 2 to 3 minutes. Remove from heat, stir in butter, and cool to room temperature.

Meanwhile, prepare the crust: Place flour and salt in a large mixing bowl, then cut in lard until mixture is crumbly and about the texture of uncooked oatmeal. Add water, about a tablespoon at a time, tossing with a fork, just until mixture holds together. Divide pastry in half. Roll one half on a lightly floured board or pastry cloth into a circle about 12 inches in diameter. Lay rolling pin across center of pastry, gently fold half of pastry circle over rolling pin, and ease pastry into a 9-inch pan; press pastry lightly over bottom and up sides. Roll remaining pastry into an 11-inch circle. Spoon cooled schnitz mixture into pastry-lined pan, mounding it up in the center slightly. Ease top crust into place, then trim top-and-bottom-crust overhang so that it is about 1 inch larger than piepan. Roll overhang up and over onto rim, then crimp into a high fluted edge. Make decorative slashes or steam vents in the top crust. Bake pie in a moderate oven (350°) about 45 to 50 minutes or until crust is nicely browned and filling is bubbling. Cool pie to room temperature before cutting.

Almost any cookbook that contains Pennsylvania Dutch recipes will feature shoo-fly pie. Very few, on the other hand, include shoo-fly cake, which is, according to those who have tasted it, "much more delicious."

Though this shoo-fly cake recipe calls for molasses, it should be noted that in Pennsylvania Dutch country molasses is actually a dark corn syrup (called "king" syrup) or a very light golden molasses generally unavailable elsewhere. For a cake that most nearly resembles that made by the Pennsylvania Dutch, use the proportions of corn syrup and molasses listed in the recipe here. Though it may seem odd, the cake contains no eggs.

Shoo-Fly Cake

MAKES A 13 × 9 × 2-INCH LOAF

4 cups sifted all-purpose flour
1 pound light brown sugar
½ pound butter
¾ cup dark corn syrup
¼ cup molasses

2 cups boiling water
2 teaspoons baking soda

Place flour, brown sugar, and butter in a large bowl, then rub together with your fingers until mixture is uniformly crumbly. Measure out and reserve 1 cup to scatter on top of cake. Combine corn syrup, molasses, boiling water, and soda and stir into crumbs in bowl, mixing just until fairly smooth. Pour into a greased 13 × 9 × 2-inch baking pan, scatter reserved cup of crumbs on top, then bake in a moderate oven (350°) about 45 minutes or until cake begins to pull from sides of pan and a finger, pressed lightly into top of cake, leaves a print that vanishes slowly. Cool cake upright in its pan on a wire rack, then cut into large squares and serve.

&

Crumb cakes, a Pennsylvania Dutch specialty, are made by rubbing flour, brown sugar, and butter to crumbs, then mixing sour milk or buttermilk with half of the crumbs and scattering the rest on top of the batter. When baked, there is a rich moist cake underneath a crunchy crumb blanket.

Nothing Crumb Cake

MAKES A 9 × 9 × 2-INCH CAKE

1½ cups firmly packed dark brown sugar
2½ cups sifted all-purpose flour
¼ cup each lard and butter or ½ cup butter
1 teaspoon baking soda
½ teaspoon salt
½ cup sour milk or buttermilk
1 egg

Place sugar, flour, lard, and butter in a large bowl and rub together with your fingers until uniformly fine and crumbly. Measure out half of mixture and reserve to sprinkle on top of batter. Stir baking soda and salt into sour milk, then mix into "crumbs" remaining in bowl. Beat in egg. Pour batter into a well-greased 9 × 9 × 2-inch baking pan, then scatter remaining crumb mixture over the top. Bake in a moderate oven (350°) 40 to 45 minutes or until cake feels spongy to the touch and crumb topping is tinged with brown. Let cake cool upright in its pan 10 minutes before cutting into squares and serving.

Not the usual crisp, rolled sugar cookie, but a soft drop cookie made with *brown* sugar instead of granulated, then flavored with freshly grated lemon rind and mace. These are a brick-oven favorite at the Pennsylvania Farm Museum.

Soft Sugar Cookies

MAKES ABOUT 6 DOZEN COOKIES

4 cups sifted all-purpose flour
1 teaspoon baking soda
1 teaspoon cream of tartar
¾ cup butter
3 cups firmly packed light brown sugar
3 eggs
1 cup buttermilk
½ teaspoon finely grated lemon rind
½ teaspoon ground mace
Granulated sugar

Sift together the flour, baking soda, and cream of tartar and set aside. Cream the butter and sugar until light; beat in eggs. Add sifted dry ingredients alternately with buttermilk, beginning and ending with dry ingredients. Mix in lemon rind and mace. Drop by rounded teaspoonfuls onto lightly greased baking sheets, spacing cookies about

1½ inches apart. Bake in a moderately hot oven (375°) 8 to 10 minutes until cookies are lightly ringed with brown. Remove at once to wire racks to cool and, while still hot, sprinkle lightly with granulated sugar.

Spinning, weaving, candle dipping, and soap making are a few of the homely arts demonstrated at the Pennsylvania Farm Museum. Here, more for interest than for use, is the museum's recipe for making soap.

Homemade Soap

20 pounds fat (obtained from butchering sheep, cattle, or hogs)
4 gallons water
4 pounds caustic soda (lye)
1 pint salt

Put fat and water in a large iron kettle, add caustic soda, and heat. Allow to come to a boil. Boil slowly 2½ hours; add 1 pint salt (or more if necessary) until it separates. Boil ½ hour longer.

Meadowcroft Village
Avella, Pennsylvania

*I*t wasn't their great-great-grandfather's log cabin, or the one-room schoolhouse where three generations of their family had been taught, that prompted brothers Delvin and Albert Miller to begin the restoration now known as Meadowcroft Village. Both of these structures were already on the eight-hundred-acre Miller farm in western Pennsylvania. It was the condemnation of an old covered bridge that spurred the Millers to action, although both admit that for some time they'd considered building a Pennsylvania pioneer village that would preserve fragments of a fast-disappearing era.

The bridge, built in 1870 over Toms Run in Pine Bank, Greene County, had become known as the "kissing bridge," because lovers rumbling through in their buggies had been shielded from public view. But it was slated for destruction, to be replaced by a modern span. The Millers moved it to their farm, and the work of building Meadowcroft Village was begun.

Today the village, operated as an educational and historical community by the Meadowcroft Foundation, numbers thirty-two historic buildings that span more than one hundred years of early Pennsylvania life. The Miller brothers call it a "dispersed rural community." It is built around the 1834 schoolhouse, George Miller's log house built after he first settled the farm in 1795, and the covered bridge. Visitors can wander through two completely stocked general stores, a blacksmith shop, a smokehouse, a cobbler's shop, a trapper's cabin, and various old log homes during their nostalgic journey backward in time.

"Smokers and chewers will please spit on each other and not on the stove or floor," advises a sign hanging above the cracker barrel and checkerboard at the Meadowcroft General Store, a building housing the shelves, counters, Post Office, and furnishings of the old Fowler Store once located in nearby West Virginia. The Sugar Loaf Country Store down the road contains a complete line of merchandise from Sugar Loaf, New York, including collections of high button shoes, buggy whips and heaters, sulfur matches, candles, and corn planters.

The Blacksmith Shop features an anvil said to have been used by John Chapman, the legendary "Johnny Appleseed," and is well stocked with wood and leather bellows as well as with other tools of the smithy's trade.

A recent acquisition to the ever-growing village is the 1778 log home of Robert McCready, a western Pennsylvania pioneer educator and civic leader who fought in local skirmishes against the Indians.

Meadowcroft—the name is derived from Meadow Lands, Delvin Miller's present horse farm, and Bancroft Farm, the name of the original Miller holdings—also boasts a collection of carriages and racing sulkies, perhaps the best such collection anywhere.

The village serves not only as a living memorial to the American heritage, but as a study in wildlife and conservation. The Miller brothers' grandfather, T. A. Miller, sold some four hundred acres of the original farm for mining, and became wealthy in the process. But strip mining scarred the area. Now Albert Miller, a naturalist, botanist, agronomist, geologist, and historian, and his brother have seen that this damage has been repaired. Wildlife abounds, flowers and trees have been replanted, and the land once again is untouched by the indiscretions of an industrial age.

&

Every October at Meadowcroft Village there's a Corn Husk Festival, held to commemorate the October harvest of early pioneer days. There are husking bees, with everyone pitching in, and there are demonstrations in crafts and cooking—all based upon corn, corn cobs, and corn husks. The three recipes that follow are Corn Husk Festival favorites.

Corn Oysters

MAKES ABOUT 1 DOZEN

1 cup sifted all-purpose flour
1 teaspoon baking powder
1 tablespoon sugar
½ teaspoon salt
2 eggs, beaten until frothy
¼ cup milk, at room temperature
1 tablespoon melted butter or bacon drippings
1¼ cups cooked and drained whole kernel corn (sweet corn is best)
1 cup vegetable oil (for frying)

Sift the flour with the baking powder, sugar, and salt into a medium-size mixing bowl. Combine the eggs with the milk and the melted butter or bacon drippings, pour into the dry ingredients, and stir briskly to mix. Add the corn and mix in lightly. Heat the vegetable oil in a large, heavy skillet until very hot—a bit of the corn oyster batter dropped in the hot oil should sizzle vigorously. Drop the batter by rounded half tablespoons into the hot oil, spacing well so that the mounds do not touch one another. Fry 3 to 4 minutes on each side until a rich golden brown, drain on paper toweling, and serve. Good as is, better still accompanied by plenty of butter and maple syrup or Corn Cob Syrup (recipe follows).

Who would think to cook with corn cobs? Pennsylvania frontier women would and did. They made jelly out of corn cobs, for example, and they also made this Corn Cob Syrup, which, they maintained, was almost as good as maple syrup. Certainly it was less costly and less complicated to make.

Corn Cob Syrup

MAKES ABOUT 3 CUPS

6 fresh, clean field corn cobs (with all the kernels removed)
1 quart water
1½ cups firmly packed dark brown sugar

Break the corn cobs into small chunks (about 1½ inches long) and place in a large, heavy saucepan. Add the water, bring to a boil, then boil, uncovered, 45 minutes. Discard the cobs and strain the cooking liquid through a fine sieve into a quart-size measuring cup. You will need 3 cups liquid for the syrup—if there is slightly more, pour out the excess. Place the corn cob liquid and the brown sugar in a clean, heavy saucepan and stir until sugar is almost dissolved. Bring to a slow boil, then boil, uncovered, about 10 minutes or until the syrup is slightly thickened, about the consistency of maple syrup. Serve as you would maple syrup—over waffles or pancakes.

You must use stone- or water-ground corn meal for this recipe. It has the floury texture needed to hold the hush puppies together as they deep fat fry. Modern enriched corn meal simply won't work because it sputters and flies apart in the deep fat.

Hush Puppies

MAKES ABOUT 2 DOZEN

2 cups stone-ground or water-ground corn meal (white meal
  is preferable)
3 tablespoons sugar
1 teaspoon baking powder
1 teaspoon salt
1 cup boiling water (about)
¼ cup unsalted butter
Vegetable oil for deep fat frying (you will need about 6 cups)

Combine the corn meal, sugar, baking powder, and salt
in a large mixing bowl. Slowly pour in the boiling water,
stirring briskly, to make a batter about the consistency of
biscuit dough—soft but firm enough to shape with the
hands. Add the butter and stir until melted. Heat the
vegetable oil in a deep fat fryer to a temperature of 375°
(use a deep fat thermometer). Drop in the hush puppy
batter by heaping teaspoonfuls, shaping the dough each
time on the spoon to make a smooth oval cake. Deep fry
the hush puppies, 6 to 8 at a time, 3 to 4 minutes until a
deep nut brown. Keep the temperature of the deep fat as
nearly as possible at 375° so that the hush puppies will
not only brown nicely but also cook straight through to
the center. Drain on paper toweling and serve hot with
fried fish or fried chicken.

Harpers Ferry National Historical Park

Harpers Ferry, West Virginia

*F*ew American towns as beautiful as Harpers Ferry have had an uglier history. Some of the ugly scars remain—of that drizzling October night in 1859 when abolitionist John Brown and a band of eighteen men raided the town and its arsenal, of the Civil War years when Stonewall Jackson took the town together with nearly thirteen thousand Union soldiers, the Federal Armory and its stockpile of weapons.

But Harpers Ferry today possesses once again the serenity and beauty that lured settlers there more than two hundred years ago. One of the first to come (in 1747) was a millwright named Robert Harper, who was so enchanted by the mountain valley, cradled as it was between the Shenandoah and Potomac Rivers, that he bought out two squatters on the spot, paying them sixty-five dollars for their cabin, their corn patch, and their canoe. Harper opened a ferry service across the Potomac (hence the name Harpers Ferry), and, to take advantage of the water power, he built a mill. Other settlers soon trickled into the valley, Harpers Ferry became industrialized, and in 1796, Congress, at the urging of President George Washington, established a gun factory there. The first arms were manufactured in 1801, and by 1810 production had increased to ten thousand muskets a year. By 1819, the Hall Rifle Works, under government contract, was mass-producing breech-loading flintlock rifles and, to stockpile those arms, a U.S. armory of twenty buildings was built on the south bank of the Potomac.

Harpers Ferry was becoming a strategic town—to John Brown, who viewed it as a refuge for runaway slaves, and, a few years later, to Confederate and Union troops that slugged it out in the streets.

The Civil War virtually destroyed Harpers Ferry, and if the town did not die, it never fully recovered.

Today the dozen remaining historic buildings and landmarks have been made into a National Historic Park, and the Park Service's new "living history" program has revitalized the town and re-created life as it was in Harper's Ferry before the Civil War. Staff interpreters in period dress move busily about, intent on their daily chores. The old Blacksmith Shop has been reactivated, the Dry Goods Store, an Apothecary, the Recruiting Office, the Tavern. And at the Harper House up on the hill (built by Robert Harper between 1776 and 1782 and the town's oldest structure), there are demonstrations in cooking, needlepoint, and gardening.

The battle sites are here too (Arsenal Square, John Brown's Fort), but they are mute reminders of the town's grim history. Elsewhere life goes on as it did some hundred and fifty years ago. You can visit the old Stagecoach Inn, the Master Armorer's House (now a museum where the story of gunmaking is told), you can visit the Point, where the Shenandoah and Potomac Rivers meet, climb the Stone Steps, hand carved in the nineteenth century to link the upper and lower towns, and you can climb higher still to Jefferson Rock for a majestic view of three states (Maryland, Virginia, and West Virginia).

The rock is named for Thomas Jefferson, who stood there in 1783, gazed out across the mountains and river-carved valleys, and proclaimed the view "worth a voyage across the Atlantic."

And so it is. So, too, is Harpers Ferry, for to prowl up and down its slopes, to tour the restored and refurbished buildings, to talk with the costumed interpreters, is to understand how this serene mountain town found its place in the history books.

🪶

Food is cooked daily in the Harper House at Harpers Ferry—to feed the staff and, sometimes, to demonstrate nineteenth-century cooking methods to visitors. As park technician Deborah K. Mehrkam explains it: "Each day the interpreters from the shops in the restoration arrive at noon at the Harper House to sit down for the family meal. The menu is varied, including meats, vegetables, lots of stews and soups, and always some type of hot bread. Visitors who have climbed the steps to visit Harper House are startled to see such a sight, but are quickly made to feel at home when offered a taste of the meal. This is not a commercial enterprise and we do not serve meals to the public; however, visitors are often invited to taste. Those foods that are not available in our garden, the ladies shop for at the Dry Goods Store, returning with lard, beans, flour and sugar. They can also be seen strolling (in period dress) to the chicken house on Shenandoah Street before Sunday dinner to pick out a tender fryer or tough old rooster that must be stewed."

One of the favorite recipes prepared by the ladies at Harper House is Okra Soup. "We don't measure anything," they say. "We just make soup." The following recipe is based upon their description.

Okra Soup

MAKES ABOUT 12 SERVINGS

8 cups chicken stock
2 cups minced, cooked chicken meat (the ladies at Harpers
    Ferry use carcass trimmings and leftover scraps)
4 medium-size yellow onions, peeled and chopped

2 sweet green peppers, cored, seeded, and chopped
6 large ripe tomatoes, peeled, cored, and chopped (reserve
    juice)
4 cups sliced fresh okra (use tender young pods and slice
    about ½ inch thick)
3 cups cooked long-grain rice
1 tablespoon sugar (about)
Salt to taste
Cayenne pepper to taste

Set the chicken stock, chicken meat, onions, peppers, tomatoes and their juice to simmer in a big, heavy kettle over medium heat (at Harpers Ferry, the women make soup on a wood stove). Simmer, covered, about 1½ hours, then uncover soup and let bubble gently about 1 to 1½ hours longer—it doesn't really matter how long the soup simmers because it just gets richer and richer. Moreover, you don't have to watch the pot if you keep the heat fairly low. Add the okra, cover, and cook about 10 minutes, just until the okra is tender (don't overcook or it will become slimy). Add the cooked rice, enough sugar (1 tablespoon or more) to mellow the tartness of the tomatoes, and salt to taste (the amount of salt needed will vary according to the saltiness of the chicken stock). Just before serving, add cayenne pepper—just until the soup is as "hot" as you like it (¼ teaspoon makes a nippy but not fiery soup). Ladle into big soup bowls and serve with squares of fresh baked corn bread.

No one knows why there are so many mulberry bushes at Harpers Ferry. Or who planted them or when. Perhaps some early settler intended to go into the business of making silk (silkworms feed upon the leaf of a particular species of mulberry). But mulberries have thrived in this mountain valley for well over a hundred years, as proved by this ad in the October 16, 1838, edition of the *Harper's Ferry Constitutionalist*: "Morus Multicaulis For Sale." *Morus multicaulis* is the mulberry, and in summer the mulberry bushes at Harpers Ferry hang heavy with fruit. The grackles stuff themselves with mulberries and so, too, do members of the National Park Service staff at Harpers Ferry. One of the great specialties at historic Harper House is Mulberry Muffins. "They are delicious," says park technician Deborah K. Mehrkam, "and you always know when we've been eating them by the purple stain the berries leave on our hands and mouths."

Mulberry Muffins

MAKES ABOUT 1½ DOZEN

2¼ cups sifted all-purpose flour
¼ cup sugar
3½ teaspoons baking powder
⅛ teaspoon salt
1 cup mulberries, washed and patted dry (fresh blueberries
    may be substituted)
1 egg, beaten lightly
1 cup milk, at room temperature
¼ cup melted butter

Sift the flour, sugar, baking powder, and salt together into a large mixing bowl. Add the mulberries and toss lightly to dredge. Combine the egg, milk, and melted butter. Make a well in the center of the dry ingredients, pour the liquid mixture in all at once, and stir just enough to moisten the dry ingredients (no matter if there are a few lumps here and there). Spoon batter into well-greased muffin pan cups, filling each no more than two-thirds full. Bake in a hot oven (425°) 20 minutes or until muffins pull from sides of muffin pan cups and are touched with brown on top. Serve oven-hot with plenty of butter.

Apples, like mulberries, are abundant at Harpers Ferry, and during the fall harvest, hostess-guides at Harper House make whopping caldrons of apple butter to demonstrate the old-fashioned method to tourists. Here, in their own words, is how it is done.

COPPER KETTLE APPLE BUTTER

"We peeled 5 to 6 bushels of Stayman apples grown in a local orchard and cooked them into a sauce the day before we were to make the apple butter. Cooking the apples on the wood stove yields about 18 gallons of sauce. The next morning we started our fire outside the kitchen with the help of the Blacksmith and put the sauce on to cook in a large copper kettle. We then added 18 quarts of apple cider and when that was hot, added 36 pounds of sugar. It is necessary to stir this mixture constantly with a long-handled wooden apple butter stirrer or the butter will stick and burn. We cooked this down until about a half hour before it was ready—the only way you can tell when it is ready is to have someone there who has made apple butter before. We added 18 teaspoons each of cinnamon, allspice and ground cloves and cooked about a half hour longer. When the apple butter was done, we put it into Mason jars or crocks for storage. This recipe yielded about 30 to 35 gallons of apple butter. It took us all day long to make it, but it was worthwhile. We baked biscuits while the apple butter was cooking and served samples to our visitors. The remainder we will use with our hot breads at meals next summer."

The South

Colonial Williamsburg
Virginia

The most famous of America's restored and reconstructed historic villages, the most impressive, and one of the largest, Colonial Williamsburg stretches almost one full mile along Duke of Gloucester Street from the restored Sir Christopher Wren Building (1690) on the College of William and Mary campus to the reconstructed Capitol. There are eighty-eight fully restored and preserved eighteenth-century buildings here and more than fifty faithful reproductions that have risen from the rubble of structures destroyed during Tidewater Virginia's march of progress. Once Virginia's capital had been moved from Williamsburg to Richmond (in 1779), Williamsburg became a backwater, disused and decaying. As late as 1926 one of its residents described the town thus:

"Williamsburg on a summer day! The straggling street ankle deep in dust, grateful only to the chickens ruffling their feathers in perfect safety from any traffic danger. The cows taking refuge from the heat of the sun under the elms along the sidewalk.

"Our city fathers, assembled in friendly leisure, following the shade of the old Court House around the clock, sipping cool drinks and discussing the glories of the past. Almost always our past."

Williamsburg's past proved to be its salvation, for that past, painstakingly re-created, is today one of America's most popular tourist attractions.

Architectural purists and historians have sneered at Colonial Williamsburg, claiming that it sprang full-blown from the drawing boards in the 1930s, helped along by lavish infusions of Rockefeller money. But they generalize too much. Williamsburg rests upon solid historic foundations. And it re-creates the gracious eighteenth-century life of the capital city of the royal colony of Virginia in a way that today's Americans can relate to, understand, and enjoy.

This is no ghost town. It hums today as yesterday with artisans and craftsmen plying their trades. There are more than twenty authentic craft shops in Williamsburg, manned by artisans in colonial dress. Here you can see the gunsmith at work, the wigmaker, the milliner, the weaver, the spinster, the bookbinder, the printer, the baker, and the candlestick maker. Here you can dine by candlelight in one of three historic taverns: Christiana Campbell's, where George Washington once dined and where balladeers now stroll among the tables; Josiah Chowning's; the King's Arms (such a favorite of Baron von Steuben that in 1781 he ran up a bill of nearly three hundred dollars). These taverns today serve a mixture of English and colonial fare typical of that of eighteenth-century Williamsburg—smoky-red Virginia hams, sweet Tidewater oysters and peanuts, velvety spoon bread, crunchy sweet-tart watermelon rind pickles.

American independence found its beginnings at Williamsburg in the House of Burgesses, where such patriots as George Washington, Thomas Jefferson, and Patrick Henry spoke out for freedom. You can visit the reconstructed Capitol today, where these men once sat, you can tour the opulent Governor's Palace, the grim Gaol. You can relax upon the public greens, stroll the shady sidewalks of Duke of Gloucester Street, savoring the leisurely pace of eighteenth-century Virginia. You can watch fife-and-drum drills, musket firings, and at

Christmas time caroling by candlelight. You can even stay, if you make arrangements, at one of Williamsburg's historic cottages, faithfully restored and furnished.

Nowhere in America will you find a grander-scale restoration than at Williamsburg, or one that offers more to see and do. To savor Williamsburg fully, you must give it three days at least. And, better still, a week. Then strike out at your own pace, prowl about, poke about. You will rediscover one of the most important chapters in early American history and live, for a few days at least, in a bygone era of grace and gentility.

Meat in the early days of Williamsburg usually meant ham, a smoky-salty mahogany-hued Virginia ham. What distinguished Virginia hams from all others—and does to this day—is that the hogs were turned loose to root the Tidewater peanut fields. The exercise made the hogs lean, and the peanut diet gave their flesh a unique nut-like flavor. These qualities, combined with a salty cure and long, slow smoking over hickory fires, produced the dark red, firm-fleshed hams that Queen Victoria relished so much she had a standing order for them at Buckingham Palace. Virginia hams are not difficult to cook—but they are tedious, requiring about two days. They are best, by the way, served cold, carved tissue thin, and, according to Virginians, sandwiched into small baking powder biscuits.

Williamsburg Ham

MAKES 10 TO 12 SERVINGS

1 Virginia ham, weighing 10 to 12 pounds
¾ cup firmly packed light brown sugar
1 cup soft fine bread crumbs
2 tablespoons light corn syrup
⅓ cup melted butter (about)
Whole cloves

With a stiff brush, scrub the ham well in tepid water to remove excess salt and bits of mold (these are harmless). Rinse ham well and soak overnight in a very large kettle of water. Next day, again scrub the ham in tepid water and rinse. Place the ham in a very large, heavy oval kettle (saw off the hock, if necessary, in order to fit the ham into the kettle). Add enough cool fresh water to cover the ham, bring to a simmer, cover, and cook 8 to 9 hours, changing the cooking water twice during this period (this makes for a less salty ham). When the ham is tender enough to pierce easily with a fork, remove from cooking water and cool overnight. In the morning, cut away the rind and trim outer covering of fat to a thin layer—about ¼ inch. Mix together the brown sugar, bread crumbs, and corn syrup, then add enough melted butter to hold all together. Pat crumb mixture firmly over fat surface of ham, score in a crisscross pattern with a sharp knife, and stud the center of each square with a clove. Bake ham, uncovered, in a large, shallow roasting pan in a moderate oven (350°) 45 to 50 minutes until crumb coating is nicely browned. Cool to room temperature before serving.

This tart coleslaw is a specialty of the King's Arms Tavern in Williamsburg. The recipe calls for diced sweet red pepper—which gives the slaw dots of bright color. Red peppers, however, are not as widely available as sweet green peppers, so if you are unable to find them, use the green peppers instead. Or, if you have the time, simply let the green peppers stand at room temperature for two or three days. They will turn orangey-red.

King's Arms Cabbage and Pepper Slaw

MAKES 6 SERVINGS

6 cups coarsely shredded cabbage
¼ cup thinly sliced celery

¼ cup thinly sliced onion
¼ cup diced sweet red pepper
½ cup cider vinegar
1 teaspoon sugar
½ teaspoon salt
⅛ teaspoon pepper
1 teaspoon celery seeds
½ cup vegetable oil

Place the cabbage, celery, onion, and sweet red pepper in a large mixing bowl and toss well. Mix the vinegar with the sugar, salt, pepper, and celery seeds, stirring until the sugar and salt dissolve. Add the oil and mix vigorously to blend. (An easy way to do this is to mix the dressing in a jar with a close-fitting lid; to mix, simply shake the jar hard.) Pour the dressing over the slaw and toss well to mix. Refrigerate for several hours, then toss well again just before serving.

Spoon bread is nothing more than a savory corn bread custard eaten with a spoon. There are in Tidewater Virginia as many recipes for spoon bread as there are cooks, and you will find it featured on virtually every hotel and restaurant menu in Williamsburg, each version differing slightly from the others. This old Virginia recipe is particularly moist and soufflé-like. Serve it in place of—or in addition to—potatoes.

Old Virginia Spoon Bread

MAKES 4 TO 6 SERVINGS

2⅓ cups light cream
¼ cup unsalted butter
5 teaspoons sugar
¾ teaspoon salt
1 cup sifted, stone-ground white corn meal
4 eggs, separated

1 teaspoon baking powder
Pinch of white pepper

Heat together just until scalding hot—do not boil—the cream, butter, sugar, and salt. Remove from heat and briskly mix in the corn meal, continuing to stir until thick. Beat the egg yolks lightly with the baking powder and pepper. Blend a little of the hot mixture into the yolks, then stir back into pan. Beat the egg whites to soft peaks and fold into the corn meal mixture as gently as possible so as not to break down their volume. Pour into a buttered 2-quart casserole or soufflé dish and bake uncovered in a moderately hot oven (375°) 30 to 35 minutes until puffed and golden brown. Rush to the table and serve. Be sure to put out plenty of fresh sweet butter, salt, and a pepper grinder so everyone can season his spoon bread the way he likes it.

An old Southern favorite, spicy with just a touch of lemon. Double the recipe, if you like, so that you will have more pickles to show for the hours of slow cooking.

Williamsburg Lodge Watermelon Rind Pickle

MAKES ABOUT 4 PINTS

2 pounds peeled and trimmed watermelon rind, cut in 1-inch cubes
¼ cup salt dissolved in 4 cups cold water (brine)
8 cups cold water (about)
2 pounds sugar
2 cups cold water
2 cups cider vinegar
1 lemon, sliced thin and seeded
1 tablespoon crushed stick cinnamon
1 tablespoon crushed whole cloves
1 tablespoon crushed whole allspice

Place the watermelon rind in a large enamel kettle, pour in brine, cover, and soak overnight. Next day, drain the brine from the watermelon rind. Rinse the kettle, return rind to kettle, add the 8 cups cold water (more if needed to cover the rind), and boil rind until tender, about 1 to 1½ hours (add more water as needed to cover the rind). In a separate large enamel kettle, make a pickling solution by bringing to a boil the sugar, 2 cups cold water, vinegar, and lemon slices. Tie the crushed spices in several thicknesses of cheesecloth and drop into the kettle. Drain watermelon rind well, add to the pickling solution, and simmer slowly, uncovered, until the rind becomes clear and syrup is fairly thick, 1½ to 2 hours. Remove spice bag. Ladle boiling hot pickles into 4 hot sterilized pint-size preserving jars, filling to within ¼ inch of the top, and screw on lids to seal. Process 10 minutes in a boiling water bath. Cool, then store pickles on a cool, dark, dry shelf.

Jamestown Festival Park
Jamestown, Virginia

Come to Jamestown by water if you can; that is, by ferrying across the James River from the little town of Scotland on the south bank, for only then will you see Jamestown as the English settlers saw it in 1607. This is wild country, more swampland than woodland, ensnarled with honeysuckle, smilax, and poison ivy.

The Englishmen could scarcely have picked a less hospitable spot. It was a mosquito breeding ground, as stifling under a summer land breeze as wet cotton wool. It was a land bitter in winter, its dampness numbing straight to the marrow. It was a backwater menaced by malaria and hostile Indians.

But this is the land the English chose to settle, coming ashore in May of 1607 after a wallowing ocean voyage of many weeks aboard the *Susan Constant*, the *Godspeed*, and the *Discovery*.

You see replicas of these three ships as your ferry nears the Jamestown shore. Mere toys, they seem, about a third the size of the river ferry, and, to see them bobbing in the James's ripples, you marvel that they could have crossed the Atlantic with one hundred and four passengers crammed above and below decks.

But cross it they did, bringing fivescore Englishmen and boys who would establish England's first permanent colony in America. The miracle of Jamestown is that it survived. The settlers were not a plucky lot. Nor were they accustomed to hard labor. As Captain John Smith complained, they were "ten times more fit to spoil a commonwealth than either begin one, or but help to maintain one...a plaine soldier that can use a pickaxe and a spade is better than five knights."

And try as Captain Smith did to convince the Virginia Company of London to send masons and carpenters and "diggers up of trees," later ships brought more colonists of the same ilk—gentlemen of leisure who had been lured to the New World by promises of treasure in the forests and mountains.

Smith organized the settlers, assigned duties and tasks, and under his leadership the first Virginia gentlemen built a triangular palisade of logs (a defense against both the Indians and the Spaniards, who, having settled at St. Augustine, were making forays up and down the South Atlantic coast).

That early log encampment has been re-created at Jamestown Festival Park, the triangular stockade (James Fort) together with some eighteen daub and wattle shelters. Guides here, in showy Elizabethan dress, explain what life was like in those early days—the growing and harvesting of crops, the preparation and preservation of food, and encounters with Indians.

In the woodlands just outside the stockade stands a replica of Chief Powhatan's lodge, a tall quonset-hut-shaped structure woven of twigs and grasses, and the guides here, Indians all (descendants, in fact, of those early tribes), provide the Indian point of view.

In jolting contrast to these rustic structures loom three enormous modern pavilions (it is through these that you enter Jamestown Festival Park). Their contemporary architecture and a series of exhibits dramatically trace man's progress in the New World.

Jamestown Festival Park stands about one mile from the actual landing site, where only the ivy-shrouded skeleton of Jamestown's first church (1639) stands as a ghostly memorial to those first settlers. However, a 1608 glasshouse has been reconstructed nearby on the site of the original, and glass blowers, tending their earthen furnace and demonstrating the art of glass blowing, help dispel the gloom of those church ruins. The area has been returned to wilderness by the National Park Service, and as you drive the woodland trail, you return in both mind and body to the birthplace of English America.

Had it not been for an abundance of fish and shellfish in the inlets, bays, and rivers of Tidewater, Virginia, America's first permanent English settlement at Jamestown may well have failed. But there *was* plenty of seafood. Captain John Smith reported one day that, while exploring the lower reaches of Chesapeake Bay, the fish "were lying so thicke with their heads above the water" that their boats could scarcely navigate through them. Having no fishing lines or nets, the Englishmen tried to scoop the fish out of the water with skillets. But their catch was poor, Captain Smith noted, because the fish would not leap into the skillets. As for shellfish, oysters appeared to be the favorite. In the beginning, they were probably eaten raw, boiled or pan-roasted in the shell over campfires. But later, when Englishwomen had been imported to Jamestown, oysters were prepared in the more elaborate ways of England. They were simmered into chowders or scalloped with onions and butter and cracker crumbs.

Jamestown Scalloped Oysters

MAKES 4 TO 6 SERVINGS

1 quart shucked oysters, drained
¾ cup oyster liquor
½ cup butter
2 tablespoons finely minced green pepper

2 tablespoons finely minced onion
½ clove garlic, peeled and crushed
2 tablespoons flour
1 teaspoon salt
⅛ teaspoon pepper
1 tablespoon lemon juice
1¼ cups fine soda cracker crumbs

Pick over oysters, removing any fragments of shell, then warm the oysters in the oyster liquor over low heat just until their skirts ruffle, 3 to 4 minutes. Meanwhile, melt the butter in a small skillet and sauté the green pepper, onion, and garlic 3 to 4 minutes until limp. Blend in the flour, salt, pepper, lemon juice, and 1 cup of the cracker crumbs. Stir into the oysters, turn into a buttered 6-cup casserole, and sprinkle with remaining ¼ cup cracker crumbs. Bake in a moderately hot oven (375°) 20 to 25 minutes or until bubbling and lightly browned.

Squashes were one of the foods American Indians gave the world, and at Jamestown the Virginia colonists were introduced to both the hard-skinned winter squashes and to such delicate summer varieties as yellow squash and the flat, round, fluted, pale green cymlings (also known as pattypans). This simple way of preparing cymlings was no doubt learned from the Indians, although the use of salt pork was probably an English refinement. Indian women would have been more likely to fry their cymlings in bear grease.

Fried Cymling Squash

MAKES 6 TO 8 SERVINGS

8 small tender cymlings
⅛ pound salt pork, cut in small dice
1 small yellow onion, peeled and minced
Salt
Pepper

Peel the cymlings and quarter; set aside. Fry the salt pork slowly in a large, heavy skillet until most of the fat has cooked out and only crisp brown bits remain. Add the cymlings and onions and fry slowly, stirring now and then, until squash is tender. Season to taste with salt and pepper and serve.

In the beginning, the Jamestown colony faltered, and for some years it looked as if it, like Sir Walter Raleigh's earlier ill-starred colony at Roanoke Island, North Carolina, would founder. But by 1619, twenty-two burgesses had come to sit in America's first legislative body, and a year later, in 1620, the first large number of "Virginia maides" had arrived to set up housekeeping in the four-acre settlement in the wilderness. They came bringing English household remedies and recipes, and it is then that a Virginia cuisine began to evolve. It was heavily English at first, but gradually, as the young English-women learned to prepare the New World foods, it became a mixture of American Indian and English and remains largely so today. The following recipes for Sally Lunn and Syllabub, taken from the Jamestown Foundation files, reflect the early English influence, although the Sally Lunn recipe has been updated to take advantage of quick-rising, modern dry yeast.

Miss Emma Lou's Sally Lunn Bread

MAKES A 10-INCH TUBE LOAF

2 packages active dry yeast
¼ cup warm water
½ cup butter
⅓ cup sugar
3 eggs, beaten until frothy
1 cup lukewarm milk
1 teaspoon salt
4 cups sifted all-purpose flour

Soften the yeast in the warm water and set aside. Cream the butter and sugar until fluffy and light, then beat in eggs. Combine the milk and yeast mixture; stir salt into flour. Add flour and milk mixture alternately to the creamed butter-sugar-and-eggs, beginning and ending with flour. Cover with cloth and set in a warm, dry spot to rise until double in bulk, about 1 hour. Stir down, then pour into a well-greased 10-inch tube pan, spreading dough as evenly as possible. Cover with cloth and let rise in a warm spot 30 to 40 minutes until again double in bulk. Bake in a moderate oven (350°) 45 to 50 minutes until nicely browned and loaf sounds hollow when thumped with the fingers. Let stand upright in pan on a wire rack 10 minutes, then turn out of pan. Serve warm with plenty of fresh sweet butter.

Records indicate that there was no shortage of spirits among Jamestown colonists, even in earliest years. Cream, however, was a far greater luxury, as were fresh oranges. But once both were available, Syllabub, a frothy English whipped-cream dessert laced with sherry and brandy, was served forth at Christmas and other festive occasions.

Syllabub

MAKES 6 SERVINGS

6 navel oranges
1 pint heavy cream
½ cup sifted confectioners' sugar
2 egg whites
2 tablespoons cream sherry
2 tablespoons brandy

Peel the oranges, section, and chill well. When ready to serve, whip the cream with ¼ cup of the confectioners' sugar until stiff. Beat egg whites with remaining ¼ cup sugar to stiff peaks. Fold whipped cream into beaten whites, then sherry and brandy. Drain orange sections and arrange in 6 large goblets. Mound syllabub on top and serve.

Old Salem
Winston-Salem, North Carolina

*T*o those unfamiliar with the South, Old Salem may come as a surprise. You must forget, first of all, visions of white-columned mansions massed with gardenias and camellias; forget, too, the live oak allées trailing tatters of Spanish moss.

Old Salem is an altogether different South, a staunch red brick village even down to its sidewalks, located in the heart of North Carolina's biggest tobacco town. It is no replica or re-creation; it is the authentic restoration of mid-eighteenth-century Salem, a Registered National Historic Landmark.

Salem was founded in 1766 by the Moravians, a pious Germanic people who funneled down the Appalachian valleys from Bethlehem, Pennsylvania, into the rolling Piedmont of North Carolina. The first Moravians arrived in November of 1753 and took refuge in an abandoned log cabin on a 98,985-acre site sold to the Brethren by Lord Granville of England. Straightaway they set about building their town, which they named Bethabara, meaning "House of Passage," for they intended this site to be a temporary one. Within three years, Bethabara had become a bustling community, looked upon by the Indians as a place "where there are good people and much bread."

While living at Bethabara, the Moravians carefully planned their central town, and on January 6, 1766, the first tree was felled for the first building. Their town would be called "Salem," meaning "Peace," and for the next six years the Moravians labored to build it. By 1772 the principal buildings had been completed and the citizens of Bethabara pulled up stakes and moved to Salem, a congregation town in which both economic and spiritual affairs were guided by the church. The congregation was divided into "choirs" according to age, sex, and marital status and housed accordingly. Salem's artisans —weavers, spinners, potters, tinsmiths, gunsmiths, cobblers, and cabinetmakers—soon became known for the quality of their work, and Salem gained a reputation as a cultural, industrial, and educational center.

As the town prospered, the surrounding countryside became more populous, and in the mid-nineteenth century a new town sprang up just north of Salem. Winston, it was called, and many of the Moravians moved there. Salem fell into disuse, but because the Moravians had built so sturdy a town, its buildings withstood years of neglect and many remained intact at the end of World War II. It was at this time, when a local grocery announced plans to put up a supermarket in Salem, that local citizens united to block the modern encroachment and preserve the old. By 1950 Old Salem, Incorporated, had been organized to restore the eighteenth- and early-nineteenth-century Moravian congregation town.

They have done their work well. Old Salem today is pin-neat and proud, its half-timbered red brick buildings and clapboard homes lined up along the red brick sidewalks of Main Street. Only seven of the forty-three historic buildings are open to the public (others are lived in by local residents), but to visit these seven is to respect the industry and artistry of those early Moravian settlers. At the Single Brothers House (the older part of which dates to 1769) craftsmen carry on crafts in the old tradition, crafts that were taught years ago to the Moravian youths who came to the house to live and to learn.

The basement kitchen and dining hall have been restored and costumed guides explain in detail what life was like at the Single Brothers House. One of the most popular buildings at Old Salem is Winkler Bakery (1800), where the old brick ovens are fired every day with hardwood for the baking of Moravian sugar cakes, breads, and cookies (these are offered for sale, and both local residents and tourists line up daily to buy the yeasty loaves and crisp gingery cookies). Other exhibit buildings at Old Salem include the Miksch Tobacco Shop (1771), the Boys School (1794), the Market-Fire House (1803), which served as both meat market and fire station, the John Vogler House (1819), home of Salem's silversmith and clockmaker, and the Salem Tavern (1784), where George Washington once slept. At the Salem Tavern Dining Rooms (built in 1816 as an annex to the tavern) you can sample at lunch or dinner the hearty German fare for which the Moravians were famous (the tavern's Sauerbraten and two specialties of the Winkler Bakery follow).

Also not to be missed on any tour of Old Salem are the Home Moravian Church (1800); God's Acre (1771), the burial ground where the Moravian Easter Sunrise Service is conducted each year; Salem Academy and College (1805); and the Museum of Early Southern Decorative Arts at the far end of Main Street, where fifteen rebuilt period rooms trace the evolution of architecture and interior decoration during the South's first hundred and fifty years.

Save for the occasional car and the comings and goings of Old Salem's twentieth-century residents, it is difficult, as you wander the handmade brick sidewalks, hear the hundred-and-eighty-year-old clock chime the hours from the spire of the Home Moravian Church, and sniff the heady scent of yeast breads baking, to believe that beyond these few blocks exists the skyscraping Southern city of Winston-Salem.

In the brick-floored basement kitchens of the Single Brothers House you can see the eighteenth-century cooking utensils used to prepare meals for the unmarried men of Old Salem who lived at the house. And just a couple of blocks down Main Street at the Salem Tavern Dining Rooms (circa 1816) you can sample—by sunlight or candlelight—some of the same hearty German-style foods they relished, among them this beer-laced sauerbraten.

Salem Tavern Sauerbraten

MAKES 6 SERVINGS

3 pounds top round of beef, in one piece
2 cups cider vinegar
1 cup beer
2 teaspoons pickling spices
1 large bay leaf
1 large yellow onion, peeled and chopped
4 peppercorns, bruised
1 garlic clove, peeled and sliced
2 teaspoons salt
3 tablespoons melted beef suet
3 tablespoons flour mixed with ½ teaspoon salt and ¼
    teaspoon pepper
¾ cup fine gingersnap crumbs

Trim excess outer fat covering (suet) from beef and save to use later in browning the beef. Place beef in a large, shallow glass or ceramic bowl; mix together vinegar, beer, pickling spices, bay leaf, chopped onion, peppercorns, sliced garlic, and salt and pour over beef; cover and refrigerate for 3 days, turning beef in marinade twice each day. Remove beef from marinade and pat dry. In a large, heavy kettle, melt the reserved fat trimmings; pour off drippings, measure out 3 tablespoons and return to kettle. Rub beef well with the 3 tablespoons seasoned flour and brown on all sides in the drippings over a fairly quick heat. Strain the marinade and pour over beef; bring to a full boil, then lower heat so that liquid just ripples, cover, and simmer beef 1½ to 2 hours until a kitchen fork will pierce it easily. Lift beef to a hot platter and keep warm. Measure the cooking liquid, then return 3 cups of it to the kettle. Whisk in the gingersnap crumbs and heat and stir until thickened and smooth; pour into a gravy boat. To serve, carve the beef in thin slices and ladle some of the gravy on top.

Some of the best breads you will ever taste are baked in the giant wood-fired ovens at the Winkler Bakery (circa 1800) on Main Street in Old Salem. An Easter time favorite, which townspeople line up early to buy lest the supply run short, is Moravian Sugar Cake, a spongy-light, yeast-raised coffee cake with puddles of melted butter, brown sugar, and cinnamon on top.

Moravian Sugar Cake

MAKES TWO 13 × 9 × 2-INCH LOVES

2 medium-size potatoes, peeled and cubed
1½ cups water
6 tablespoons butter
6 tablespoons lard (hog lard, not vegetable shortening)
1 scant cup sugar
2 eggs
2 teaspoons salt
2 packages active dry yeast softened in ¼ cup warm water
5½ cups sifted flour

Topping:
¼ cup butter (about)
¼ cup light brown sugar (not packed down)
Ground cinnamon
¼ cup heavy cream (about)

Boil the potatoes in the water in a covered saucepan about 15 minutes until very tender. Drain off cooking water and reserve. Mash potatoes well until light and fluffy but add no seasoning; measure out 1 cup and set aside—when measuring the mashed potatoes, just spoon them *lightly* into the measuring cup—do not pack down. Cream the butter, lard, and sugar until very light, then beat in the eggs, one at a time. Beat in the mashed potatoes and when creamy mix in 1 cup of the reserved potato cooking water and the salt. Test temperature of the mixture—it should be warm but not hot. If too hot, let cool a bit, then mix in the softened yeast. Stir in the flour, about 1 cup at a time, beating well after each addition. When all the flour has been mixed in and you have a nice soft dough, cover with a dry cloth and let rise in a warm spot 2 hours or until doubled in bulk.

Punch dough down in the bowl and beat a minute or so to reduce the volume. Divide dough in half and pat out in two well-buttered 13 × 9 × 2-inch loaf pans. The dough will be springy and you will have to persist, with well-buttered hands, to flatten the dough over the bottoms of the pans. Cover each pan with a dry cloth, set in a warm spot, away from drafts, and let rise again until doubled in bulk, about 2 hours.

When dough is puffy and light and has risen to within about a half inch of the tops of the pans, punch holes down in the dough with your thumb, index and third fingers bunched up. It's best to do this in an orderly pattern, making five evenly-spaced rows, three holes each, across the 9-inch side of the dough. Cut butter into little chips about the size of kidney beans and drop one into each hole. Scatter brown sugar lightly across the top of each loaf, then sprinkle with cinnamon. Finally drizzle cream over the top of each loaf. Bake loaves in a hot oven (400°) 20 to 25 minutes until richly browned. Remove to wire racks and let cool about 5 minutes. To serve, cut in large squares and put out lots of fresh sweet butter for spreading.

The trick to these brittle ginger cookies is to roll them very, *very* thin—so thin that you can almost read a newspaper through them. First of all, choose a cold, clear day for making the cookies and have your kitchen fairly cold, too. Otherwise, the dough will be difficult to transfer to baking sheets. It helps to roll the cookies on a floured marble slab instead of a board because the coldness of the marble will keep the dough firm. And it helps, too, to have cold hands—so keep a bowl of ice water handy so you can dip your fingers in whenever they are warming and softening the cookie dough too much. At Christmas time in Old Salem, these cookies are made in a variety of shapes and sizes—animals, stars. bells, and circles fluted about the edge. The circles, obviously, are easiest to cut and transfer intact to baking sheets.

Moravian Christmas Cookies

MAKES 10 to 12 DOZEN TISSUE-THIN COOKIES

2 cups molasses
1 cup firmly packed dark brown sugar
½ cup lard, melted and cooled (hog lard, not vegetable
   shortening)
½ cup butter, melted and cooled
1 teaspoon ground cinnamon
½ teaspoon ground cloves
½ teaspoon ground ginger
½ teaspoon baking soda
4½ cups sifted flour

Mix molasses and sugar well, then beat in lard and butter. Sift the spices and soda with 1 cup of the flour and mix in. Add remaining flour, about 1 cup at a time, mixing thoroughly after each addition. Cover bowl of dough and let stand in a cool spot 8 to 10 hours or overnight to season. Take up about ¼ or ⅓ of the dough, pat quickly into a flat round, then roll on a floured board or marble slab with a floured rolling pin into a circle about as thin as a piece of paper. Cut out in circles or any other shapes you fancy, using floured cookie cutters, transfer with a floured spatula to well-greased baking sheets and bake in a moderate oven (350°) 10 to 12 minutes until lightly browned about the edge and cookies seem firm to the touch. Let cool on baking sheets about a minute, then, using a spatula, life to wire racks to cool. Roll and cut the remaining dough the same way, doing only a small amount of it at a time and keeping the remaining cool until you are ready to roll it. The scraps can be rerolled, too, but the cookies won't be as tender after the second or third rolling because they will pick up extra flour from the board and rolling pin.

Oconaluftee Indian Village
Cherokee, North Carolina

*T*he first Indian most tourists see as they drive into the little Smoky Mountain town of Cherokee is the brave in buckskins and feathered headdress posing for snapshots. He may be Cherokee, but he is not dressed as one. He wears the Sioux war bonnet, looks very much like the Indian on the nickel because this is how White Man visualizes the Indian.

To see what the Cherokee are really like—or rather, what they were like some two hundred and fifty years ago—you must leave the tourist gimcrackery of downtown Cherokee and head for the Oconaluftee Indian Village nearby. Here, in this authentic re-creation of a seventeenth- and eighteenth-century Cherokee community, you will see properly dressed Cherokee, the men in straight-cut trousers and bright overblouses reminiscent of those worn by Russian cossacks, the women in long, gathered cotton skirts and full-sleeved shirtwaists. It is not ceremonial dress they wear, because what Oconaluftee portrays is the day-to-day life of a Cherokee village.

Here you will see ears of corn over smoldering fires to parch, strings of green beans set in the sun to dry (they will later be made into that Cherokee favorite, Leather Britches Beans, the recipe for which follows). You will see pumpkins and squash, too, all foods the American

Indian gave the world. You will see women making corn into hominy (by boiling it in water and a mixture of wood ashes), pounding dried corn into meal and flour, dyeing willow slats with the juices of berries and roots and barks. And you will see them weave baskets in traditional Cherokee patterns and coil ropes of native clay into bowls and pots.

The men of the village are busy too, making dugout canoes with fire and ax, fashioning blowguns out of green river cane, tailing locust darts with thistle, feathering arrows, chipping flint into arrowheads, carving wooden spoons and combs, hollowing out gourds for dippers and ladles.

The cultural and geographic center of Oconaluftee Indian Village is the domed, seven-sided council house, hand-hewn out of logs and furnished as it would have been centuries ago with animal furs and hand-woven blankets. Its function today is to provide a glimpse of the social life of the Cherokee and to demonstrate the role and ritual of the medicine man.

Oconaluftee Indian Village stands on the Cherokee Reservation deep in the Great Smoky Mountains, ancient homeland of the Cherokee. It's a forested mountain village, and the Cherokee homes are not tipis or dugouts or lean-tos but the square structures of woven cane and clay used by the earliest Cherokee and the sturdy log cabins of later generations, very much like those frontiersmen built as they pushed west over the Appalachians to the prairie lands beyond.

Cherokee life, the Oconaluftee visitor learns, was civilized and comfortable two and a half centuries ago. The Cherokee were woodsmen with a deep understanding of and reverence for nature, they were knowledgeable herbalists (as the Cherokee Botanical Garden near Oconaluftee proves), and they were artisans of uncommon skill (exhibits at the Museum of the Cherokee Indian show just how skilled).

Oconaluftee Indian Village capsulizes for the visitor a day in the life of the Cherokee, and the outdoor drama

Unto These Hills, performed in summer at the Mountainside Theatre, traces their history from the arrival of De Soto in 1540 to their banishment, in the late 1830s, to the Indian Territory of Oklahoma in what has become known as "The Trail of Tears."

Cherokee recipes, for the most part, are simple and earthy—too earthy, sometimes, for white man's palate. But a number of them are excellent by anyone's standard, among them *S-Que-Wi*, which is nothing more than cabbage and sweet green pepper browned together in meat drippings.

S-Que-Wi (Cherokee Cabbage)

MAKES 4 TO 6 SERVINGS

1 small cabbage, cut into bite-size chunks
3 tablespoons bacon or pork drippings
1 small green pepper, cut in small, thin strips
1 teaspoon salt
⅛ teaspoon pepper

Fry the cabbage in the bacon or pork drippings in a large, heavy kettle over moderately high heat just until cabbage begins to wilt and brown slightly—8 to 10 minutes. Add the green pepper and continue to fry and stir until the raw green color goes out of the pepper. Clap the lid on the kettle, turn the heat down low, and let cabbage "wilt" 10 to 15 minutes. It should be nicely glazed with the meat drippings, touched with brown here and there, but still somewhat crisp. Add salt and pepper, toss well to mix, and serve.

Each year the Cherokee would grow enough fruits and vegetables to last them through the bitter winter months. Fresh fruits and vegetables would not keep fresh, of course. So the women would dry them, either in the sun or over smoking fires. Green beans were picked young—just as soon as the pods matured—then spread out in the sun to dry. Afterwards, they were threaded onto strings, hung from the rafters, and cooked as needed. Drying changes the flavor and texture of green beans. After a few days in the hot sun, they yellow, shrivel, and toughen, which accounts, perhaps, for the name "Leather Britches Beans." Not everyone will like beans prepared this way, but Southerners invariably do.

Leather Britches Beans

MAKES 6 SERVINGS

1½ pounds fresh young green beans or pole beans
2 quarts cold water
⅓ pound fatback or salt pork, cut in ½-inch cubes
Salt and pepper to taste

Wash the beans in cool water, snap off the tips, but leave the beans whole. Spread them out, one layer deep, on baking sheets or trays, then set up on two sawhorses (or on a table) in the yard in the hot sun. Let the beans dry for 3 to 4 days, bringing them in each night so that the dew doesn't dampen them, and of course bringing them in, too, should it rain. When properly dry, the beans will be olive-drab in color, shriveled and leathery. To cook, place the beans in a large saucepan, cover with the cold water, and let soak overnight. Next day, add the fatback or salt pork to the saucepan, bring to a simmer, cover, and let bubble slowly about 3 hours (Cherokee women let the beans cook all day). Check the pot occasionally and add more water if it threatens to boil dry—you want plenty of "pot likker" to sop up with corn bread. Taste the beans and add salt and pepper to taste (the amount of salt needed will vary according to the saltiness of the fatback or salt pork). Ladle beans into soup bowls and serve accompanied by fresh-baked corn bread.

Bread to the Cherokee was corn bread, sometimes nothing more elaborate than a thick mush of meal and water baked in hot ashes or stuffed into the hollow curve of a piece of hickory bark, then stood before the fire to bake. Cherokee women today still bake corn breads daily, but they often add a bit of baking powder or meat drippings for a somewhat lighter texture and tenderer crumb. The following recipe is a Cherokee staple, used to sop up the "pot likker" of Leather Britches Beans or boiled turnip greens. If fried in a skillet the bread becomes Corn Pone; if baked in hot coals, Ash Cake. Try whichever method appeals to you most. Or try them both. These are heavy breads, remember, but the Cherokee would have them no other way.

Corn Pones and Ash Cakes

MAKES 6 SERVINGS

1½ cups corn meal (preferably stone-ground white meal)
1½ teaspoons baking powder
½ teaspoon salt
3 tablespoons meat or bacon drippings
¾ cup cold water

Stir together the corn meal, baking powder, and salt in a medium-size mixing bowl. Briskly mix in the meat or bacon drippings and water and stir just enough to make a stiff dough. This, then, is the basic mix. Shape and cook by either of the methods that follow:

To make corn pones: Shape the dough into 6 round, flat cakes (pones) about ½ inch thick. Heat about 2 tablespoons meat or bacon drippings or lard in a very large, heavy iron skillet just until it begins to smoke. Add the pones, reduce heat slightly, and brown well—about 10 minutes on each side. The pones will be crisp and brown outside, chewy inside.

To make ash cakes: To bake these the Cherokee way,

you will need about 4 dozen large green oak, maple, or sassafras leaves. You will also need a hearth and a good bed of hot coals. First, wash the leaves well and pat very dry. Rake the coals to one side of the hearth so that you have a clean space. Lay down about half of the leaves to make a smooth covering. Quickly shape the dough into 2 flat, round loaves no more than an inch thick, set them side by side on the bed of leaves, cover completely with the remaining leaves, then pile all the hot coals on top. Bake 40 minutes, then rake a few coals to one side and test one of the loaves—it should be browned outside but moist, almost dough-like inside. If not done—the time needed will vary according to the quantity and hotness of the coals—re-cover with coals and bake 10 to 15 minutes longer. Rake away the coals, lift the loaves from the bed of leaves with a long-handled pancake turner, and serve piping hot.

An Additional Old North Carolina Recipe

If you should be touring Old Salem in North Carolina or the Oconaluftee Indian Village at Cherokee, stop at any one of the small town farmers' markets or women's exchanges where local foods and crafts are sold and ask for a Brown Sugar Pound Cake. It isn't sold at either of these restored villages, but it *is* an old Southern recipe and an unusually good one. It has much the same firm-moist texture as plain pound cake, and a rich caramel flavor with plenty of pecans or walnuts baked into the batter. One of the best Brown Sugar Pound Cakes packaged for sale is that at the Women's Exchange in Pinehurst, North Carolina, about an hour and a half's drive southeast of Old Salem through the pottery country of Moore County. The potteries at Seagrove and Jugtown are well worth a visit if you want to see old-fashioned earthenware and stoneware hand thrown, glazed, and fired much as it was centuries ago when the Scots first settled in the red clay hills of North Carolina's Piedmont area.

Brown Sugar Pound Cake

MAKES A 10-INCH TUBE CAKE

3 cups sifted all-purpose flour
½ teaspoon baking powder
¼ teaspoon salt
¾ cup butter, at room temperature
¾ cup vegetable shortening
1 pound light brown sugar
1 cup sugar
5 large eggs
1 cup milk
1½ teaspoons vanilla
1 cup chopped pecans or walnuts

Sift together the flour, baking powder, and salt and set aside. Cream the butter and vegetable shortening until very light, add brown sugar gradually, creaming all the white until fluffy, then add the plain sugar the same way and cream until very light. Beat in the eggs, one at a time. Add the sifted dry ingredients alternately with the milk, beginning and ending with the dry ingredients and beating after each addition only enough to blend. Stir in vanilla and nuts. Pour into a well-greased and floured 10-inch tube pan and bake in a moderately slow oven (325°) for 1¾ to 2 hours or until cake begins to pull from sides of pan and the top springs back slowly when pressed with a finger. Cool cake upright in its pan on a wire rack 10 minutes, then invert and turn out on the wire rack. Let cool to room temperature before cutting.

Charleston, South Carolina

The Old South at its best—moonlight . . . magnolias . . . and more historic mansions per square mile than perhaps anywhere else in America.

There is about Charleston an in-limbo unreality: horse-drawn buggies clop down shade-dappled streets; secret gardens overclimb their high brick walls, spilling wisteria petals upon the sidewalks; Spanish moss runs amok in the live oaks; three- and four-story town houses, seemingly deserted, stare seaward through lacy iron balconies. Charleston's somnolence reaches deep into the surrounding Low Country, where stands of cypress rise from black-water swamps, camellias big as oaks engulf plantation homes, and once-productive rice paddies give way to salt grasses.

Nowhere in America is there a stronger sense of, or pride in, times past. Charleston's past was one of affluence and elegance, for its people amounted to New World landed gentry, profiting from both soil and sea.

Charleston is a sea-borne city, cradled by the rivers Ashley and Cooper on their meander to the Atlantic. Its history began in 1663, when King Charles II rewarded a clutch of close friends by designating them Lords Proprietors of Carolina. Seven years later settlers set forth from England to establish a colony, stepped ashore on the western bank of the Ashley River, and began building there a town called at first Albemarle Point, then Charles Towne in honor of the King.

The riverbank site was a temporary one, and within ten years, a "Grand Modell" had been laid out on Oyster Point with 335 lots and grand boulevards intersecting a market square in the Continental manner (the two original boulevards are today Meeting and Broad Streets).

Within a few decades, Charleston had become a busy seaport with ships lined up along the East Bay Street wharves loading cargoes of lumber and hemp; then, as Charleston plantations flourished, rice, indigo, and cotton. Homeward-bound ships arrived with holds full of European luxuries, and Charleston became a sort of "little London" in the New World semitropical wilderness.

But all was not peace and prosperity in Charleston. Down the years it withstood fires, a serious earthquake, twenty hurricanes, and a series of wars (the opening shot of the Civil War, or War Between the States, as Southerners choose to call it, was fired on Fort Sumter at the entrance to Charleston Harbor).

That war left Charlestonians poor, if not impoverished, which may well have been the city's saving grace. There simply was no money to gussy up with Victorian frills the once grand homes whose architectural styles ranged from Georgian to Adam to Regency to Classic Revival. So the homes stood untouched, many of them until after World War II. The majority have now been restored, but in a manner faithful to their original styles. So what the visitor sees, as he ambles along the streets, is a virtually intact colonial and antebellum city.

Charleston's tour map pinpoints fifty historic sites and buildings, among them the exquisite Adam-style Nathaniel Russel House, completed in 1809 at a cost of $80,000; the Heyward-Washington House (circa 1770); the Dock Street Theatre (opened in 1736 and America's first building designed exclusively for theatrical performances); the Joseph Manigault Mansion (1802), another fine example of the Adam style; and the William Rhett House (built in 1712; it is Charleston's oldest dwelling and remains a private home).

There is enough in Charleston to spellbind the history buff for a week at least. But plantation homes and country gardens beckon too: Middleton Place Gardens and Stableyards (of which more later); the watery wilderness of Cypress Gardens, classified as "one of the great gardens of the western world"; Boone Hall Plantation (used for location shots in *Gone with the Wind*); and Magnolia Gardens, considered by Baedeker at the turn of the century one of three double-starred attractions in the United States (the other two were Grand Canyon and Niagara Falls). Finally, at Charles Towne Landing, site of the first permanent settlement, there is a three-hundred-acre exhibition park that looks, at its remote river's edge, much as it did when the first English settlers disembarked more than three hundred years ago.

The Mills Hyatt House is a loving re-creation of the Mills House, circa 1853, Charleston's once grand "grand old hotel." It is, of course, modern, but its public rooms, filled with antiques, and its façade, hung with frilly wrought-iron balconies in the manner of the original Mills House, reflect the leisurely, luxurious life style of antebellum Charleston. So, too, does the food served at the Barbadoes Restaurant, entered through either the hotel's lobby or a fountain-splashed, gardenia-scented courtyard. Among Chef Lindner's specialties are these two Christmas Time recipes, roast rack of venison and sautéed mushrooms. Deer, in early plantation days, roamed the Low Country forests and is hunted today by bow and arrow on one of the offshore islands near Charleston.

Mills House Roast Venison with Juniper-Red Currant Sauce

MAKES 6 SERVINGS

1 rack of venison, weighing 5 to 6 pounds
Short, thin strips of larding fat
1 quart milk
Salt
Pepper
1 cup water

Juniper-Red Currant Sauce:
4 carrots, peeled and sliced
2 medium-size yellow onions, peeled and chopped
½ celery rib, chopped
1 tablespoon juniper berries
1 bay leaf, crumbed
2 tablespoons melted larding fat or bacon drippings
¼ cup water
½ cup dry red wine
5 cups chicken stock or broth
4 crushed peppercorns
½ cup red currant jelly
2 tablespoons heavy cream
Venison drippings
Salt to taste
3 tablespoons flour blended with ¼ cup cold water

With a larding needle, pique the surface of the rack of venison with thin, short strips of chilled larding fat. (To pique means, simply, to tuft the surface of the meat with short strips of fat, a technique rather like hooking a rug.) Place venison in a large bowl, pour in milk, and let soak 24 hours in the refrigerator, turning venison in the milk occasionally.

Also a day ahead, begin preparing the Juniper-Red Currant Sauce: In a heavy saucepan, sauté the carrots, onions, celery, juniper berries, and bay leaf in the melted larding fat or bacon drippings about 10 minutes until lightly browned; add water and wine and simmer, uncovered, about 5 minutes; add chicken stock and peppercorns and boil gently, uncovered, 1 hour. Smooth in currant jelly and simmer 15 minutes longer. Strain liquid and chill overnight (discard the solids in the strainer).

When ready to roast the venison, remove from the milk and rub generously with salt and pepper. Stand roast on its rib ends in a large, shallow roasting pan and roast, uncovered, in a very hot oven (450°) 15 minutes; pour in the 1 cup water and continue roasting, basting often with pan drippings, 20 to 25 minutes longer for rare and 35 minutes for medium rare (venison is best rare, as it toughens and dries with longer cooking). Remove roast from oven and let stand at room temperature 15 minutes before serving so that the juices will settle in the meat and make carving easier.

Heat the chilled sauce mixture to serving temperature, stir in the cream and venison drippings, scraping up any browned bits on the bottom of the roasting pan, then season to taste with salt. Briskly mix a little of the hot sauce into the flour-water paste, then stir back into pan and cook and stir until thickened and smooth, about 3 minutes.

Arrange the venison on a heated platter and garnish, if you like, with crab apples and ruffs of parsley or watercress. Pour the sauce into a heated sauceboat and pass separately.

At the Mills Hyatt House, these sautéed mushrooms are served with roast rack of venison. But they are equally good with roast pork, turkey, or capon.

Mills House Sautéed Mushrooms, Bacon, and Onions

MAKES 4 TO 6 SERVINGS

5 slices bacon, snipped crosswise with kitchen shears into
    julienne strips

1 large yellow onion, peeled and minced
1½ pounds mushrooms, wiped clean and sliced
Salt
Pepper

Brown the bacon in a large, heavy skillet until crisp; drain bacon on paper toweling. Measure the drippings and return 3 tablespoons to the skillet. Add the onion and sauté 5 to 8 minutes until golden; add mushrooms and sauté, stirring now and then, about 5 minutes until lightly browned. Season to taste with salt and pepper and serve.

Shrimp abound in the waters in and around Charleston, South Carolina—sweet, chunky shrimp which Charleston cooks prepare in countless ways. Pickled Shrimp are a hot weather favorite, and the recipe that follows comes from *Harriott Horry's Receipt Book*, now in the possession of the South Carolina Historical Society.

The society printed extracts from the book in its quarterly and prefaced the receipts with this information:

Harriott Pinckney Horry, daughter of Chief Justice Charles Pinckney and his wife Eliza Lucas and sister of Charles Cotesworth Pinckney and Thomas Pickney of Revolutionary fame, was born August 7, 1748, and died December 19, 1830. Harriott Horry Ravenel in her biography *Eliza Pinckney* presents a clear picture of the young Harriott, her charm, education, and accomplishments. Letters of the young woman quoted therein frequently refer to Mr. (Daniel) Horry, and finally she confesses to a friend that she has been so teased about him that she feels restraint in his presence: "I believe I look so simple when he is in Company, that he thinks me half an Idiot." The handsome young widower evidently did not so regard her, for their marriage took place on February 15, 1768, at St.

Philip's, Charleston, and the young bride departed for her husband's home, Hampton Plantation, on the Santee, about forty miles away. Just a few weeks after her daughter's marriage, Eliza Lucas Pinckney wrote to her son-in-law: "I am glad your little wife looks well to the ways of her household, I daresay she will not eat the bread of Idleness, while she is able to do otherwise." Harriott Horry's receipt book gives ample proof that she ate no "Bread of Idleness" for it attests to her industry in all phases of her domestic duties.

The small cookbook, bound in russet leather and inscribed simply, "Harriott Horry, 1770," was presented to the South Carolina Historical Society by Mrs. Francis B. Stewart. The first fifty-nine pages of the book are devoted to recipes, the remaining pages to household hints and medical remedies.

Here then, as she wrote it, is Harriott Horry's recipe for pickling shrimp, and, following it, a modern-day method.

TO PICKLE SHRIMPS

Boil your Shrimps in strong salt water till the shells will easily peel off, take them out and put them to cool while you prepare the following pickle: Take, of the liquor the shrimps were boiled in and strong vinegar, equal parts (a quantity fully sufficient to cover the shrimps). To this put some black pepper, All spice and cloves coarsely pounded, and boil it till it is strong of the spice, then strain and set to cool. Pick your shrimps and put them in a pot with a blade or two of mace and a few cloves and pour the pickle cold over them. Should the weather be very hot, add a little salt.

We suggest, when making the pickle, that you do not pound the spices as they tend to darken the pickle and subsequently the shrimp.

Pickled Shrimp

MAKES 4 SERVINGS

2 pounds raw shrimp in the shell
2 quarts water, mixed with 1 tablespoon salt
1½ cups cider vinegar
12 whole allspice
16 peppercorns
24 whole cloves
2 blades of mace

Boil the shrimp in the 2 quarts salted water 8 to 10 minutes, just until they turn bright pink. Drain, reserving 1½ cups of the cooking liquid. Rinse shrimp in cool water, shell, and devein. Combine reserved cooking liquid with the vinegar, 8 of the whole allspice, the peppercorns, and 16 of the cloves. Boil vigorously 10 minutes, then strain liquid through several thicknesses of cheesecloth and cool. Pour over shrimp in a medium-size mixing bowl, drop in remaining 4 whole allspice, 8 whole cloves, and the blades of mace. Cover and let marinate in the refrigerator 10 to 12 hours before serving. Stir occasionally so that the shrimp marinate evenly. Serve cold as an appetizer or as a main course.

🦐

Only the south wing of the red brick plantation house remains, the house built in 1741 by Henry Middleton above the Ashley River near Charleston (the main house was burned at the end of the Civil War). But that wing, the Middletown Place Gardens and Plantation Stableyards are today a Registered National Historic Landmark. The gardens are America's oldest landscaped gardens and contain the New World's first camellias, brought in 1783 at the request of Henry Middleton's son Arthur, one of the signers of the Declaration of Independence. Arthur Middleton, and succeeding generations of Middletons, have continued beautifying the gardens so that today they are as impressive as any anywhere on earth. Green velvet lawns stair-step down the slopes from the ruins of the main house to mirror lakes spread out like butterfly wings, and just across from these lakes a hillside massed with thirty-five thousand azaleas explodes in springtime into a conflagration of reds and pinks. Sheep graze underneath live oaks trailing beards of Spanish moss, peacocks swagger and preen about the restored Stableyards. The red brick outbuildings here have been renovated and given over to craft demonstrations: candledipping, spinning, weaving, ironworking, and carpentry to show what life was like on an eighteenth- and nineteenth-century Southern plantation. And just a stone's throw from the Stableyards, perched above one of the lakes, stands the small plantation kitchen, where visitors can sample old South Carolina cooking at its best.

🦐

These biscuits can be made successfully with vegetable shortening and milk, but the old Southern way of using lard and buttermilk results in flakier, more flavorful biscuits.

Middleton Place Gardens Cheese Biscuits

MAKES ABOUT 16 BISCUITS

3 heaping tablespoons lard or vegetable shortening (about ⅓ cup)
2 cups sifted self-rising flour
½ cup coarsely grated sharp Cheddar cheese
¾ cup buttermilk or milk

With a pastry blender or two knives, cut the lard or shortening into the flour until the texture of coarse meal; stir in the cheese. Make a well in the center, pour in the buttermilk or milk, and mix briskly with a fork just until the dough clings together. Turn onto a lightly floured board, knead three or four times, then roll out about ½ inch thick. Cut into rounds with a biscuit cutter and arrange on an ungreased baking sheet. Bake in a very hot oven (450°) 10 to 12 minutes until puffed and touched with brown. Serve piping hot with lots of fresh sweet butter. Or cool, split, and sandwich together with small slices of baked country ham.

A housewifely hint from *Harriott Horry's Receipt Book*:

TO WASH SILK STOCKINGS

Take weak lye such as is used for washing clothes. Wash the stockings in it cold very clean with soap, then soap them well, put them in clean lye and boil them 'till all the old blue comes out. Then chop up some soap and put it into a pint of lye. Put it on the fire and let it boil till the soap is melted, then take it off and add to it 2 large spoonfulls of liquid blue, strain it and put in the stockings, while it is scalding hot. Rub them well in it, then take them out and rub them again well with the hands, then let them hang in the shade 'till about half day, then mangle [smooth] them.

A pint of Lye with 2 spoonfulls of blue will do about 4 or 5 pair of stockings.

And a medicinal tip:

TO MAKE CASTOR OIL PLEASANT

Take 2 Oz Castor oil, 2 Oz rose or plain water, 2 Lumps Sugar, the yolk of 1 new laid Egg. Rub the oil, Sugar and Egg together well, then add the rose water. Take a spoonful or the whole at a dose.

Historic St. Augustine
St. Augustine, Florida

J amestown (1607) and Plymouth (1620) are the dates and places so firmly fixed in our minds as the beginnings of colonial America that we tend to forget St. Augustine, when in fact the Spaniards had settled there forty-two years before Captain John Smith led his band of Englishmen to the shores of Virginia and fifty-five years before the Pilgrims reached Plymouth Rock. On September 8, 1565, Don Pedro Menéndez de Avilés, amid booming artillery, blaring trumpets, fluttering pennons, and the cheers of six hundred Spanish settlers, stepped ashore on the northeast coast of La Florida ("The Land of Flowers"), which had been sighted, named, and claimed for Spain some fifty years earlier by Ponce de León.

This was not Spain's first attempt to colonize Florida. It was the seventh, six earlier attempts having failed. When word reached Philip II of Spain that the French had established a fort near the mouth of the St. Johns River in northern Florida, he named Menéndez Governor of Florida and instructed him to drive out the French and any other interlopers he found in Spain's corner of the New World. Menéndez succeeded, and because his sighting of the Florida coast occurred on the feast day of St. Augustine, he named the proposed settlement in honor of that saint. The Spaniards set about building their town at once, and it remains today the oldest permanent European settlement in the continental United States.

The odds against St. Augustine's survival were overwhelming. English corsairs, including Sir Francis Drake, repeatedly pillaged the town. And as English settlers spread through the South, they made numerous attacks against Castillo de San Marcos, the massive stone fortress built at St. Augustine by the Spaniards. Governor James Moore of Carolina led one such siege (unsuccessfully), and some years later General James Oglethorpe of Georgia led another (also unsuccessfully). In 1763, however, the English did gain control of St. Augustine, not by defeating the Spaniards but by agreeing to a swap: recently conquered Havana for St. Augustine. For twenty years England ruled St. Augustine, then, as the result of another treaty, it returned to Spanish rule and remained there another thirty-seven years.

The American Revolution had come and gone, the nineteenth century had dawned, the United States of America was pushing its boundaries west and south. Spain finally sold Florida to the young republic, and in a full-dress military ceremony on July 10, 1821, United States troops took possession of the territory Menéndez had begun building two and a half centuries earlier. The Spanish soldiers left Florida, never to return. St. Augustine became American. But not Americanized.

Indeed, to wander the walled streets of Historic St. Augustine today, to stroll past the flat-roofed Gallegos House (representative of the first Spanish period), the two-story, wooden-balconied Ribera "fine" House, reconstructed on its original eighteenth-century foundations, the one-room "house of boards" known as the Gomez House, "the shell-rock" Triay House with its shingled, steep-gabled roof, the more elegant Salcedo House with its white stuccoed kitchen house directly behind, the Old Spanish Inn, is to realize how much a melting pot America was—and is.

The twenty-eight buildings at Historic St. Augustine, some of them restored, some of them reconstructed, echo not only the Spanish colonial influence but also the English, for the Preservation Board's intent was not "to freeze the history at any particular period," but rather to show St. Augustine as a living, growing community.

It is indeed that. Cooking smells waft out onto St. George Street from the kitchen of the Gallegos House, where demonstrations are given. There may be breads proofing or baking—rough, nourishing breads made with whole-grain flours. Or there may be peppery fish stews or bean soups bubbling in giant caldrons over an open fire.

In the dirt-floored Blacksmith Shop, a smithy, descended from St. Augustine's early Minorcan settlers, forges iron tools and hardware in the eighteenth-century manner (many of them are for sale). Just next door a leathercraftsman tools saddles, bridles, harnesses, belts, boxes, and book covers while, directly across Cuna Street, an artisan demonstrates the casting of pewter at the William Sims Silversmith Shop, a small house-cum-shop typical of those built by English refugees from the American Revolution.

There are costumed hosts and hostesses everywhere about Historic St. Augustine to answer the visitor's questions and put him in touch with the reality of yesterday. A yesterday spread out over a dozen or so blocks of St. Augustine and two and a half centuries of its history —from 1565, when Menéndez first marched ashore, to 1821, when St. Augustine, along with the rest of Florida, joined the United States.

The Gallegos House, just inside the city gates at Historic St. Augustine, is a simple flat-roofed, two-room house, and to step into its cool dimness from the glary Florida sunlight is to step back some two hundred and fifty years in time, to sense what life was like for a Spanish colonial family in the 1720s. The East Room is now the kitchen, and it is here that old Spanish recipes—among them peppery bean soups, yellow rice, thick fish chowders, and rustic yeast breads—are prepared on a primitive wood-fired stove much as they were when the original Gallegos House was built.

Un Caldo Gallegos Bueno (A Good Gallegos Soup)

MAKES 6 TO 8 SERVINGS

1 pound boned beef chuck cut in very small pieces (about ½-inch cubes)
¼ cup olive oil
1 large Spanish onion, peeled and chopped
2 cloves garlic, peeled and minced
1 sweet green pepper, cored, seeded, and minced
1 to 2 hot red chili peppers, cored and minced, or ½ to 1 teaspoon crushed dried red chili peppers
1 cup dried garbanzo beans (chick-peas), soaked overnight in 2 cups cold water
5 cups cold water
1 tablespoon salt
¼ teaspoon crushed cumin seeds
1 small cabbage, coarsely shredded

Brown the beef well in the olive oil in a large, heavy kettle over fairly high heat. Turn the heat down to moderate, add the onion, garlic, green and red peppers, and fry, stirring now and then, until lightly browned and limp —about 10 minutes. Add the garbanzo beans and their soaking water, the 5 cups water, the salt, and cumin seeds. Bring to a simmer, cover, and let bubble 1½ to 2 hours until the beans and beef are very tender. Add the cabbage, pushing down into the liquid, cover, and cook just 10 to 15 minutes longer—the cabbage should be tender but still crisp. Mix the cabbage well into the soup and serve steaming hot.

🍃

Zarzuela, in Spanish, means "musical drama," and this piquant fish dish, as cooked at St. Augustine, is dramatic if not musical. It is of Catalan origin and was no doubt brought to the New World by Spanish colonists.

Zarzuelas de Pescado
(Fish Fillets in Spicy Tomato Sauce)

MAKES 6 SERVINGS

3 tablespoons olive oil
3 garlic cloves, peeled and minced
1 large Spanish onion, peeled and minced
1 medium-size sweet green pepper, cored, seeded, and minced
4 large firm-ripe tomatoes, peeled, cored, and chopped (reserve juices)
1 teaspoon crushed dried red chili peppers
½ teaspoon ground cumin
½ teaspoon leaf oregano, crushed
¼ teaspoon rubbed sage
1 teaspoon salt
1½ cups dry white wine or fish stock
2 teaspoons raw sugar (if needed to mellow tartness of tomatoes)
6 fillets of mullet, red snapper, or flounder

Heat oil in a large, heavy kettle over moderately high heat about a minute, add garlic, onion, and green pepper, and sauté, stirring now and then, 8 to 10 minutes until onion is lightly browned and limp. Add tomatoes and their juices, chili peppers, cumin, oregano, sage, salt, and wine and simmer, uncovered, stirring occasionally, about 20 to 25 minutes to mellow flavors. Taste and add raw sugar if too tart. Gently lay fish fillets down in sauce and cook about 10 minutes longer, just until fish will flake at the gentle probing of a fork. Serve fish on a bed of boiled white or brown rice and top with plenty of the tomato sauce.

Use the heaviest kettle you have because you want the water to boil down and every grain of rice to stand unto itself. If the water cooks down too fast, the rice will burn and be gummy—and it will in less than the heaviest kettle.

Arroz Amarillo con Chorizos
(Yellow Rice with Sausages)

MAKES 6 TO 8 SERVINGS

2 tablespoons olive oil
6 chorizos (or other peppery small link sausages), diced
10 scallions, minced (include some of the tops)
¼ teaspoon crushed saffron mixed with 1 tablespoon hot
    water
5½ cups water
2 bay leaves
1 to 1½ teaspoons crushed dried red chili peppers (depending
    on how hot you want the rice)
1 teaspoon salt
2 cups brown rice

Heat the oil in a large, heavy kettle, add sausages and scallions, and fry, stirring now and then, about 8 to 10 minutes until lightly browned. Add saffron, water, bay leaves, chili peppers, and salt and bring to a full rippling boil. Stir in rice, set lid on kettle askew, adjust heat so water boils gently, and cook about 35 minutes until most of the water has boiled away. Stir once, then cook rice, uncovered, about 10 minutes longer until all the water has cooked down. Serve steaming hot as a main dish.

Crusty brown rounds of bread made with unbleached and whole wheat flours, raw sugar, and olive oil.

St. Augustine Sponge Bread

MAKES 2 LARGE ROUND LOAVES

2 packages active dry yeast, softened in ½ cup warm but not
    hot tap water
½ cup raw sugar or light brown sugar (not packed down)
2 cups warm but not hot water
5 cups sifted unbleached flour (about)
1½ teaspoons salt
2 tablespoons olive oil
1½ cups unsifted whole wheat flour

Combine softened yeast, raw sugar, warm water, and 2 cups of the unbleached flour in a large bowl and beat until smooth. Cover with a cloth, set in a warm spot, and let rise about 30 minutes until very light and spongy. Stir in salt and olive oil, then mix in whole wheat flour and 2½ cups unbleached flour. Again cover with cloth, set in a warm spot, and let rise until doubled in bulk, about 45 minutes. Turn out on a very well-floured board (dough will be soft and sticky) and knead in about ½ to ¾ cup unbleached flour until dough is elastic and no longer sticky (keep your hands and the board well floured). Knead vigorously about 10 minutes, flouring the board and your hands as necessary. Divide dough in half, knead each half about 25 to 30 times, then shape into round loaves about 5 inches across. Place in greased layer cake pans, cover with cloth, and let rise in a warm spot until doubled in bulk, about 45 minutes. Bake in a hot oven (400°) about 30 minutes until richly browned and loaves give a hollow sound when thumped with your fingers. Remove from pans and let cool on wire racks at least 10 minutes, then cut into wedges and serve.

Shakertown
Pleasant Hill, Kentucky

'Tis the gift to be simple, 'tis the
   gift to be free,
'Tis the gift to come down where we
   ought to be.
And when we find ourselves in the
   place just right
'Twill be in the valley of love and
   delight.

—Old Shaker Song

"*The* valley of love and delight" was heaven, for there was fraternal love only in the nineteen celibate Shaker communes that flourished in New England and the Midwest during the nineteenth century. Surely there could have been little delight in the arduous days the Shakers spent, devoting "their hands to work and their hearts to God."

Still, the Shakers believed that their very abstemiousness, diligence to work, and equal sharing among Sisters and Brethren were establishing for them God's Kingdom on Earth. There is no denying, certainly, that their willingness to work rewarded them with sturdy homes and substantial food.

The Shakers lived comfortably. Just how comfortably is best seen, perhaps, at Shakertown, the restored Shaker commune at Pleasant Hill, bosomed in the bluegrass country of Kentucky twenty-five miles south of Lexington.

The Shakers came to this "pleasant hill," as they called the bluff above the Kentucky River palisades, in 1805 and remained there for one hundred and five years, building a community of fine frame and masonry homes, building, too, a reputation for hospitality and the best public dining room in the Kentucky heartland.

Word spread and soon the fashionable people of the countryside began driving over in horse-drawn carriages to break bread at the Shaker's table. "Winter Shakers" came too, the homeless and hangers-on whom the Shakers welcomed into their circle, sheltered, and fed through the cold months, only to see these new "converts" depart with the first flush of spring.

The Shaker faith, an offshoot of the Quaker sect, was not an easy one to embrace. Its rules were rigid: celibacy, confession of sins, isolation from the world, and communal ownership of property. Its Sisters and Brethren dressed drably (artifice was anathema to the Shakers), they slept in the same houses but in distinctly separate quarters reached by separate staircases. Husbands and wives were separated upon embracing the Shaker beliefs, and lived ever afterward as Brothers and Sisters. The only moments of joy and merriment appeared to occur, at least to the curious who came to eavesdrop on the Shakers, during the religious service itself, when men and women joined in a large circle, chanting, dancing, shouting—shaking the sins from their bodies, which gave rise to the name "Shakers."

Life otherwise was ordered, uncluttered, serene, characteristics all embodied in the Shaker architecture, which is probably the purest and most practical in America.

Shakertown today, with its twenty-five fully restored early-nineteenth-century buildings and homes, is perhaps the single most important showcase of Shaker design in America. Here you will see functional architecture at its best, clean of line, devoid of arabesques and frills. But it is not a black-and-white town-scape you see at Shakertown, for the Shakers developed rich, mellow colors—earthy reds and yellows, soft slate blues—with which they relieved the raw whiteness of paint and plaster both inside and out. They were master engineers and craftsmen, able to construct, via intricate trussing, rooms of awesome size without supporting pillars or archways. The Meeting House room in which the Shakers performed their ritual singing and dancing, measures forty feet by sixty feet, the size of a small gymnasium, and yet it contains not a single column, an astonishing architectural feat for 1820. The Shakers also elevated built-ins to high art, as can be seen in the skylighted, cupboard-lined storage room at the Centre Family Dwelling House (1824–34).

Every room, indeed every wall, at Shakertown is banded with a molding of polished wood, studded with wooden pegs. The molding is set about six feet from the floor and it was the rack upon which everything was hung—hats, cloaks, lamps, even chairs, which meant that the Sisters could go about cleaning and polishing the floors without having to shove furniture around.

Everywhere about Shakertown you see proof of the Shakers' industry and artistry—in the staved wooden washtubs and vats at the East Family Wash House (1825); at the East Family Sisters' Shop (1855) where the spinning, weaving, and sewing were done; at the Cooper's Shop (remodeled in 1847) where the Brethren made and sold as many as two thousand cedar pails, buckets, and butter churns in a single year; at the Shoemaker's Shop (1835), at the East Family Brethren's Shop (1845), where broom handles were manufactured, garden seeds boxed, and medicinal herbs packaged and labeled, at the Preserve Shop (1859), where the Sisters put up thirty tons of the famed Shaker "sweetmeats" each year, to be sold, along with other Shaker items, to the "World" at large; at the Carpenter's Shop (1815), and at the Tanyard Brick Shop (1823), where rawhide was tanned for harness, saddles, and shoes.

The grounds at Shakertown, like the buildings, are open and spacious. But they are ordered, too, marked off by picket fences and dry stone walls. There is a livestock exhibit—of Leicester sheep, Durham dairy cows, chickens, ducks, geese, horses, for the Shakers were knowledgeable agriculturalists and husbandrymen as well as architects and engineers. Few of us are aware of what we owe the Shakers. It was they who invented the flat broom, the clothespin, the cut nail, the washing machine, and the circular saw.

What is most unique about Shakertown is that nine of the historic buildings have been converted into guesthouses so that you can actually stay the night at Shakertown, sleeping, perhaps, in one of the original bedrooms of the Brethren or of the Sisters. And at the Trustees' House, you can tuck into a hearty breakfast, Shaker-style, or a lunch, or a dinner by candlelight.

You will find at Shakertown the same gracious hospitality for which the Shakers were famous a hundred years ago. And you will also find the same bountiful meals, cooked and served with love, just as they were in the days of the shy, gentle Shaker Sisters.

"Let a stranger visit your country and enquire for your best specimens of agriculture, mechanics and architecture, and sir," said Kentucky State Senator Robert Wickliffe in 1831, "he is directed to visit the Society of Shakers at Pleasant Hill." He might also have added that Pleasant Hill was the place to sample some of Kentucky's finest fare, for Shaker women were known far and wide as uncommonly good cooks. They grew their own herbs, fruits, and vegetables, tended the poultry and dairy cows, and three times a day dished up simple, sustaining meals for the five hundred celibate Brothers and Sisters who, during the nineteenth century, lived at Pleasant Hill. Today, the recipes for which the Shaker women were famous a hundred years ago are served at the Trustees' Office dining rooms at the restored Shaker village at Pleasant Hill. And for those who would try them out at home, they have been gathered together by Elizabeth C. Kremer, director of the dining rooms, in a small paperback cookbook called *We Make You Kindly Welcome*. Included here are five of those recipes.

Country Meat Loaf

MAKES 6 TO 8 SERVINGS

1½ pounds ground lean beef
1 egg, lightly beaten
½ cup finely chopped onion
2 tablespoons diced celery
2 tablespoons minced green pepper
1½ teaspoons salt
¼ teaspoon pepper
1 cup tomato juice (the Shakers would have used home-
    canned)
¾ cup uncooked oatmeal

Mix together lightly with a fork the beef, egg, onion, celery, green pepper, salt, and pepper. Stir in tomato juice, then oatmeal, using as light a touch as possible so that the meat loaf will not be heavy. Shake into a large round loaf on a foil-lined shallow baking pan. Bake in a moderate oven (350°) 1½ hours. To serve, cut in thin wedges.

&

The Shakers at Pleasant Hill excelled as husbandry-men. They imported Berkshire hogs and Bakewell sheep to Kentucky and in the early 1870s owned more pure-bred shorthorn cattle than any cattle rancher or breeder in America. Pork was popular at Pleasant Hill, both smoky country-cured ham and fresh pork. The recipe below was made originally of pork tenderloins (and is today at Pleasant Hill), but since they are virtually impossible to buy in modern-day supermarkets, we have taken the liberty of substituting boned and rolled pork loin roast. The results are very much the same.

Pork Loin and Cream Gravy

MAKES 4 TO 6 SERVINGS

1 rolled pork loin roast, weighing about 2 pounds
3 tablespoons pork roast drippings
3 tablespoons flour
2 cups milk
1 teaspoon salt
⅛ teaspoon pepper

Roast pork loin in a shallow, open roasting pan in a moderate oven (350°) 2 hours. Remove from oven, slice about ¾ inch thick, keeping slices intact. Place the pork roast drippings in a very large, heavy skillet and blend in the flour. Add milk and heat and stir until thickened and smooth, 3 to 5 minutes. Stir in salt and pepper. Place pork slices down in the cream gravy and simmer slowly 15 to 20 minutes, basting occasionally. Serve the pork topped with plenty of the gravy.

A summertime favorite at Pleasant Hill—cool, crisp, and tart. Like most slaws, this one "seasons" and improves on standing in the refrigerator.

Shakertown Coleslaw

MAKES 4 TO 6 SERVINGS

4 cups finely shredded cabbage
¼ cup finely grated carrot
¼ cup finely chopped celery
¼ cup finely chopped onion
½ teaspoon salt

½ cup Country Dressing (recipe follows)
¼ cup mayonnaise

Place cabbage, carrot, celery, onion, and salt in a large bowl and toss to mix. Blend country dressing with mayonnaise, pour over slaw mixture, and toss well again to mix. Refrigerate until ready to serve.

This sweet-tart salad dressing owes its bite to dry mustard. Shaker women grew their own mustard, as they did all of their herbs, dried the seeds, and ground them to powder to use in cooking.

Country Dressing

MAKES ABOUT 1 CUP

1 teaspoon dry mustard
2 tablespoons sugar
¼ teaspoon salt
2 tablespoons flour
½ cup cold water
2 egg yolks, lightly beaten
¼ cup cider vinegar
2 tablespoons butter

Mix together the mustard, sugar, salt, and flour and set aside. In the top of a double boiler, beat the water with egg yolks and vinegar. Stir in mustard mixture, set over simmering water, and cook and stir until thickened, 3 to 4 minutes. Mix in the butter and, when it melts, use to dress coleslaw or lettuce salads.

One of the best pies you will ever eat is this one served at the Trustees' House at Pleasant Hill, Kentucky. Unlike lesser pecan pies, it does not stint on butter, eggs, or pecans. No flour is added to thicken the filling—the eggs do it alone. It's a rich, *rich* pie, so cut the pieces small.

Pleasant Hill Pecan Pie

MAKES A 9-INCH PIE

3 large eggs, lightly beaten
1 cup light corn syrup
1 cup firmly packed light brown sugar
⅓ cup melted butter
⅛ teaspoon salt
1 teaspoon vanilla
1 cup pecans (halves or coarsely broken nutmeats)
1 9-inch unbaked pie shell

Stir together eggs, corn syrup, brown sugar, melted butter, salt, and vanilla until well blended. Mix in pecans. Pour into unbaked pie shell, then bake in a moderate oven (350°) about 1 hour or until crust is lightly browned and filling puffy and of a jelly-like consistency (it should quiver slightly as you nudge the pan in the oven, but it will thicken somewhat as the pie cools). Let pie cool to room temperature before cutting.

The Midwest

Hale Farm and Western Reserve Village
Bath, Ohio

By the turn of the nineteenth century, New England had become both populous and prosperous, "Mad Anthony" Wayne had chased the Indians west of the Cuyahoga River in what is now Ohio, paths had been cleared across New York and Pennsylvania, the westward push was on.

Yankee farmers began loading their families and belongings into covered wagons and rumbling overland to begin new lives in the Connecticut Western Reserve, the northeast corner of Ohio to which Connecticut still laid claim. One such Yankee farmer was Jonathan Hale, who in 1810 left Glastonbury, Connecticut, for the wilderness of the Cuyahoga Valley. To his astonishment he discovered that the woodlands he had bought had already been cleared. Or, rather, that several acres of them had, that crops had been sown, and that the squatter responsible for it all had built himself a log cabin. Being an honest man, Hale could not in good conscience evict the squatter without compensating him for the groundwork he had done. So he turned over to the squatter his own horses and wagon, then waved him on his way. Hale and his family moved into the squatter's cabin and lived there for the next sixteen years. Things went so well for Hale in the Western Reserve that in 1826 he began building an impressive three-story red brick home on a rise over-looking the pastures and fields. It is that home, bequeathed to the Western Reserve Historical Society in 1958 by the great-granddaughter of Jonathan Hale, that forms the nucleus of Hale Farm and Western Reserve Village.

Today this re-created village is growing as early farm villages of the Western Reserve grew in the first half of the nineteenth century. Indeed, a stroll along the dusty village streets is a sort of short course in the history of the Western Reserve. It shows, for example, how the first frontiersmen in the Ohio wilderness were the farmers who cleared the fields and planted the crops, how, as they prospered, tradesmen were attached to the community. Blacksmiths and carpenters, at first, then saw millers and grist millers.

The Hale Farm is worked today as Jonathan Hale worked it. Fields are planted with Indian corn, flax, and other mid-century crops. Sheep, horses, and cows graze the pasturelands. In the village there are blacksmiths at work, woodworkers, chandlers, weavers, spinsters, and on occasion women in nineteenth-century farm dress, demonstrating the art of fireplace cooking.

Though Western Reserve Village never existed as such, it is composed of historic buildings, all rescued from the wrecking ball, trucked to the village from nearby towns, faithfully restored and furnished. There is the Saltbox, built in 1830, a strong reminder that many of the Western Reserve's settlers were Connecticut Yankees. There are the Greek Revival Jagger House (circa 1845), the Log School (1816), the Law Office (1825), the high-steepled Baptist Meeting House (1852), the Grist Mill (1851), the Franklin Glassworks (1824–32), the Land Office (1832), and the Stow House (1850). The village sprawls, New England style, about a grassy common. It is a young village, a developing village, local history repeating itself.

Nestled behind a picket fence, the white frame Jagger House (a proud Greek Revival structure built about 1845) stands beside Western Reserve Village green against a backdrop of evergreens. Like so many of the restored buildings at Hale Farm and Village, it was rescued from destruction and moved to the restoration site from nearby, in this case from the village of Bath. The great-granddaughter of the original owner works today at the Hale Farm, conducting classes called "A Day in the 19th Century" for Cleveland Community College and preparing old Ohio recipes over an open fire or in a fireplace oven. The three recipes given here are all from the Jagger family, recipes that were served from 130 years ago in the Jagger House.

Grandma Jagger's Beef Stew

MAKES 6 TO 8 SERVINGS

2 pounds boned beef chuck, cut in 1-inch cubes
3 tablespoons lard
6½ cups boiling water
2 cloves garlic, peeled and crushed
2 large yellow onions, peeled and sliced
1 tablespoon salt
1 teaspoon sugar
1 teaspoon freshly ground black pepper
1 tablespoon paprika
Pinch of ground cloves
6 medium-size potatoes, peeled and diced
6 carrots, peeled and diced
6 small yellow onions, peeled and quartered
4 tablespoons flour blended with 5 tablespoons cold water

Brown the beef well on all sides in the lard in a large, heavy kettle. Add the boiling water, garlic, sliced onions, salt, sugar, pepper, paprika and cloves, cover, and simmer 1½ to 2 hours until meat is tender. Add potatoes, carrots, and quartered onions, cover, and simmer 1 hour longer. Spoon a little of the hot liquid into the flour-water paste, then stir quickly back into kettle and cook, stirring constantly, until thickened and no raw flour taste remains, about 5 minutes. Ladle into soup plates and serve.

Lemony and rich.

Jonathan Apple Bread

MAKES A 9 × 5 × 3-INCH LOAF

2 cups sifted stone-ground unbleached flour
1 teaspoon baking powder
1 teaspoon baking soda
¼ cup butter
¾ cup sugar
2 eggs, beaten until frothy
2 cups finely chopped, peeled, and cored Jonathan apples (or McIntosh)
1 tablespoon finely grated lemon rind
¾ cup chopped pecans or walnuts
2 tablespoons melted butter

Sift together the flour, baking powder, and soda and set aside. Cream the butter and sugar until pale and light, then beat in eggs. Add the sifted dry ingredients alternately with the chopped apples, beginning and ending with dry ingredients. Stir in the lemon rind and nuts and spoon into a well-greased 9 × 5 × 3-inch loaf pan. Bake in a moderate oven (350°) 50 to 60 minutes or until loaf begins to pull from sides of pan and top seems springy to the touch. Brush top with melted butter. Cool loaf upright in pan on a wire rack 10 minutes, then turn out on rack and cool to room temperature before slicing.

Extra dark and spicy, with caraway seeds adding both crunch and flavor. If you are unable to find stone-ground flour, use regular unbleached flour or all-purpose flour.

Caraway Gingerbread

MAKES ABOUT 12 SERVINGS

2½ cups sifted stone-ground unbleached flour
1½ teaspoons baking soda
1 teaspoon salt
1 teaspoon ginger
¾ teaspoon nutmeg
½ teaspoon mace
½ teaspoon allspice
½ teaspoon cloves
1 teaspoon caraway seeds
½ cup butter
½ cup firmly packed light brown sugar
1 cup light molasses
2 eggs
1 cup buttermilk

Sift together the flour, soda, salt, ginger, nutmeg, mace, allspice, and cloves. Stir in caraway seeds and set aside. Cream the butter until light, add brown sugar, and continue creaming until fluffy. Mix in the molasses and ½ cup of the flour mixture. Beat the eggs in one at a time. Add the remaining flour mixture alternately with the buttermilk, beginning and ending with flour and beating well after each addition. Pour into a greased and floured 13 × 9 × 2-inch baking pan and bake in a moderate oven (350°) 35 to 40 minutes or until gingerbread begins to pull from sides of pan and top seems springy to the touch. Cut into large squares (about 3 inches) and serve. Good hot or cold.

Au Glaize Village

Defiance, Ohio

*A*u Glaize is one of America's newest restored and re-created villages (it was begun in 1966), and it is also one of the busiest. Busy, not only because it seems to be springing up overnight (there are already ten buildings on the forty-acre tract and four more to come), but also because it is a "please touch" museum, a place where visitors are encouraged to pick up and examine the museum pieces, to join in the activities of the day, whatever they may be—a barn raising, perhaps, apple butter or sorghum making, wheat threshing, candle dipping. People come not only to ride the historic Au Glaize Village Railroad, but also to help split rails. They come to watch the weavers work and, perhaps, to add an inch or so of weft to the warp themselves.

There is plenty to see and do: at the operating Cider Mill, the Cane Mill, the Village Blacksmith's, the Village Cook Shed, the Jewel Railroad Station. There's Dr. Cameron's Office to visit, the Sherry School, the Kieffer Cabin, St. John's Lutheran Church. Most of these buildings are historic (circa 1860–90), having been transferred from elsewhere about Defiance County to their present location three miles southwest of the city of Defiance. Soon to be added to the village are a grist mill, a tavern, a sawmill, and a broom factory. And for the 1976 Bi-Centennial, the Defiance County Historical Society aims to cover an eighty-acre tract adjoining Au Glaize Village with a full-scale replica of historic Defiance (dating from 1670 to 1812) and, in the Maumee Valley Heritage Festival Park hard by Au Glaize, to reconstruct Fort Defiance, Fort Au Glaize, a Shawnee village, a French mission, and a number of traders' cabins.

Meanwhile, visitors and Defiance Countyites must content themselves with the activities at Au Glaize Village. Not that there is any shortage of events, among them the Maumee Valley Frontier Days, the Harvest Demonstration, the Johnny Appleseed Festival, the Thanksgiving Turkey Shoot, the Antique Car Meet, the Antiques Flea Market.

At Au Glaize Village, history is learned by reliving it. And no one considers it a dull course.

One of the most popular pioneer recipes prepared at Au Glaize Village is this bean soup, which is served at both the Fort Defiance North-South Skirmish and Old-Fashion Harvest Time, held in July, and at the Johnny Appleseed Festival in late September. Early pioneers would have made the soup with whatever dried beans or vegetable tag ends they had on hand instead of following a particular recipe. The Au Glaize version is rich and thick, a meal in itself. You can make it with ham bones, ham hocks, or, for an even huskier soup, with coarsely ground smoked ham. The recipe makes a whopping kettleful, but the soup freezes well in quart-size containers.

Mixed Bean Soup

MAKES ABOUT 2 GALLONS (8 QUARTS) OR ENOUGH
FOR 20 TO 25 SERVINGS

1 pound dried baby lima beans, washed and sorted
1 pound dried navy or pea beans, washed and sorted
5 quarts cold water (about)

½ pound dried lentils, washed and sorted
½ pound dried green split peas, washed and sorted
3 pounds ham bones or 1 pound ham hocks or 1½ pounds
    coarsely ground smoked ham
3 large yellow onions, peeled and chopped
4 celery stalks, diced
4 carrots, peeled and diced
3 bay leaves
16 peppercorns
2 teaspoons salt (about)

Place lima and navy beans in a very large bowl, add 3
quarts water, and soak overnight. Next day, pour off and
measure soaking water; add enough additional water to
total 5 quarts. Place soaked beans in a very large, heavy
kettle (at least 2½ gallons); add the 5 quarts water, the
lentils, split peas, ham bones, hocks, or ground ham,
onions, celery, carrots, bay leaves, and peppercorns.
Bring to a simmer and cook, uncovered, stirring occasionally, 3½ to 4 hours, until quite thick and all flavors
are blended. Taste for salt and season as needed (the
saltiness of the ham will vary). Remove ham bones or
hocks if used, cut off any clinging bits of meat, and return to kettle (most of the meat will have already fallen
from the bones). Serve piping hot. Or, if you prefer, cool
to room temperature, ladle into quart-size freezer cartons, and freeze. When reheating the frozen soup, you
will probably have to add about 1 cup of water to each
quart of frozen soup, as the soup seems to thicken up in
the freezer.

Au Glaize Village is not a "stroll through" museum. It
is the "pitch in and help" variety. Hundreds of visitors,
for example, came to watch the erection of an original
Black Swamp cabin, hand-hewn of white oak logs, then
they stayed to help chop. Hundreds more have split
rails, skimmed cooking sorghum, fashioned candles, or
stirred apple butter in a giant copper caldron. In August,
when the annual "Frontier Days" is in full swing at Au

Glaize Village, there will be vast cast-iron kettles of Indian Corn Stew to stir and, later, to taste at one of the village's "taste tables." In the old days, the stew was made with venison, and is today whenever venison is available. But very lean beef, Au Glaize volunteer cooks say, makes excellent corn stew too.

Indian Corn Stew

MAKES 6 SERVINGS

1 pound coarsely ground venison or lean beef
1 large yellow onion, peeled and chopped
1 medium-size green pepper, cored, seeded, and chopped
3 cups fresh cream-style sweet corn, cut from the cob (for 3 cups, you will need 6 to 8 ears of corn; to cut from the cob cream-style, score down the center of each row of kernels with a sharp knife, then scrape pulp and milk from cob with the knife)
4 large ripe tomatoes, peeled, cored, and cut in thin wedges
2 teaspoons sugar
1½ teaspoons salt

Brown the venison or beef in a fairly large, heavy kettle, adding, if necessary to keep meat from sticking to kettle, about a tablespoon of bacon drippings or butter. Add onion and green pepper and brown lightly also. Stir in all remaining ingredients, adjust heat so mixture simmers gently, cover, and cook 1½ to 2 hours or until about the consistency of chili and flavors are well blended. Ladle into soup bowls and serve.

A hearty meat and vegetable stew that simmers lazily for hours. It's served on "Railroad Days" at Au Glaize Village. Make it with venison if you have it, otherwise with lean ground beef. Like Mixed Bean Soup, this makes a huge kettleful. Freeze what you can't eat right away to enjoy later.

Mulligan Stew

MAKES 1½ GALLONS (6 QUARTS), ENOUGH FOR 16 TO 20
HEARTY SERVINGS

2 pounds coarsely ground venison or lean beef
3 large yellow onions, peeled and chopped
1 green pepper, cored, seeded, and chopped
4 stalks celery, cut in fine dice
4 carrots, peeled and cut in fine dice
6 medium-size potatoes, peeled and cubed
2 large white turnips, peeled and cubed
½ small cabbage, cored and shredded
½ cup shelled green peas
2 quarts cold water
4 teaspoons salt (about)
¼ teaspoon pepper (about)

Brown venison or beef in a 2-gallon heavy kettle over
fairly high heat, adding about 1 tablespoon bacon drippings or butter, if needed, to keep meat from sticking to
the kettle. Add all remaining ingredients, bring to a simmer, cover, and cook 1½ hours. Uncover and simmer
very slowly about 1 hour longer, stirring now and then.
Taste for salt and pepper and add more, if needed, to suit
your taste. Ladle into large soup bowls and serve. Cool
leftover stew to room temperature, ladle into quart-size
freezer containers, and freeze.

Au Glaize Village lies in the Johnny Appleseed country of northern Ohio, and the village has its own operating cider mill. In early autumn when the Johnny
Appleseed Festival is held, hundreds of visitors throng in
to lend a hand at stirring the apple butter, cooked out-
doors in immense copper kettles. The recipe here is one
that has been used at Au Glaize for eight years. It was
also demonstrated at both the Ohio Folk Festival at the
Ohio State Fair and at the Smithsonian Festival of American Folk Life in Washington, D.C.

Old-Fashioned Apple Butter

MAKES ABOUT 6 PINTS

1 gallon apple cider
4 quarts peeled, cored, and sliced apples (about 7 pounds; for
     best flavor, use Jonathan, Winesap, McIntosh or Pippin
     apples)
1 pound granulated sugar
1 cup dark brown sugar
1 tablespoon ground cinnamon
1 teaspoon ground cloves
1 teaspoon ground allspice

Pour the apple cider into a large (about 4-gallon) heavy
enamel kettle, set on to boil, then boil, uncovered, until
volume is reduced by half. Add the apples, a few at a
time, stirring all the while. Boil, uncovered, until all
pieces of apple disappear and mixture is thick and glossy.
You'll have to stir constantly lest the mixture "catch on"
(stick). Stir in the granulated sugar, brown sugar, cinnamon, cloves, and allspice and remove apple butter from
the fire. Continue to stir until sugars are completely dissolved. Ladle hot into hot, sterilized pint-size preserving
jars, filling to within ⅛ inch of the top. Seal, process for
10 minutes in a simmering water bath; cool, then store
on a cool, dry shelf.

Conner Prairie Pioneer Settlement
Noblesville, Indiana

"Conner's Prairie," it was called at first, after William Conner, who had set up a fur trading post in 1802 on the banks of the White River, twenty miles north of what is now Indianapolis and four miles south of Noblesville.

This was Indian territory at the turn of the nineteenth century, and it was with the Delaware and other tribes that Conner traded. He had grown up among the Delaware Indians, spoke their language, and had, in fact, married a Delaware chief's daughter.

The Indians, however, were soon to lose their territory, the forested prairies crisscrossed by clear rushing streams. These lands were now the American frontier into which settlers were rumbling by the wagonload, and they were lands on their way to statehood. William Henry Harrison, then Governor of the Indiana Territory, found a valuable aide in William Conner, a man who could scout the wilderness, interpret at Indian councils, help pave the way for statehood.

Statehood came to Indiana in 1816, and yet the northern two-thirds of it remained Indian territory. It wasn't until two years later that a treaty was signed in which the Delaware and other tribes agreed to release their vast wilderness to settlers and to move themselves west of the Mississippi.

With them went Conner's Delaware wife and their six children, and with them, too, went the fur trappers. Conner's fur business was doomed. But, being a resourceful man, he simply restocked his post—with the food staples and general merchandise the incoming settlers needed. He also married one of the settlers and by 1823 had become successful enough to replace his rustic log house with a fine brick mansion—the first of its kind in the territory—which overlooked a vast prairie planted with grain. Conner's brick house was more than a home, however. It was the area's first post office and, in addition, a courtroom where the local circuit court held session until county buildings were put up in the new county seat of Noblesville nearby.

Conner had, in fact, founded Noblesville, and in 1837 he moved his second wife and their seven children there, leaving his fine brick mansion to a succession of occupants. They abused it, the house fell into disrepair, and it wasn't until 1933 that someone set about restoring it. That someone was Eli Lilly (of the pharmaceutical house). Lilly did more than restore the hundred-year-old brick mansion, he furnished it with period pieces, and he brought onto the grounds a collection of historic log buildings that depicted pioneer life on the Indiana prairie —a barn, a cabin, a trading post much like that Conner had operated, a distillery, and a spring house. Lilly opened his restoration, but only to friends and private groups.

In 1964, however, the restored village and grounds were given to Earlham College to be operated as a historic landmark, and for the first time the public was invited.

The public came and has continued to come in increasing numbers because everything about Conner Prairie Pioneer Settlement is authentic. Each restored building, each piece of furniture, each accessory, the foods prepared daily at both the Conner House Kitchen and the Blacksmith's House Kitchen during the village season (from the first Tuesday in April through the last Sunday in October), and also for three weekends at Christmas time during the "closed season" so that visitors can share a "Traditional Christmas at Conner Prairie."

Six new restored buildings have been recently added to Conner Prairie, and the village now has its first two resident artisans, a potter and a blacksmith. More restored buildings are to come: a doctor's office and house, a church, a cemetery, a working farm (circa 1825), a grist mill on the White River near where Conner set up his fur trading post.

The village is growing just as early Indiana villages grew some hundred and fifty years ago. And already it has become a working microcosm of frontier Hoosier life.

"If well made, no directions will be needed for eating." That is what Henry Ward Beecher, the celebrated New England Congregational minister, said of Hoosier Biscuit, a recipe he included among the notes he wrote about his ten-year stay in Indiana during the late 1830s and early to mid-1840s. The recipe, obtained from the Indiana State Library, is one of the many early Hoosier recipes demonstrated in two restored kitchens at Conner Prairie Pioneer Settlement—the Conner House Kitchen and the Blacksmith's House Kitchen. This particular recipe is prepared in the blacksmith's kitchen. The biscuits have an unusual texture, rather like English muffins. They are hard and crispy outside, but soft and chewy inside. And they have a rich, yeasty flavor. Henry Ward Beecher was right. "No directions will be needed for eating" except to say, perhaps, that you should split the biscuits while they are piping hot and tuck in a fat chunk of butter. Here, then, is the recipe just as Beecher wrote it, followed by a modern adaptation.

HOOSIER BISCUIT

Add a teaspoonful of salt to a pint of new milk, warm from the cow. Stir in flour until it becomes a stiff batter, add two great spoonfuls of lively brewer's yeast; put it in a warm place and let it rise just as much as it will. When well raised, stir in a teaspoonful of saleratus (baking soda) dissolved in hot water. Beat up three eggs (two will answer), stir with the batter, and add flour until it becomes tolerable stiff dough; knead it thoroughly, set it by the fire until it begins to rise, then roll out, cut to biscuit form, put in pans, cover it over with a thick cloth, set by the fire until it rises again, then bake in a quick oven.

Hoosier Biscuit

MAKES ABOUT 2½ DOZEN

2 cups milk, scalded and cooled to lukewarm
1 teaspoon salt
2 tablespoons active dry yeast
6½ cups sifted all-purpose or unbleached flour (about)
1 teaspoon baking soda dissolved in ¼ cup hot water
2 eggs, beaten until frothy

Place the milk in a warm large mixing bowl, stir in salt and yeast, and mix until both are dissolved. Stir in 3 cups of the flour, 1 cup at a time, to make a stiff batter. Cover with a clean dry cloth and set in a warm spot, away from drafts, to rise for about 1½ hours, or until doubled in bulk. Stir the batter down, mix in the baking soda solution and then the eggs. Mix in the remaining 3½ cups flour, 1 cup at a time, to form a stiff dough (it will still be slightly sticky). Turn dough out onto a well-floured board, sprinkle top lightly with flour, and flour your hands also. Knead the dough hard for about 5 minutes, just until it is springy and satiny-smooth, adding a little extra flour as needed to keep the dough from sticking to the board and to your hands. Place in a buttered large mixing bowl, and turn dough in the bowl so that it is buttered all over. Cover with cloth and let rise 45 minutes in a warm spot, away from drafts, until not quite doubled in bulk. Punch dough down, turn out onto a lightly floured board and roll out to a thickness of ½ inch. Cut into rounds with a floured 2½-inch biscuit cutter, then place biscuits ½ inch apart on ungreased baking sheets. Again cover with cloth and let rise about 1 hour in a warm spot—just until the biscuits have about doubled in height. Bake in moderately hot oven (375°) until lightly browned on top, about 15 minutes. Serve piping hot with plenty of butter.

Christmas time at Conner Prairie Pioneer Settlement is a busy time with more cooking and baking going on than usual. Here is one of the seasonal favorites—apple slices fried in a sweet, wine-laced batter. The original version calls for the apple slices to be cooked inside two layers of rich batter, a method that may work well enough on a spider (a griddle with feet) set on the hearth. But a method that is not particularly suited to modern-day ranges. So I have altered the recipe slightly, suggesting that the apple slices be dipped in batter and then browned. The taste, however, remains the same.

Apple Frazes

MAKES 6 SERVINGS

3 large not too tart cooking apples (McIntosh, Jonathan, or
    Winesaps are good varieties to use)
3 tablespoons butter
Flour (for dredging apple slices)

Batter:
3 eggs

2 egg yolks
4 tablespoons sugar
1 cup sifted all-purpose flour
½ teaspoon ground nutmeg
3 tablespoons heavy cream at room temperature
3 tablespoons dry sherry
1 tablespoon melted butter

Topping:
Melted butter
Granulated sugar or sifted confectioners' sugar

Core the apples, peel, and slice about ⅜ inch thick. Brown lightly on both sides in the butter in a large, heavy skillet over moderately high heat, allowing 1 to 2 minutes per side; drain apple slices on paper toweling.

To prepare the batter: Beat the eggs, egg yolks, and sugar in an electric mixer at high speed until very thick and light—about 3 minutes of hard beating should do it. Stir together the flour and nutmeg; combine the cream, sherry, and melted butter. Then add the flour mixture to the beaten eggs alternately with the combined liquids, beginning and ending with flour. Dredge the apples lightly on both sides with flour (simply dip them in a small bowl of flour, shaking off any excess flour), then dip in the batter to coat evenly. Fry on a lightly greased, hot large griddle over moderate to moderately high heat, just until lightly browned on each side. This will take about 1 to 2 minutes on each side—the slices are ready to turn when small holes appear in the surface of the batter. Serve the frazes griddle-hot and top each with a generous ladling of melted butter and with a heaping teaspoon of granulated sugar or thick dusting of sifted confectioners' sugar.

The cooking varies daily at Conner Prairie; thus the visitor may see anything from turkey, goose, or suckling pig being spit-roasted in a hearth to fresh horseradish being grated by "tearful" hostesses for Indiana sauce.

Here is the recipe just as it was provided by Conner Prairie. It comes, they say, from a small book located in the Manuscript Division of the Indiana State Library. *Mrs. Collins' Table Receipts—Adapted to Western Housewifery*, the book is called. And it was published in 1851 by Jno. R. Nunemacher, City Bookstore, No. 2 Main Street, New Albany, Indiana.

INDIANA SAUCE

One ounce of scraped horseradish, one ounce of mustard, one of salt, half an ounce of celery seed, two minced onions and a half ounce of cayenne; add a pint of vinegar; let it stand in a jar a week, then pass it through a sieve, and bottle it up securely. This sauce is excellent for game or broiled cutlets.

New Harmony, Indiana

This National Historic Landmark in the Golden Rain Tree country of southwestern Indiana is the site of two early-nineteenth-century experiments in communal living. The first (1814–24) was undertaken by Father George Rapp and a group of Harmonists (also called Rappites) from Württemberg, Germany, who had defected from the liberalism of the German Lutheran Church. The second commune (1824–26) was composed of a band of free thinkers led by Robert Owen, a Welsh industrialist and social reformer.

The two groups could scarcely have been more dissimilar. The Rappites, having spent ten prosperous years in eastern Pennsylvania, pushed west to the banks of the Wabash to prepare a place where they might await the Second Coming of the Lord. Indeed, they looked upon their commune as an annex of heaven on earth.

The Rappites were celibate, a dedicated and hardworking group of men and women. They built their village with astonishing speed and care because they had devised a way of standardizing measurements, prefabricating parts and mass-producing homes (a method that is today the foundation of the construction industry). "Harmonie" is what they named their commune, and, to ward off evil, they marked every doorway with the sign of the cross.

Life did appear harmonious at New Harmony although the rules set forth in the Articles of Association were strict: "To have everything in common, to submit to the regulations of the congregation, to work for the good of the group."

The sowing and harvesting of crops were done communally, the tending of livestock, even the cooking (the recipes that follow are early Rappite ones).

Life at New Harmony was rigorous, certainly by today's standards. The Rappites were awakened about five in the morning, they breakfasted at six, then set about their chores. Aside from three hearty meals a day, they took "lunch" about nine in the morning and "*vesper brodt*" in midafternoon. The curfew rang at nine in the evening after the night watchman had completed his rounds, chanting:

"Again a day is past and a step made nearer to our end. The time runs away and the joys of Heaven are our reward."

Perhaps. But the millennium did not occur, as expected, while the Rappites toiled at New Harmony. And after ten years on the Indian frontier, they retreated to Economy, Pennsylvania, where their sect survived for another seventy-eight years.

In 1825, Father George Rapp sold New Harmony to Robert Owen, who believed that men of all nations might achieve happiness through education.

"If we can not reconcile all opinions," Owen said, "let us endeavor to unite all our hearts." Unlike Rapp, however, Owen was not a religious man; indeed, he considered religion "so many geographical insanities." But the Rappite commune suited his purposes exactly, standing as it did in the Indian wilderness—free from social order, ready for the establishment of a "new moral world."

The way to achieve that "new moral world," Owen believed, was to educate and mold young children. Thus, infants—girls as well as boys—were taken from their homes at the age of two and boarded at New Harmony. Owen's plan was to instill reason in these children rather than factual knowledge. But the Owen Experiment was shorter-lived than the Rappite one. It lasted two years only.

The end of the commune, however, did not spell the end of New Harmony. A number of scientists and educators stayed on and ultimately made significant contributions to the development of America. It was here that the first free public school system in America was established, here that the first free library was founded, the first infant school, the first kindergarten, the first trade school, the first women's club with a written constitution (Owen afforded women equal rights), the first civic dramatic club. And it was here, too, that the first Geological Survey of the United States was headquartered.

Today, twenty-five of the old Harmonist buildings remain at New Harmony, and ten of them have been fully restored. They are proud, straight houses built of clapboard or brick, so sturdy that even today none leans with the west wind. Among them are the Opera House (built by the Rappites but converted into an opera house by Owen), Harmonist Dormitory Number Two (where unmarried men were domiciled), the Old Fauntleroy Home, the Harmonist Fort-Granary, the Poet's House, the Barrett-Gate House (the lower floor of which was the first building raised at New Harmony), the Dye House (one of the first such plants west of the Appalachians where the Rappites processed both fabrics and wallpapers), and the Labyrinth or Maze (this a reproduction), planted by the Rappites to symbolize the various paths offered to Man as he traveled the road of life.

Though both New Harmony communes failed to achieve their ultimate goals, each made substantial contributions to young America. And to visit New Harmony today is to understand something of the dreams of Father George Rapp and Robert Owen, and to realize how those dreams have touched our own lives.

The baking of cakes and breads at New Harmony was a communal effort, and the community ovens, scattered throughout the village, were fired on certain days for the weekly baking. In addition, each home contained its own small brick oven, to the right of the fireplace, which was used for small baking—usually of roasts and meats such as this savory Sausage Loaf. This is a frugal loaf, surprisingly filling and rich. You will have best results with it if you use a lean sausage meat because if the sausage is too fat the loaf will not hold together properly as it bakes.

Sausage Loaf

MAKES 6 TO 8 SERVINGS

1 pound lean sausage meat
2 cups unseasoned mashed potatoes
1 medium-size yellow onion, finely chopped
2 eggs, lightly beaten
½ teaspoon rubbed sage
½ teaspoon salt
¼ teaspoon leaf thyme, crumbled
¼ teaspoon freshly ground pepper
½ cup uncooked rolled oats (the quick-cooking variety works well)

Mix together well the sausage meat, mashed potatoes, onion, eggs, sage, salt, thyme, and pepper. Shape into an oblong loaf on a sheet of wax paper, then roll loaf in the rolled oats to coat evenly all over. Transfer to an ungreased baking sheet, reshaping loaf if needed, and bake, uncovered, in a moderate oven (350°) about 1 hour and 45 minutes until nicely browned. Remove loaf from oven and let stand at least 15 minutes before slicing.

Pickled Eggs are very much like what the Pennsylvania Dutch call "Red Beet Eggs," eggs mixed with pickled beets. But the Rappites, like the Pennsylvania Dutch, were German and, in fact, found their way to the banks of the Wabash after having lived for ten years in Pennsylvania.

Pickled Eggs

MAKES 4 TO 6 SERVINGS

1 cup beet juice
1 cup cider vinegar
½ teaspoon salt
½ teaspoon ground cloves
¼ teaspoon ground mace
¼ teaspoon ground allspice
6 hard-cooked eggs, shelled

Place beet juice, vinegar, salt, cloves, mace, and allspice in a small saucepan and bring to a boil. Meanwhile, place hard-cooked eggs in a quart-size preserving jar. When beet mixture boils, pour into jar over eggs, screw lid down tightly, and cool to room temperature, then place in refrigerator and let stand 2 to 3 days before serving. Every now and then, turn the jar upside down so that the eggs will absorb the pickled-beet flavor and color evenly. Serve cold as an appetizer or snack.

Here are two very old recipes, written just as they appear in the *Rappite Cookbook*.

PEACH LEATHER

Peel very ripe peaches, mash and roll out on a flat platter. Cover with netting and set in a hot sun to dry. When completely dry, cut into strips and store. Food was often dried on the roof. This is eaten like candy.

SUN PRESERVES

Add 1 quart sugar to 1 quart strawberries. Cover and let stand overnight in a cool place. In the morning, bring to a boil and cook for 8 minutes. Pour onto a large platter and cover closely with a piece of glass. Set in the sun until the juice thickens and jells. Cool completely and seal in jars and glasses.

From an early New Harmony cookbook comes this old home remedy.

Whooping Cough Remedy

1 sliced lemon
¼ pint flaxseed
2 ounces honey
2 tablespoons pulverized sugar
1 quart water

Mix together. Simmer, not boil, four hours. Strain when cool. If there is less than a pint after simmering, add hot water to make a pint. Keep in cool place.

Dose: 1 tablespoon four times a day and one after each severe fit of coughing. It is said to cure in four days if given when the child first whoops.

Lincoln's New Salem
New Salem State Park, Illinois

*C*arl Sandburg, Lincoln's most famous biographer, once said: "New Salem was Lincoln's Alma Mater...the six years he spent there amounted to his college education."

There is no question, certainly, that those six years marked the turning point in his career, for it was an aimless, rawboned youth who arrived in New Salem in 1831, a youth, Lincoln once said of himself, "who could make a few tracks with a pen." But it was a mature man of purpose who left New Salem in 1837 for Springfield twenty miles away to embark on a career of statesmanship and law.

Oddly, New Salem scarcely outlived Lincoln's stay there, for in 1839 the county seat was transferred from it to nearby Petersburg. And so what Sandburg described as a "no hick town" declined rapidly. Decay set in and before long New Salem virtually crumbled to dust.

It remained a forgotten dot on the map until the early 1900s, when Lincoln's stature began to grow. In 1906 William Randolph Hearst, lecturing at the Old Salem Chautauqua, became interested in preserving the old townsite. He bought it, transferred it in trust to the Chautauqua Association, and eleven years later the Old

Salem Lincoln League was formed at Petersburg to carry forth research and keep interest in New Salem alive. In 1931, the Illinois General Assembly appropriated funds for the permanent improvement of the site, and it was then that reconstruction of the old town began.

Today New Salem looks much as it did when Lincoln lived there, serving at various times as a storekeeper, a flatboatman, a postmaster, a private and captain in the militia, a state legislator. It's a rudely simple town, sprawled along one grassy main street in wooded country crisscrossed with split rail fences but uncluttered by commercialism. At one end of town stands Clary's Grove, where Lincoln wrestled rough-and-tumble Jack Armstrong to the ground (they remained friends ever afterward) and where Lincoln enlisted in the Black Hawk Indian War.

At the heart of New Salem you see the Berry-Lincoln Store, where Lincoln served as postmaster, and nearby the famous Rutledge Tavern (Lincoln slept in the loft of the original). Way at the end of the town, down the hill and across the road, there is the saw and grist mill that Jame Camron and James Rutledge built. Rutledge was Ann's father, the young girl who was Lincoln's sweetheart and whose untimely death forever wedded her name to Lincoln's in legend and in poetry. Time seems to stop at the Rutledge-Camron mill, engulfed as it is by hardwoods. The Sangamon River flows silently by on its way to the Illinois, and it was here that Lincoln boarded a flatboat for New Orleans, a trip that forever affected his life. In New Orleans, Lincoln visited the slave auctions, and the sight of those slave blocks stirred in him a loathing for slavery. "If ever I get a chance to hit that thing," he is quoted as having said, "I'll hit it—and hit it hard."

It was at New Salem, however, that Lincoln began seriously to educate himself, poring over books by the light of a fire made from cooper's shavings at the Onstot Cooper Shop (this, by the way, is the only original building at New Salem. It was built in 1835, moved to Petersburg two miles away in 1840, then returned to New Salem in 1922). All of the other buildings are reproductions, but flawless in their authenticity. There are twelve timber houses; the Rutledge Tavern; ten shops, stores, and industries; and a school where church services were held. All have been furnished with items of the 1830s, some of which had actually belonged to the townspeople of New Salem. Here you will see wheat cradles, candle molds, cord beds, flax shuttles, wool cards, dough and corn meal chests; a doctor's office equipped with mortars and pestles, early surgeon's instruments, medicine chests, and old textbooks; a cobbler's shop outfitted with awls and rasps and pewter and earthenware lined up along shelves above the hearth. At the Hill-McNamar Store, counters and cupboards bulge with calico bolts, crocks, jars, utensils, and other general merchandise typical of Lincoln's time.

The village has been so painstakingly re-created that early plants indigenous to the area have been brought in—red haw, Osage orange, wild crab and plum, witch hazel, wild gooseberry and blackberry. All the trees and shrubs and herbs that Lincoln would have recognized.

This then, is the town Abraham Lincoln loved, the town where he first left an imprint upon the pages of American history. His presence lingers there—today as yesterday.

🐚

Abraham Lincoln, for the most part, was both unknowing and uncomplaining about food. He would eat almost anything set before him without comment and, his biographers have noted, would often forget to eat at all unless summoned several times to table. But there were exceptions. Lincoln did enjoy a good strong cup of coffee and once, when served a questionable steaming beverage, remarked to the waiter: "If this is coffee, please bring me a cup of tea, but on the other hand, if this is tea, please bring me a cup of coffee." Lincoln also liked steak, and in his Illinois days could buy for ten cents enough to feed half a dozen people. His favorite steak recipe is said to be this one, an unlikely mixture of steak, mustard, and coffee. It is a recipe with Swedish overtones (Swedes often roast beef under bastings of coffee or braise pot roasts in coffee), but there were in Lincoln's time many Swedish immigrants in Illinois. Lincoln apparently liked his steak "well done," for an old recipe calls for browning the steak in plenty of butter, then covering the skillet and cooking it fifteen or twenty minutes longer. It's easy enough, however—not to mention *advisable*, with steak costing twenty to thirty times what it did in Lincoln's day—to reduce the cooking time so that the steak is "rare" or "medium" or however *you* like it.

Abe's Butter-Browned Steak with Coffee-Mustard Sauce

MAKES 4 SERVINGS

4 club, shell, or strip steaks cut about 1 inch thick
2 tablespoons butter
Salt and pepper to season
4 teaspoons spicy prepared mustard
⅔ cup strong hot coffee

Brown the steaks quickly on both sides in the butter in a very large, heavy skillet and, if you like them very rare, remove at once to a hot platter and keep warm. For medium-rare or medium, turn the heat under the skillet to low and let the steaks cook slowly 5 to 8 minutes longer, then remove to platter. Sprinkle steaks with salt and pepper and spread each with 1 teaspoon mustard. Pour coffee into skillet and bring quickly to a simmer, scraping up browned bits on bottom of skillet. Pour over steaks and serve.

While serving in the Illinois Legislature, Lincoln spent much of his time traveling about the state (he was first elected in New Salem in 1834 and served four two-year terms). At a small hotel operated by Mrs. Nancy Breedlove (records fail to say where in Illinois the hotel was), Lincoln was served this soft, tart lemon custard pie and liked it so much he asked Mrs. Breedlove for the recipe. She gladly obliged. The recipe, it is said, remained a favorite of Lincoln's and was served with great success at the White House.

Meringue-Topped Tart Lemon Custard Pie

MAKES AN 8-INCH PIE

Crust:
1 cup sifted all-purpose flour
¼ teaspoon salt
¼ cup lard
3 to 4 tablespoons cold water

Tart Lemon Custard Filling:
1 cup sugar
1 tablespoon cornstarch
Pinch of salt
Finely grated rind of 1 large lemon
Juice of 1 large lemon
⅔ cup water
4 egg yolks
1 egg
2 tablespoons melted butter

Meringue:
4 egg whites
3 tablespoons sugar

Prepare the crust: Place flour and salt in a large, shallow mixing bowl and stir well to mix. Add lard and cut in with a pastry blender or 2 knives until texture is that of uncooked oatmeal. Add water, a few drops at a time, mixing briskly with a fork until dough holds together. Turn out on a lightly floured board and roll into a thin circle about 11 inches in diameter. Fit pastry into an 8-inch piepan, roll overhang under even with rim and crimp.

To make the filling: Mix sugar with cornstarch and salt; stir in lemon rind and juice and water. Beat egg yolks in, one at a time, then beat in whole egg. Blend in melted butter. Pour into unbaked pie shell and bake in a moderately slow oven (325°) 30 to 35 minutes until bubbly and beginning to thicken. Remove from oven and let stand on counter 10 minutes. Raise oven temperature to very hot (450°). Beat egg whites until frothy, then continue beating, adding sugar gradually, until meringue peaks softly. Spread gently over lemon filling, making sure meringue touches crimped edges of crust all around. Return to oven and bake 2 to 3 minutes until meringue is tipped with brown. Cool to room temperature before cutting.

"Best I ever ate," is what Abraham Lincoln had to say about this velvet crumbed white cake made with finely grated blanched almonds. No small praise, considering Lincoln's unconcern for food. It is a recipe Mary Todd's family obtained from a Lexington, Kentucky, caterer named Giron, who had created the recipe in 1825 on the occasion of Lafayette's visit to Lexington. Mary served the cake often during the Lincolns' Illinois days and later at the White House. In those days, the almonds would have been painstakingly grated by hand, one at a time. They can be done in a trice today in an electric blender or better still, with one of the small rotary hand graters, which gives the grated nuts a fluffiness akin to that of flour. One can only wonder what Mary Todd Lincoln's reaction to such modern gadgets would be.

Mary Todd Lincoln's White Almond Cake

MAKES A 9-INCH TUBE CAKE

¼ pound blanched whole almonds (about)
3 cups sifted cake flour
1 tablespoon baking powder
½ pound unsalted butter
2 cups sugar
1 cup milk
1 teaspoon vanilla
½ teaspoon almond extract
6 egg whites
Pinch of salt

Grate enough of the almonds in a rotary hand grater to
total 1 cup exactly (do not pack the nuts in the measure)
or grate them, a few at a time, in an electric blender at
high speed; set nuts aside. Sift the flour with the baking
powder and set aside. Cream the butter until very light,
then add 1¾ cups of the sugar gradually, creaming all the
while until fluffy. Add the sifted dry ingredients alternately with milk, beginning and ending with the dry ingredients. Fold in the grated almonds, the vanilla, and
almond extract. Beat the egg whites with the salt and
remaining ¼ cup sugar to soft peaks, then fold gently but
thoroughly into the batter. Pour into a well-buttered and
floured 9-inch tube pan and bake in a moderate oven
(350°) about 1 hour or until cake begins to pull from sides
of pan and a finger, pressed lightly into the top of the
cake, leaves an imprint that vanishes slowly. Cool cake
upright in its pan on a wire rack 10 minutes, then loosen
cake around edges of pan with a spatula and turn out on
a rack. Cool thoroughly before cutting. The cake is a rich
one—rather like a white pound cake—and needs no
frosting.

Stonefield Village
Cassville, Wisconsin

*T*he horse-drawn omnibus carries you through the arches of a covered wooden bridge, and back three-quarters of a century into the heart of a sleepy little farm village at the crossroads of America.

This is Stonefield Village, a hamlet nestled beside the Mississippi River in southwestern Wisconsin, which tells the story of early rural life in America.

Stonefield was the name given by Nelson Dewey, Wisconsin's first governor, to the rock-studded two-thousand-acre farm he established along the bluffs of the Mississippi near Cassville. Dewey built Gothic stone barns, and a hundred-thousand-dollar palace in the wilderness, three stories high, with Gothic dormers, broad balconies, hot air heat, and other conveniences unusual in that day. It was the showplace of Wisconsin.

Dewey practiced law from his farm and raised a variety of crops and livestock, employing at times as many as fifty hands who did everything from building stone fences to making furniture, wine, butter, and fine Wisconsin cheeses. Dewey became wealthy, but the panic of 1873 wiped him out, and that same year a fire gutted much of his beautiful mansion. On July 20, 1889, he died, alone, of a paralytic stroke.

In 1936, the State of Wisconsin acquired seven

hundred acres of the old farm for the Nelson Dewey State Park and set about restoring and refurnishing the Dewey homestead.

Now visitors to Stonefield Village can see life as it was in those simpler days. They can watch a blacksmith at his forge, a printer at his press, a clerk at his desk.

Stonefield Village is not modeled after any particular town. Instead, it is a composite of all the little Midwestern villages that grew up to serve the farming and mining interests of the late 1800s.

Stonefield Village is a product of many hands. Businesses and people from throughout the state have proudly contributed time, energy, and material to the project—even to the Douglas County woman who gave to the general store some flypaper she had saved for more than sixty years.

"This village," said Ray Sivesind, supervisor of the State Historical Society's Office of Sites and Markers, "will not be a decorative arts exhibit. We are trying to portray a way of life; we are not merely setting up exhibits."

The goal is not lost on the thousands of visitors who go to Stonefield each year from the beginning of May through October, who squeeze into the desks at the schoolhouse, examine the high button shoes in the general store, and try their hands at the press in the office of the *Gazette*.

Everything the self-sufficient village needed has been re-created at Stonefield: a butcher shop, a drugstore, a bank, the village church, a firehouse. There are also a photograph gallery, a cheese factory, a railroad station, all frozen in time. And there is the museum, chronicling the history of Wisconsin agriculture.

Here is life as it was lived seventy-five years ago, in an easier time, a simple life, a sustaining life, almost within reach.

Among the recipes demonstrated at Stonefield Village during the 1890 Craft Days is this nutmeg-flavored sour cream cookie. The original recipe calls for lard (rendered hog fat), but you can, say Stonefield Village cooks, substitute vegetable shortening. Lard, however, gives the cookies a mellower flavor. The amount of flour the recipe requires will vary according to the type of lard or shortening used. A soft lard makes a soft dough, and thus more flour will need to be added so that the cookies can be rolled and cut. The cookies are more soft than crisp and they are not particularly sweet. The recipe makes a huge amount, but the dough can be frozen, then rolled and baked as needed.

Old-Fashioned Sour Cream White Cookies

MAKES ABOUT 7 DOZEN COOKIES

1 cup lard or vegetable shortening
1¾ cups sugar
2 eggs, lightly beaten
2 cups thick sour cream (commercial sour cream works well)
5 to 5½ cups sifted all-purpose flour
2 teaspoons baking powder
1 teaspoon baking soda
1 teaspoon ground nutmeg (preferably freshly ground)
½ teaspoon salt
Sugar (topping)

Cream the lard or vegetable shortening with the sugar until very light and fluffy; beat in the eggs and sour cream. Sift 4½ cups of the flour with the baking powder, soda, nutmeg, and salt and stir into creamed mixture. Then work in as much of the remaining 1 cup of flour as necessary to make a dough stiff enough to roll. Divide dough into 4 equal parts, wrap each in foil or plastic food wrap, and chill at least 24 hours. (Or, if you prefer, freeze all or part of the dough to roll and cut later; you will need to let the dough stand at room temperature about 30 minutes until it is soft enough to roll.) Roll only about ¼ of the dough at a time, keeping the remainder frozen or refrigerated. Roll on a well-floured pastry cloth to a thickness of ¼ inch, then cut out with a floured 2-inch round cookie cutter. Arrange cookies 1½ inches apart on ungreased baking sheets, sprinkle lightly with sugar, and bake in a moderately hot oven (375°) 10 to 12 minutes until faintly ringed with tan. With a wide spatula, transfer cookies at once to wire racks to cool.

For those who live on farms and would cook the way our forefathers did, here are two early Wisconsin recipes provided by the State Historical Society of Wisconsin. Neither has been tested or updated for two reasons: The recipes are exceedingly special, requiring quantities and ingredients generally unavailable, and, second, setting the recipes down in present-day terms would destroy their old-fashioned charm. Both, however, have been used successfully for decades by Wisconsin farm women who lived in rural communities much like Stonefield Village. The first, *Blodklub*, is a savory Scandinavian pudding made from pork blood ("the blood must be fresh-caught from the pig carcass during the butchering process," a recipe headnote advises). The second recipe is for old-fashioned sweet-sour pickles made—and kept—in a giant earthenware crock.

Blodklub (Blood Pudding)

1½ cups raw barley
9 cups fresh pork blood
3 cups oatmeal
2 cups graham flour
4 cups white flour
3 tablespoons salt
½ cup finely cut suet
Pepper to taste

Boil barley in salted water until tender. Cool and mix with other ingredients to a waffle batter consistency. Fill small cloth bags about ¾ full and tie shut. Boil in water for 2 to 3 hours. Serve hot with butter and sugar.

Sweet-Sour Pickles

Clean 300 small cucumbers and use whole—or use any size cucumbers and cut in about 300 pieces. Place in a large pan and sprinkle ⅔ cup coarse salt through them. Cover with boiling water.

The next day wipe dry and place in an earthen jar. Pour over cucumbers a mixture of ¼ gallon cold vinegar, 4 large tablespoons of dry mustard, 4 large tablespoons of sugar and 4 tablespoons salt. Stir well. Cover with ¼ cup pickling spices. Put in a cool place. Weigh out 3 pounds of sugar and each morning, add one handful of sugar to the pickles and stir each time. When sugar is all added, pickles are ready to use. Cover jar and store in a cool place. Use pickles as needed.

At one of Stonefield Village's annual 1890 Craft Days, women demonstrated this authentic washday "receipt," included here in its original spelling.

Grandma's Receipt for Doing the Family Wash

1. bild a fire in back yard to heet kettle of rain water
2. set tubs so smoke won't blow in eyes if wind is pert
3. shave one hole cake of lie soap in biling water
4. sort things, make three piles. 1 pile white. 1 pile cullord. 1 pile work britches and rags.
5. stur flour in water to smooth, then thin down with biling water.
6. rub dirty spots on board, scrub hard, then bile. rub

cullord, but don't bile—just rench and starch

7. take white things out of kettle with broom handle, then rench blew and starch.
8. spred tea towels on grass
9. hang out old rags on fence
10. pore rench water on flower beds
11. scrub porch with hot soapy water
12. turn tubs upside down
13. go put on a clean dress—smooth hair with side combs—brew cup of tee—set and rest and rock a spell and count blessings.

Lumbertown, U.S.A.
Brainerd, Minnesota

"*N*othing fake." That's the motto of this re-created 1870s–1880s lumber town on the shores of Gull Lake in the heart of Minnesota's tall timber. A hundred years ago the rasp of saws and thump of axes echoed through the evergreens here. And Gull Lake and the network of lakes and waterways surrounding it were jammed with logs on their way to the saw-mills of nearby Gull River and Brainerd. Today this is more leisure country than lumber country—except at Lumbertown, U.S.A.

Building Lumbertown was no small feat. It all began a little more than ten years ago when Mr. and Mrs. W. J. Madden of Brianerd decided to preserve for America what had been one of early Minnesota's liveliest and most lucrative industries. So on forty acres of lake flats, they began to plan a replica of an old lumbertown as faithful to the era and area as careful research could make it.

Lumbertown, U.S.A., is the result of a lot of legwork and love. The Maddens sought the advice of both the county and state historical societies, then spent months traveling throughout northern and central Minnesota, scouting for historic buildings and furnishings that could be incorporated into Lumbertown.

Today there are more than thirty buildings at Lumbertown, some of them faithful replicas, others late-nineteenth-century buildings that were uprooted, trucked overland to the townsite, and restored. One of the most interesting, perhaps, is the square-hewn log cabin (circa 1873), pegged with dowels and chinked with swamp clay and moss. Its interiors gleam with whitewash (a hundred years ago, twenty-five cents would buy enough whitewash to cover an entire house). Whitewash, it should be added, wasn't brushed around for purely cosmetic reasons. It had a more practical function—it killed bugs, bedbugs, in particular, which were a perennial lumber camp pest. The log house, two stories high, is furnished as it might have been a hundred years ago. The kitchen table is set, but with the cups and plates turned upsidedown, so that grit and dust, sifting down from the floor above as people clomp about, does not fall into them. In olden days, the tableware was not turned right-side-up until after everyone had gathered at the table and grace had been said.

Another of Lumbertown's historic buildings is the Little Red Schoolhouse, built in the 1880s in a community nearby. It, like many other lumber country schools, was known as a "tough" school, for many of its students, strapping farmers or lumberjacks most of the year, were more than twenty years old and "tough" for a teacher to keep in line.

Sandy streets and boardwalks meander through Lumbertown, U.S.A., past the old print shop, which, with its antique Washington Press, is the only completely restored nineteenth-century printing shop in Minnesota; past Maggie's Millinery Shop, where there's a luscious red velvet hat, feathered with ostrich plumes (its label reads, "Nicollet Avenue, Minneapolis, 1860, made in France"), past the General Store (its antique merchandise and furnishings came from an old general store on Cedar Lake); past the Old Ice Cream Parlor, where oldfashioned ice cream is dished up in lumber camp portions; past the operating Saw Mill, the Fire Fighting

Museum, the lake front where the replica paddle-wheeler *Blueberry Queen* is moored. You can cruise Gull Lake on the *Queen*, or you can climb aboard the Lumbertown Express, an authentic reproduction of the first Northern Pacific Railroad train, for a run through the evergreen forests.

It all looks very much as it did a hundred years ago. And the only thing missing, perhaps, are the cries of "T-I-M-B-E-R!"

Wild rice isn't rice at all but a wild grass native to the Minnesota and Wisconsin lake country. It is a food so precious that the Chippewa and Winnebago who gather the wild rice customarily travel about with small pouches of it lest they run short of money. In bartering, they say, it is as good as gold. Bartering is perhaps how the lumber camp cooks of the North Woods acquired their supplies for this husky—yet surprisingly sophisticated—main dish.

Baked Ham, Wild Rice, and Mushrooms North Woods Style

MAKES 6 SERVINGS

1 cup wild rice, washed
2¼ cups water mixed with 1 teaspoon salt
1½ cups diced cooked ham
4 tablespoons bacon drippings
¼ pound mushrooms, wiped clean and sliced thin
1 celery rib, diced
1 cup chopped onion
3 tablespoons flour
2½ cups milk
⅛ teaspoon salt
⅛ teaspoon pepper
½ cup fine dry bread crumbs mixed with 1 tablespoon melted
    butter

Boil the wild rice gently in the salted water in an uncovered saucepan about 25 minutes until firm-tender and all water has been absorbed. Meanwhile, brown the ham in 2 of the tablespoons bacon drippings in a large skillet, about 5 minutes. Add mushrooms, celery, and onion and stir-fry slowly about 10 minutes. Spoon all into a 16-cup casserole. Blend the flour with the remaining 2 tablespoons bacon drippings in a small saucepan; add milk, salt, and pepper and cook, stirring constantly, until thickened and smooth. Pour into casserole. When rice is done, add to casserole and toss all lightly to mix. Top with buttered crumbs and bake, uncovered, in a moderate oven (350°) 30 to 35 minutes until bubbly and touched with brown.

Cookies, in a lumber camp, are apt to be made with whatever odds and ends there are on hand. In this case, leftover morning coffee. These cookies are spicy, thin, and crisp; the dough freezes well, so it can be kept on hand, rolled, cut, and baked as needed.

Lumberjack Cookies

MAKES ABOUT 8 DOZEN COOKIES

¾ cup butter or vegetable shortening
1 cup sugar
½ cup molasses
2 egg yolks
½ cup boiling strong coffee
1 teaspoon ground ginger
1 teaspoon ground cinnamon
½ teaspoon ground cloves
2 teaspoons baking soda
¼ teaspoon salt
4 cups sifted all-purpose flour

Cream butter and sugar until light, then beat in molasses and egg yolks. Mix coffee with ginger, cinnamon, cloves, soda, and salt and stir into batter. Mix in flour, about a cup at a time. Chill dough several hours or until firm enough to roll, then roll out about a fourth of the dough at a time to a thickness of ⅛ inch on a lightly floured board and cut with a floured 2-inch cutter. Arrange cookies 1 inch apart on ungreased baking sheets and bake in a moderate oven (350°) 10 to 12 minutes until firm to the touch and lightly browned around the edges. Transfer at once to wire cookie racks to cool.

The Amana Colonies
Amana, Iowa

*T*he seven historic villages of the Amanas are unique in America. Here, in these quiet towns just twenty-three miles from Cedar Rapids, live some eighteen hundred people bound together for the common good. Theirs is a heritage of flight from religious persecution, of a new start in a new country, of a simple life style, of decency and honesty.

The people of the Amanas, rebels from the ritual worship and intellectual theology of the Lutheran Church in eighteenth-century Germany, settled first around Buffalo, New York. But they soon needed more room, and so in 1854 they looked westward. Here, along the Iowa River, they found the rich soil, the timber, the sandstone, limestone, and brick clay necessary for building a new community. The first village, Amana, was laid out in 1855. Subsequently, six more were built in the medieval manner, with houses clustered together and enveloped by farmland.

These were a farming people, growing the wheat that they baked into breads in hickory-stoked ovens, raising hogs that would be turned into sausages and fine smoky hams, growing fruits and vegetables and herbs.

But the Amana people were superb craftsmen, too, making wagons and cabinets, weaving woolens and printing calicos. The Amana Society was virtually self-supporting and all property was held in common. Religious life unified the people, and, having no entertainment, no indulgences of dress or sport, they turned their creativity to food.

By the late 1920s, improved communication and transportation, not to mention the Depression made isolated communal living difficult. So in June of 1932, the old order gave way. Today, their industries include the giant Amana Refrigeration Plant, but they also include the making of woolens, furniture, clocks, wine—and food—the time-honored way.

While boys in the cities of Iowa were learning the ways of industry and finance, Amana boys were learning the intricacies of curing a ham, of baking bread, of distilling a mild rhubarb wine called *Piestengel*. Amana foods today, fresh from the fields and local kitchens, remain free of preservatives and artifice, and they possess an honest, down-to-earth flavor uniquely their own. They have been collected into a small cookbook, *Amana Colony Recipes*, by the Ladies Auxiliary of the Homestead Welfare Club, Homestead, Iowa. All of the recipes included here except German Breslauer Steaks were adapted from that book. These are, the book says, "Family-size recipes of the foods prepared and served in the Amana Villages for over a century."

A visitor to Amana country will not hunger for history, either. It is here, in the museums for all to see and ponder. The Museum of Amana History has become the repository for Amana's treasures, for vital documents, old tools, family heirlooms, industrial artifacts, art, photographs, and books. Here you will see what an Amana church looks like, and you can view an Amana living room of a hundred years ago.

The century-old Amana "Heim" and Heritage House Museum have been restored, re-creating a portion of the Amanas' past. And the Old Colony Kitchen, the Cooper's Shop, and the Hearth Oven Museum provide quiet retreats from the hurried, cluttered, and commercial twentieth-century world.

Amana is a peaceful, pastoral place, a romantic glance backward that nourishes body and soul.

A family-style Amana favorite—veal and pork patties seasoned with onion and nutmeg, then served in a rich mushroom gravy. It is a specialty of the Seven Villages Restaurant in Williamsburg, Iowa.

German Breslauer Steaks

MAKES 6 SERVINGS

1 pound ground veal
1 pound ground pork
3 tablespoons minced chives
⅓ cup finely minced onion
1 teaspoon salt
⅛ teaspoon pepper
⅛ teaspoon nutmeg
2 tablespoons butter

Mushroom Gravy:
3 tablespoons meat drippings (from browning steaks)
½ pound mushrooms, wiped clean and sliced thin
3 tablespoons flour
1½ cups chicken broth or stock
½ cup light cream
Pinch of salt
Pinch of pepper
Pinch of nutmeg

Mix together the ground veal and pork, minced chives and onion, salt, pepper, and nutmeg; shape into 6 large, flat patties. Brown on both sides in butter in a very large, heavy skillet; remove to a plate and keep warm.

For the mushroom gravy: Pour all but 3 tablespoons

meat drippings from skillet; sauté mushrooms in drippings until they are nicely browned and begin to release their juices. Blend in flour, then add chicken broth and cream and cook and stir until thickened. Add salt, pepper, and nutmeg. Return steaks to skillet, pushing down under gravy, cover, and simmer slowly 15 to 20 minutes until "well done" in the center.

Amana cooks are more imaginative than most about preparing vegetables because they team them in unusual ways—these boiled carrots, for example, served in creamy mashed potato sauce.

Gelbe Rüben (Carrots with Mashed Potatoes)

MAKES 4 SERVINGS

½ cup minced onion
2 tablespoons lard or bacon drippings
8 medium-size carrots, peeled and sliced ½ inch thick
3 small potatoes, peeled and quartered
1¼ cups water
1 tablespoon sugar
½ teaspoon salt
Pinch of pepper

Sauté the onion in the lard or bacon drippings in a large, heavy saucepan 3 to 4 minutes until limp and golden. Add carrots, potatoes, and water, bring to a boil, cover, and cook 20 to 25 minutes until carrots and potatoes are tender. Fish out potatoes with a slotted spoon and mash well; return to pan and mix in along with sugar, salt, and pepper. Cook, uncovered, about 5 minutes longer, just until mashed potato sauce thickens up slightly.

With most Amana meat dishes so rich and filling, this tart celery salad makes a refreshing counterpoint.

Celery Salad

MAKES 4 SERVINGS

1 large bunch of celery, washed, trimmed of leaves, and sliced
    thin
1 cup water
½ teaspoon salt
⅛ teaspoon freshly ground pepper
2 tablespoons cider vinegar
¼ cup light cream

Cook celery in the water in a covered saucepan about 15
minutes until tender but still slightly crisp. Drain well,
mix with remaining ingredients, and chill several hours
before serving.

    A vanilla pudding as soft and billowing as an angel-
food cake batter. Its delicacy is unique among Amana
desserts, which run to pies, pastries, yeast cakes, and
fritters. Kiss Pudding can be eaten as is, but in Amana it
is traditionally topped with a thin chocolate sauce.

Kiss Pudding

MAKES 6 SERVINGS

3 eggs, separated
1 cup sugar
3 tablespoons cornstarch blended with ⅓ cup cold milk
3 cups scalding hot milk
1 teaspoon vanilla
Pinch of salt

Beat egg yolks and sugar in the top of a double boiler
until very light and thick; blend cornstarch-milk mixture
in well. Add scalding milk slowly, stirring briskly, set
over simmering water, and cook and stir until the consis-

tency of stirred custard—10 to 12 minutes. Remove from heat and mix in vanilla. Beat egg whites with salt to soft peaks. Blend a little of the hot mixture into the beaten egg whites, then quickly but gently fold beaten whites into the hot mixture so that no streaks of white remain. Chill several hours before serving.

Thin Chocolate Sauce

MAKES ABOUT 2 CUPS

½ cup sugar
2 teaspoons cornstarch
2 tablespoons dark Dutch-style cocoa
Pinch of salt
1¾ cups scalding hot milk
1 egg, lightly beaten
½ teaspoon vanilla

Blend together sugar, cornstarch, cocoa, and salt in a small, heavy saucepan. Stir in hot milk, set over low heat, and cook and stir until mixture has thickened—about 3 minutes. Blend a little hot sauce into the beaten egg, then stir back into pan and cook and stir over lowest heat about 1 minute. Remove from heat and mix in vanilla. Cool, then serve over Kiss Pudding (above).

The Plains and
Central States

Silver Dollar City, Missouri

Women in gingham and calico husking corn and simmering up huge kettles of stew...children moseying along the streets on the backs of burros...men chopping wood or carving it. These are only a few of the attractions offered at Silver Dollar City, a replica 1880s Ozark mountain village and mining settlement nestled in the Mark Twain National Forest just nine miles from Branson in southwestern Missouri.

There are sixty-five buildings here sprawled across fifty acres of Ozarks, and two of them are original to the location, the Wilderness Church and the McHaffie Homestead. Craft and cooking demonstrations seem to be going on everywhere about Silver Dollar City (there are two dozen different ones in all), which show how resourceful the Ozark hill people were in turning nature's bounty into no-frills food, fashions, and furnishings.

It's a bustling town with the Butterfield Stage thundering about filled with tourists, the Frisco-Silver Dollar steam engine whoo-eeeing through the woodlands, tourists climbing down for a tour of Marvel Cave or a scary look at a flooded mine. Or others climbing up to visit a house in the treetops.

It is a fascinating slice of the Ozark folk life that produced a husky food and some amusing guidelines for cooking it: "A real Ozark cook puts a touch of onion in everything but the coconut custard" . . . "A woman who can't make pickles has about as many friends as a horse has toes" . . . "A pan of lime kept in a cupboard with jams and preserves will prevent molding" . . . "Set a dish of water in the oven with cake when baking and it will seldom scorch." There were rules of Ozark etiquette, too: "Dinner is always around noon. We have supper at night" . . . "The accepted Ozark way of eatin' gravy is over a thick slice of homemade bread. Gravy over potatoes is for fancy folks."

There's nothing fancy about Silver Dollar City or its food, the best of which has been printed in a small paperback cookbook called *Country Cookin'—City Style*. The recipes that follow are adapted from that book and are those more or less representative of those demonstrated at the re-created village.

Silver Dollar City is a family place, a fascinating place, and possibly the easiest dose of American history anyone ever swallowed.

There's no nonsense about cooking in the Ozarks. Families were big and appetites bigger, making woman's work a sunup-to-sundown job. There were chickens to feed, cows to milk, gardens to weed, fruits and vegetables to gather in. Ozark women, for the most part natural-born cooks, used the "by guess and by gosh" method, adding a pinch of this or dash of that until a particular soup or stew tasted "just right" instead of cooking "by the book." Their recipes were devoid of frills, but they were flavorful and nourishing, as these four Silver Dollar City recipes prove.

Miner's Spiced Kettle of Beef and Vegetables

MAKES 8 TO 10 SERVINGS

2 pounds boned beef chuck, cut in 1-inch cubes
½ cup flour, mixed with 1 tablespoon salt and ½ teaspoon
    each pepper and paprika
2 tablespoons lard or bacon drippings
1 cup chopped onions
6 cups water
2 bay leaves, 1 clove, and 1 teaspoon mixed pickling spices
    tied in cheesecloth
3 cups peeled and chopped fresh tomatoes (or 3 cups drained,
    canned tomatoes)
2 cups diced carrots
1 cup sliced celery
3 cups diced potatoes
1 cup shelled green peas (or 1 cup frozen green peas)
1 teaspoon sugar
2 teaspoons salt
¼ teaspoon pepper
3 tablespoons cornstarch blended with ¼ cup cold water

Dredge beef cubes in the flour mixture, then brown in
the lard or bacon drippings on all sides in a very large,
heavy kettle. Add onions and brown lightly. Add water
and spice bag and simmer, covered, ½ hour. Add tomatoes, carrots, celery, and potatoes and simmer, uncovered, 1 hour. Add peas, pushing down well into stew, the
sugar, salt, and pepper and simmer, uncovered, ½ hour.
Blend a little of the hot gravy into the cornstarch mixture, stir back into stew, and heat and stir until thickened, about 3 minutes. Ladle into big soup bowls and
serve with fresh-baked biscuits or corn bread. (*Note:*
This stew freezes well.)

Poor man's "meat and potatoes" and very good, too.
In the Ozarks, the traditional accompaniment would be
boiled turnip greens and corn bread.

Hoppin' John

MAKES 4 TO 6 SERVINGS

2 cups shelled black-eyed peas (or 2 packages, 10 ounces
    each, frozen black-eyed peas)
2 (¼ inch thick) slices salt pork
1 cup boiling water
2 cups hot cooked rice
2 tablespoons butter
½ to 1 teaspoon salt (depending on saltiness of the salt pork)
¼ teaspoon pepper

Cook the black-eyed peas with the salt pork in the boiling water in a covered saucepan 30 to 40 minutes until
peas are tender. Fork in the rice, butter, salt, and pepper
and heat over lowest heat about 5 minutes to drive off
excess steam. Fluff up with a fork and serve.

In the Ozarks, baked ham wouldn't be "fittin' " without Sweet Taters and Apples. They are good, too, with
roast pork or chicken.

Sweet Taters and Apples

MAKES 6 SERVINGS

6 medium-size sweet potatoes or yams
6 medium-size cooking apples
½ cup melted butter (about)
⅓ cup light brown sugar (about)
½ teaspoon nutmeg (about)

Bake the potatoes in their skins in a hot oven (400°) 1
hour or until tender. When cool enough to handle, peel
and slice ¼ to ½ inch thick. Peel, core, and slice the
apples. Layer sliced potatoes and apples alternately in a
9 x 9 x 2-inch baking dish, scattering melted butter,

brown sugar, and nutmeg over each layer. Cover with foil and bake in a moderate oven (350°) 30 to 35 minutes until bubbling.

One of the most unusual slaws you will ever eat—red and white cabbage teamed with sauerkraut—and one of the best. It is so popular at Silver Dollar City that visitors come into the kitchen, asking for the recipe.

Hot Sweet-Sour Kraut and Cabbage Salad

MAKES 6 TO 8 SERVINGS

¼ head white cabbage, sliced fine
¼ head red cabbage, sliced fine
2 cups sauerkraut
1 tablespoon prepared mustard
2 cups mayonnaise-type salad dressing
¼ cup sugar
1 tablespoon celery seeds
¼ teaspoon salt (about)
¼ teaspoon pepper

Place white and red cabbage in a large bowl. Heat sauerkraut with mustard, salad dressing, sugar, celery seeds, salt, and pepper in a large saucepan about 10 minutes, stirring frequently; do not allow to boil. Pour over cabbage and toss well to mix. Taste for salt and add more if needed (amount will vary according to saltiness of the sauerkraut). Serve hot.

The Arkansas Territorial Restoration
Little Rock, Arkansas

*I*f the access to Interstate 30 in the heart of Little Rock weren't so thronged with fast-moving traffic, more travelers might glance across Cumberland Street at a group of old red brick and white frame buildings nestled in a tree-filled oasis. This is the Arkansas Territorial Restoration, and to enter is to step into the early-nineteenth-century Arkansas frontier.

Here, thirteen old buildings have been painstakingly reassembled to create what many consider the most authentic village restoration in America. Here trees are nature's air conditioner. Boxwoods, lovingly trimmed, line the paths, and flowers of most every description abound. The mood is calm, and here, in the middle of the city, the air seems somehow purer.

The most imposing of the structures is Hinderliter House, and here, from a great brass kettle on the hearth, one can sample on special occasions a hearty soup made from chickens and vegetables the way it was a century and a half ago. This house, built in 1819–20 as a log tavern, is perhaps the oldest building in Little Rock, and one of the oldest in Arkansas. Until 1833 it was the home of Jesse Hinderliter, who operated his grog shop and general store on the ground floor and lived upstairs.

Some historians believe that the house was also the meeting place of the last Territorial Legislature in 1835.

When Hinderliter House was remodeled in 1834, the hand-hewn oak logs were covered with hand-beaded red-heart cypress siding. All of the ceiling beams, old and new, have since been given this same hand-beaded finish.

In the center of the Territorial Restoration complex is Noland House, a mid-nineteenth-century red brick structure named after Lieutenant C. F. M. Noland. It was Noland, a lawyer and journalist, who was chosen by his fellow legislators to take the constitution to Washington for ratification when the Arkansas Territory became a state in 1836. The house has a wide porch across the back, characteristic of early Southern homes, which looks across a garden bordered with dwarf English boxwood grown from cuttings from George Washington's garden at Mount Vernon.

Farther on is Woodruff House. In 1819, William E. Woodruff, then living at Arkansas Post, founded the *Arkansas Gazette*, the oldest newspaper west of the Mississippi River. When the capital of the territory was moved to Little Rock in 1821, Woodruff and his small press followed. Three years later he built his home and printing office on this site, just two blocks north of the "little rock," a natural rock landing extending into the Arkansas River.

The printing office in Woodruff House contains a Washington hand press, restored to working order, similar to the one used by Woodruff. In the editorial room are Woodruff's original mahogany secretary and apothecary chest. And one of the house's most interesting pieces is the small cedar table made from a tree that grew near the "little rock."

Another historic structure is Conway House, a well-built frame house doweled with white oak pegs. This is a good example of the smaller Southern homes of its period and features original hand-carved mantels and doors. It is thought to have been the residence of Elias

N. Conway, territorial auditor and Arkansas's fifth—and only bachelor—governor.

Many treasures are contained in this fine old home—a massive four-poster bed with trundle used by visiting relatives, a shaving stand, a Jeffersonian bureau and tufted-back rocker used by the governor, a rare hand-etched candle lantern, a Queen Anne dining table, and Chippendale side chairs.

To take the Markham Street exit off Interstate 30, to veer to the right onto Second Street, and then into a free parking area is to begin an enlightening and pleasurable journey through the early days of the Arkansas Territory.

This bracing Mulled Cider is served at the annual Christmas Open House at the Arkansas Territorial Restoration. It is based upon an old recipe that dates to territorial days.

Mulled Cider

MAKES 12 SERVINGS

2 sticks cinnamon
12 whole cloves
2 teaspoons whole allspice
1 gallon apple cider
1 cup firmly packed light brown sugar
1 lemon, sliced thin

Tie the cinnamon sticks, cloves, and allspice in a small cheesecloth bag. Place cider in a large, heavy enamel kettle, drop in bag of spices, and add brown sugar. Simmer, uncovered, 15 minutes. Remove the bag of spices. Pour cider into a metal or heatproof punch bowl, float lemon slices on top, and serve hot.

This is the soup to make if you have plenty of rich chicken stock on hand. You can substitute canned condensed chicken broth, but the soup will not be as good as it is made with a broth in which chickens and soupbones have simmered, together with onion, bay leaf, celery leaves, parsley, carrots, thyme, and the end of a lemon. This is the way women at the Arkansas Territorial Restoration prepare it for special occasions. Their recipe calls for "lots of autumn vegetables—dried corn, okra, tomatoes [which their grandmothers "put up"], onion, herbs to taste" and then added, just before serving, fluffy Arkansas rice. Here, then, is a more specific recipe based upon the old Arkansas one.

Arkansas Chicken and Autumn Vegetable Soup

MAKES 10 TO 12 SERVINGS

2 quarts rich chicken broth or stock, skimmed of fat
2 medium-size yellow onions, coarsely chopped
½ cup diced celery
2 tablespoons minced parsley
1 teaspoon leaf thyme, crumbled
1 bay leaf, crumbled
1 strip of lemon rind about 2 inches long and ½ inch wide
   (the yellow part only)
1 quart canned tomatoes (preferably home canned)
2 cups dried corn (there is a recipe for drying corn in this
   book; see Index for page number) OR, if you prefer, 2
   cups fresh whole kernel corn
1 pound tender young okra pods, washed and sliced about ½
   inch thick
2 teaspoons salt (about)
¼ teaspoon freshly ground pepper (about)
2 cups hot fluffy cooked rice

Place the chicken broth or stock, the onions, celery, parsley, thyme, bay leaf, lemon rind, tomatoes, and dried or fresh corn in a very large, heavy kettle and bring to a simmer. Cover and simmer slowly about 1½ hours, until corn is very tender and flavors have mellowed together. Add the okra, cover, and simmer 10 to 15 minutes longer until okra is tender. Add the salt and pepper, taste, and add more of each if needed. Stir in the rice and let simmer, uncovered, for another 5 to 10 minutes. Ladle into large soup bowls and serve.

"Little Fellows" are nothing more than small lemon "chess" tarts—very lemony, very buttery, very sweet. Lemon "chess" resembles the English lemon "cheese," and some food historians believe that "chess" is a corruption of "cheese." Others maintain that "chess" comes from "chest," because these rich sweet pies were "keeping pies," always ready for the unexpected visitor, especially the visiting preacher. "Little Fellows" are often no bigger than a thimble, but a more practical size is the small individual tart. You can buy prepared tart shells, ready to fill and bake, in many supermarkets. Or you can make your own tart shells. You will need pastry for a two-crust pie (use your own favorite recipe). And you will need muffin pans in which to bake the tarts. Simply roll the pastry out as you would for piecrust, cut in circles about one inch larger in diameter than the muffin pan cups, then fit the pastry circles into the muffin pan cups, pressing against the bottom and sides to form tart shells. Do not bake until after you have added the filling.

"Little Fellows"

MAKES ABOUT 2½ DOZEN

½ cup butter at room temperature
2 cups sugar
4 eggs
1 tablespoon flour
⅓ cup lemon juice

Finely grated rind of 1 lemon
30 unbaked tart shells (about 2¾ inches in diameter and 1¼
  inches deep)

Cream the butter and sugar just enough to blend well—
mixture should not be fluffy or filling may bubble up and
boil over in the oven. Beat in the eggs, one at a time,
then stir in flour. Add the lemon juice and rind (the mixture will seem to curdle but don't be alarmed; it will
smooth out in the baking). Spoon mixture into tart shells,
filling each no more than ⅔ full. (Should you have any
left-over filling, spoon into custard cups, again filling no
more than ⅔ full, set in a small baking pan, and pour
water into pan to a depth of 1 inch. These may be baked
in the oven alongside the tarts and will be done in about
the same amount of time.) Bake tarts in a moderate oven
(350°) 30 to 35 minutes until filling is puffy and golden
and pastry lightly browned. Remove from oven, cool
tarts in their pans to room temperature, then remove
from pans and serve.

Here is a sixth-generation Arkansas receipt for
Beaten Biscuits, written in its original form. "Beaten,"
by the way, does not mean beaten with a spoon. It means
pounded with a hammer or mallet, and in days past families awoke to a rhythmic hammering as the cook "beat"
the day's supply of biscuits. Beaten Biscuits are not
often made anymore because of all the time and energy
they require. Even hostesses at the Arkansas Territorial
Restoration favor an easier-to-make hot dinner roll. But
here, for the record—and for anyone who would like to
attempt them—is the historic beaten biscuit recipe.

ARKANSAS BEATEN BISCUITS

Mix 1 quart flour, 1 teaspoon salt, 2 rounding tablespoons lard (no substitute). Make into a stiff dough
using equal parts ice water and cold milk. Work on

a kneader or beat with a mallet (1,000 licks) until smooth and glossy. When ready, the dough is unmistakably satiny and begins to blister. Roll ¼ inch thick and cut no more than 2 inches in diameter. Prick centers 3 times with a 4-tined fork. Bake at moderate heat 20–25 minutes until lightly browned.

Old Washington Historic State Park
Washington, Arkansas

*I*n the course of American history towns are born, towns boom, and towns die. Old Washington, nothing more than a country crossroads tucked into the southwest corner of Arkansas, was such a town. History touched it once—briefly—for it was here that two pioneer trails crossed: the Fort Towson Trail, running east and west, and the Chihuahua Trail (later the Southwest Trail), along which Yankees made their way into the Southwest.

Famous men traveled those trails—Sam Houston, Stephen Austin, Jim Bowie. Old Washington was a popular stopping point because of its inn and because of a blacksmith named Jim Black, who forged better knives than anyone else on the frontier. Black developed a secret process of forging and tempering, a process that died with him, a process that created the famous Bowie knife.

Old Washington may not be old as American towns go, but it is old as Arkansas towns go, having been founded in 1824. It served as the Confederate Capital of Arkansas during the Civil War (from 1863 to 1865) and in its heyday boasted a population of two thousand.

But as often happens, progress by-passed Old Washington. The railroads came, but not to Old Washington, and the old trails, no longer traveled, were overrun by weeds and brush. Traffickers on the Red River, a few miles south, used to come to Old Washington, but as the town withered, they headed elsewhere. Even highways, being flung across the countryside, seemed to by-pass Old Washington. Death set in and Old Washington, like so many other once prosperous towns, may have deteriorated into a ghost town had the Pioneer Washington Foundation not restored its historic buildings and opened them to the public: the Block-Catts House (1850), a salt box filled with period furnishings; the Old Tavern (1824) with its pioneer kitchen, taproom, and Sam Houston Room; the Gun Museum with some five hundred firearms and Bowie knives on exhibit; the Garland House (1836), home of Augustus H. Garland, who served as Governor of Arkansas and, during Grover Cleveland's administration, U.S. Attorney General; the School House; the Royston House (1845), home of Confederate General Grandison D. Royston; the Confederate State Capitol (built in 1833), and of course James Black's Blacksmith Shop (1831) where the first Bowie knife was forged.

Another old house here has been restored and made into the Pioneer Kitchen and Dining Rooms. Its rooms are filled with antiques, and the foods served (among them the recipes included here) are almost all "old Arkansas." The kinds of things "Grandma used to make," says Mrs. Inez Carr, owner and operator of the dining rooms. Her dream was to find an old house, restore it, fill it with tables where families might eat their fill of Grandma's cooking. She has made her dream come true. And, it might be added, the dreams of others who have had their fill of "heat and serve," "instants and mixes." There are no kitchen short cuts here. Just plain good food, prepared the old-fashioned way, and plenty of it.

"You will be served anytime of the day when you stop by my kitchen," promises Mrs. Carr. And after she has served you, she will send you off to tour Old Washington in a surrey with a fringe on top.

One of those old-fashioned recipes that frugally use up odds and ends of cheese and vegetables.

Arkansas Boiled Egg Pie

MAKES 6 SERVINGS

Pastry for a 2-crust 9-inch pie (your favorite recipe)
1 tablespoon butter
¼ cup finely minced onion
⅓ cup finely minced celery
1 tablespoon all-purpose flour
1¼ cups light cream
¾ cup grated sharp Cheddar cheese
½ cup cooked and drained green peas (leftovers are fine)
1 tablespoon finely minced pimiento
1 teaspoon salt
⅛ teaspoon pepper
1 tablespoon dry sherry
2 egg yolks, lightly beaten
6 hard-cooked large eggs, shelled

Roll half of the pastry out on a floured board or pastry cloth into a circle about 12 inches in diameter; fit into a 9-inch piepan, trim overhang so that it is about 1 inch larger in diameter than the rim of the pan, then roll overhang under, even with rim, and crimp, making a high fluted edge. Prick bottom and sides of pastry well all over with a fork. Roll remaining half of pastry out about ⅛ inch thick and cut into strips (for a lattice top) or, if you prefer, into large diamonds, circles, or wedges which will be placed decoratively on top of the pie (you will find these shapes easier to manage than the pastry strips). Place cutout strips, diamonds, circles, or wedges on a baking sheet and prick lightly with a fork. Weight the unbaked pie shell down by fitting a second 9-inch piepan down inside shell or by laying a piece of wax paper in the shell and filling with uncooked rice or dried beans.

Bake both the pie shell and the pastry cutouts in a hot oven (400°) 8 to 10 minutes until very lightly browned. Remove from oven, lift piepan or wax paper filled with rice or beans from pie shell. Cool pie shell and pastry cutouts while preparing the filling. Lower oven temperature to moderately hot (375°).

To make the filling: Melt the butter in a medium-size saucepan, then sauté the onion and celery in the butter about 8 to 10 minutes over moderately low heat until limp and golden but not browned. Blend in the flour, then add the cream and cook and stir until thickened, about 3 minutes. Mix in the cheese, peas, pimiento, salt, and pepper and cook, stirring now and then, until cheese melts. Stir in the sherry. Briskly mix a little of the hot sauce into the beaten egg yolks, then stir back into pan and cook and stir over lowest heat 1 minute. Remove from heat and let mellow while preparing the eggs.

Slice the hard-cooked eggs and arrange in the baked pie shell. Pour in the cheese sauce, then arrange pastry strips in a lattice pattern on top, or arrange pastry diamonds, circles, or wedges decoratively on top. Return pie to oven and bake 15 to 20 minutes at 375° until filling just begins to bubble. Remove from oven and let stand about 5 minutes before serving. Cut into wedges, making sure each person gets some of the pastry topping as well as the bottom crust.

Desperation Pudding is actually a spicy four-layer torte put together with a thick plum sauce. It's an odd mixture (the cake batter contains raw grated potato), and its name, no doubt, comes from the fact that this was a desperation attempt to stir up dessert out of odds and ends on hand. Desperation or not, the results are delicious. This is the old Arkansas recipe, just as it is prepared at the Pioneer Kitchen and Dining Rooms at Old Washington State Park.

Desperation Pudding

MAKES A 9-INCH, 4-LAYER TORTE

2½ cups sifted all-purpose flour
1 teaspoon baking soda
½ teaspoon salt
½ teaspoon ground cinnamon
½ teaspoon ground nutmeg
½ teaspoon ground ginger
¼ teaspoon ground allspice
1 cup vegetable shortening
½ cup sugar
3 eggs, separated
1 cup molasses
1 medium-size raw potato, peeled and coarsely grated
¾ cup hot water
1 recipe Plum Sauce (given below)
1 cup heavy cream, whipped until stiff with 2 tablespoons
    confectioners' sugar and ½ teaspoon vanilla

Sift together the flour, soda, salt, cinnamon, nutmeg, ginger, and allspice and set aside. Cream the shortening and sugar until light, then beat in the egg yolks. Mix in the molasses. Stir in 1 cup of the sifted dry ingredients, then mix in the grated raw potato. Add the remaining sifted dry ingredients alternately with the hot water, beginning and ending with the dry ingredients. Beat the egg whites to soft peaks and fold into the batter gently but thoroughly so that no streaks of white remain. Divide the batter evenly among 4 well-greased and floured 9-inch round layer cake pans. The batter will little more than cover the bottom of the pans, but that is as it should be. You want 4 thin layers of cake. Bake the cake layers in a moderate oven (350°) 30 to 35 minutes or until cakes begin to pull from sides of pans and a finger, pressed gently in the top of a cake, leaves an imprint that vanishes slowly. Remove cake layers from oven and cool upright in their pans on wire racks 10 minutes. Loosen edges of layers with a spatula, then invert layers on racks and lift off pans. Cool about 15 minutes, then sandwich the 4 layers together with warm Plum Sauce, letting it drip down the sides of the layers. Spread remaining Plum Sauce over the top of the torte. Cool thoroughly, then slice and serve, topping each slice with a drift of sweetened whipped cream.

Although this Plum Sauce is used as a filling for Desperation Pudding (above), it is also delicious spooned over pound cake, sponge cake, or vanilla ice cream. It will have fresher, richer flavor if made with fresh, ripe purple plums, but you can, if you like, substitute canned purple plums or greengage plums. Be certain, however, to drain the canned plums well before puréeing them in a food mill or pressing them through a sieve, otherwise the sauce will be too thin.

Plum Sauce

MAKES ABOUT 1½ CUPS

¾ cup sugar
1½ tablespoons cornstarch
½ teaspoon ground nutmeg (preferably freshly ground)
1¼ cups puréed fresh purple plums (for this amount, you will need 5 to 6 large ripe plums; simply peel them, halve, pit, and put through a food mill or press through a fine sieve)
⅓ cup unsalted butter

In a small saucepan, mix together the sugar, cornstarch, and nutmeg, pressing well with a spoon to pulverize all lumps of cornstarch. Mix in the puréed plums, set over moderate heat, and cook and stir until thickened and clear, about 3 minutes. Reduce heat slightly, add the butter and let it melt, beating hard until smooth and well blended. Cool sauce slightly, then use to fill Desperation Pudding or serve as a sauce for cake or ice cream.

An unbelievably dark and rich pie that tastes oddly of chocolate yet has no chocolate in it. It is an old Arkansas recipe, one served at the Pioneer Kitchen and Dining Rooms at Old Washington State Park. "Sorghum and/or pure sugar cane molasses were the only known kinds at the time this recipe came into being," explains Inez S. Carr, owner-operator of the Pioneer Kitchen. And the pie, certainly, is better made with light molasses instead of the dark. The peanuts used in the pie may be either raw or parched but *unsalted*. The parched nuts give the pie a richer, stronger peanut flavor, however.

Original Peanut Butter Pie

MAKES A 9-INCH PIE

1½ cups blanched, shelled raw peanuts
1 cup light molasses or sorghum molasses (or, if you prefer, dark corn syrup)
½ cup sugar
½ cup butter at room temperature
4 small eggs
A 1-inch piece of vanilla bean, minced very fine
Pinch of salt
Ground nutmeg (optional)
1 unbaked 9-inch pie shell

Spread peanuts out in a baking pan and parch in a moderately slow oven (325°)—this will take about 40 to 45 minutes. Cool the nuts, then grind very fine, or, if you have an electric blender, pulverize the nuts, a few at a time, in the blender at high speed. Firmly pack enough ground nuts in a measuring cup to total 1 cup exactly. Place the nuts, molasses, sugar, butter, eggs, minced vanilla bean, and salt in a mixing bowl and beat hard until smooth and creamy. Pour into pie shell, sprinkle lightly with nutmeg if you like, then bake in a moderately hot oven (375°) 35 minutes or until crust is lightly browned and filling set. Cool to room temperature before cutting.

Pioneer Town
Wimberley, Texas

Pioneer Town may lack the historical credentials of the majority of restored or re-created villages scattered across the United States, but it nonetheless provides a colorful glimpse of what life was like nearly a hundred years ago in a one-horse town of south central Texas.

Because it is a reproduction of an 1880s town (and makes no bones about it), Pioneer Town does smack somewhat of a movie set. Still, the furnishings in its building are genuinely antique. It's a prairie crossroads town (located on the 7-A Ranch Resort just west of the main Austin–San Antonio highway), and dust swirls through the streets as the stage rumbles in or as gunslingers stage a *High Noon*-style shoot-out. It's a seasonal town, too, in full swing only in summer, when the Opera House offers old-time melodramas and Gay Nineties shows, the Silver Spoon Cafe dishes up hearty home-style cooking, and the Ice Cream Parlor serves forth a rainbow array of sodas and shakes and sundaes.

Among Pioneer Town's other replica buildings are a print shop, a crafts shop, an old-fashioned emporium, a saloon, a Wells Fargo office, a hotel with a double-decker veranda, a depot with puffer-belly locomotive, a bank, a post office, a gunshop, a pawnshop, a blacksmith shop, and a livery stable. There's even a stockade, a hanging tree, a cemetery, and a campground with a resident medicine show man. But there are more serious exhibits, too, such as the Wagon Museum and the Pioneer Museum of Western Art.

Those who like their history straight may scoff at Pioneer Town, but those less persnickety will find it both fascinating and fun.

The pungent aroma of Mexican cooking, wafting across the Texas border, seemed to early homesteaders, rangers, and ranchers so much more exciting than their own plain fare that they began experimenting with the Mexican foods and seasonings. *Guacamole*, for example, is a Mexican original that became popular in Texas and other border states long before the rest of America adopted it as a sophisticated cocktail dip. The avocado is native to Mexico, food historians tell us, adding that its protein content is so high that in areas where both meat and fish were scarce, the Indians made it the main dish. There exist dozens of recipes for Guacamole, but this is the one served around Pioneer Town in south central Texas. It combines avocados with two other foods native to Latin America: chili peppers and tomatoes. In Texas, as in Mexico, Guacamole is more apt to be served as a salad on a bed of shredded lettuce than as a dip.

Guacamole (Avocado Salad)

MAKES ABOUT 1¾ CUPS, ENOUGH FOR 4 SERVINGS

1 clove garlic, peeled and split
2 medium-size ripe avocados, halved and pitted
⅓ cup minced onion
Juice of ½ lemon
1 to 2 small green chili peppers, minced
1 slice (¼ inch thick) cut from the bottom of a firm-ripe
    tomato, seeded and diced but not peeled

¼ teaspoon salt
2 tablespoons mayonnaise (an optional modern addition)

Rub a small wooden salad bowl with the garlic. Scoop avocado flesh into bowl, discarding any fibers. Mash avocado coarsely with a fork, then mix in onion, lemon juice, chili peppers, diced tomato, salt, and, if you like, the mayonnaise. Serve as a dip for *tostadas* (crisp, deep-fried tortillas) or corn chips, as a filling for *tacos* (Mexican tortilla sandwiches), or as a salad with shredded lettuce.

This hearty beef-and-bean stew is Tex-Mex cooking at its best and a great favorite around Pioneer Town. Non-Texans would call it chili. But Texans, never! To them, the only honorable chili is "the bowl of red," made with finely cubed beef and suet, red chili peppers, garlic, oregano, cumin, and water, but without beans, tomatoes or onions. This, then, is the sort of frugal but filling supper that ranch house cooks would prepare by the gallon. The recipe makes a lot, but the stew freezes well.

Texas Border Hot Pot

MAKES 8 TO 10 SERVINGS

1 pound dried red kidney beans, washed and sorted
10½ cups cold water
3 tablespoons lard
4 large yellow onions, peeled and chopped
4 cloves garlic, peeled and minced
2 pounds ground lean beef
1 teaspoon cumin seeds
1½ teaspoons leaf oregano
3 large ripe tomatoes, peeled, cored, and cut in thin wedges
2 tablespoons chili powder
½ to 1 teaspoon cayenne (½ teaspoon makes a "tepid" pot, 1 teaspoon a fairly fiery one)
1 tablespoon salt

Place the beans and 6 cups of the water in a large, heavy kettle, cover, and soak overnight. Next day, add 2½ more cups of the water to beans, set over low heat, and simmer, covered, 1½ to 2 hours until beans are tender. Meanwhile, melt lard in a second large, heavy kettle; add onions and garlic and sauté slowly 10 to 12 minutes until very lightly browned. Add beef, breaking up large chunks, and brown lightly. While beef cooks, place the remaining 2 cups water, cumin seeds, and oregano in a small saucepan and let boil vigorously 5 minutes; strain liquid through a fine sieve into beef mixture. Also add the tomatoes, chili powder, cayenne, salt, the kidney beans, and their cooking liquid. Stir well. Adjust heat under kettle so that mixture bubbles lazily. Then let cook, uncovered, very slowly 2 to 3 hours until mixture is quite thick and flavors have blended well. Cooking time isn't critical—in fact, range cooks would simply set the kettle on the back of the stove or over glowing coals and let it bubble away the better part of the day. Flavor is what's important—when the stew tastes right to you, it's ready to serve. Like most stews, it is better made a day ahead, refrigerated overnight, reheated slowly to serving temperature—about 20 minutes.

Pralines are a Creole adaptation of sugared almonds, a French confection named for César du Plessis-Praslin, a French diplomat. The Creoles took the old French recipe, substituted home-grown pecans for almonds, and presto! The praline. Today we think of pralines as a New Orleans specialty. And so they are. but they are also made elsewhere throughout the South, each version differing slightly from the others. Here, then, is a Texas praline, made with brown sugar.

But first a word or two of caution: Don't try to make pralines on a wet or humid day. They simply will not harden. And don't try to hurry the cooking. The brown sugar syrup must simmer *slowly*—in your biggest, heaviest saucepan—over *low* heat. It will take about 1½ hours for the syrup to reach the soft-ball stage. If you try to rush the process, the pralines may scorch. And they may also turn "gritty" as they harden.

Texas Pralines

MAKES ABOUT 1½ DOZEN PRALINES (2½-3 INCHES IN DIAMETER)

2 cups firmly packed light brown sugar
1 cup buttermilk
1 teaspoon baking soda
1 tablespoon butter
½ teaspoon vanilla
1 cup pecan halves (break any large ones in half)

Simmer the brown sugar, buttermilk and baking soda in a very large, heavy saucepan over low heat *without stirring* until the mixture reaches 240° on a candy thermometer or until a bit of syrup, dropped into a small amount of cold water, forms a soft, pliable ball. Add butter, vanilla, and pecans and beat vigorously 1 to 2 minutes, just until syrup begins to thicken (it should be about the consistency of thick honey). Drop from a tablespoon onto baking sheets lined with wax paper, making each praline 2½ to 3 inches in diameter. Cool to room temperature, then peel pralines from wax paper and serve.

Indian City, U.S.A.

Anadarko, Oklahoma

Not one reconstructed village but seven, depicting the varying life styles of the Plains Indians—Caddo, Chiricahua Apache, Kiowa, Navajo, Pawnee, Pueblo, and Wichita—all planned and developed under the supervision of the Department of Anthropology at the University of Oklahoma.

Indian City sprawls across the red hills and plains of southwest Oklahoma on a small portion of what had been the immense Kiowa, Comanche, and Apache Reservation, and it is the very spot where during the Civil War the Tonkawa Indians were massacred by a band of Shawnee and mercenaries.

Indian City today is peaceful, and to wander through first one tribal village and then another is to learn something of the social, religious, and family life of the various Plains Indians, something of their ceremonies, arts, crafts, and cooking. It is to realize, too, how different these tribes were, one from another.

The Caddo, for example, were farmers and as such built more or less permanent villages—clusters of grass-roofed "wattle and daub" houses. Village life was often a communal one, with the men providing the meat and the women drying it on racks at the community work shelter.

The Chiricahua Apache, on the other hand, were

roaming hunters, and their homes were quickly put-up brush- or grass-covered shelters called "wickiups." Looking rather like outsize molehills, wickiups provided little more than crawl space. They were built mostly for sleeping—not for the braves who bedded down out-of-doors, but for their wives and children. One of the more interesting wickiups is a sort of Indian sauna where the men of the tribe would gather to steam themselves by throwing cold water on hot stones.

The Kiowa, like the Chiricahua Apache, were a migratory tribe, but their home was the tipi. Two large tipis stand at the Kiowa Winter Camp at Indian City, fenced in by a windbreak of willow branches. The Kiowa followed the great buffalo herds across the plains, settling in only when winter snows made travel hazardous.

The Navajo were more sedentary, for the most part farmers and shepherds, and their homes, beehive-shaped hogans made of pine logs and adobe, reflect their more settled way of life. Their outdoor bake ovens were hive-shaped too, and it was here that the women of the tribe baked rough, husky loaves leavened with natural yeasts.

The Pawnee built rather more elaborate homes— earth lodges, which from the outside resemble dugouts. Inside, however, these lodges were surprisingly spacious, with poles marking off the central kitchen. At the far end of the lodge, opposite the entrance, stood the altar, the province of the family elder. And ringing the outer walls of the lodge were ledges used for sitting and, when covered with willow branches and buffalo skins, for sleeping.

The Pueblo were the master architects among Indians, for they built adobe apartment houses, sometimes several floors high, which for defense purposes were entered by scaling a series of ladders.

Among the Wichita, the women were the builders. And what builders they were, erecting out of pine poles, willow branches, and swamp grasses weatherproof community buildings of awesome size. The Council House of the Wichita at Indian City stands forty feet high, the equivalent of four stories. Teamwork not only built the Wichita villages, it also clothed and fed the tribe, for the women would gather at the Community Shelter to dry meats and vegetables, stretch and tan buffalo skins.

Indian guides (of the tribes represented at Indian City) show visitors through, explaining the function and construction of the various Indian dwellings and community centers, and explaining, too, the various tools, weapons, cooking utensils, musical instruments, games, and toys on display.

Climaxed by an exhibition of ceremonial Indian dancing, it provides a fascinating glimpse of red man's America.

A very old and basic corn soup popular among the Plains Indians. In days past, the meat used would have been buffalo or venison instead of beef, and in summer fresh corn would probably have been used instead of dried corn. But dried corn makes a better soup because it imparts a sweet, nut-like flavor. You can buy dried corn in many specialty food shops or health stores. You can also dry it easily in your own oven (directions follow).

Dried Corn Soup

MAKES 4 SERVINGS

1 pound lean, boned beef chuck, cut in ½-inch cubes
1 tablespoon bacon or meat drippings
4 cups water
1 cup dried corn
¾ teaspoon salt
⅛ teaspoon pepper

Brown the meat well on all sides in the drippings in a large, heavy saucepan over high heat. Lower heat to moderate, add water, cover, and simmer 1 hour. Add dried corn, salt, and pepper, re-cover, and simmer 1 hour longer or until both meat and corn are tender. Ladle into bowls and serve.

After harvesting their corn, Indians would dry it to use throughout the fall, winter, and spring. Their method of drying was simply to spread the corn out under the sun and let nature do the rest. Here's an oven method that works quite well provided you have an oven that will maintain a constant, very low temperature.

HOW TO DRY CORN

Husk 4 large ears of sweet corn and parboil 5 minutes in a covered kettle. Drain ears and pat as dry as possible on paper toweling. Cut corn from the cobs. Here's an easy way: Using a sharp knife and holding an ear of corn almost perpendicular to a chopping board, cut straight down along the cob, freeing the kernels. Spread the kernels out in a single layer on a baking sheet, place in a very slow oven (175°), and let dry 12 to 15 hours, stirring now and then. When properly dried, the corn should be very hard. Makes about 1 cup.

A quick, simple bread that is a Plains Indian staple. When properly fried, the chunks of bread are richly browned and crispy outside, soft and spongy inside. The important point is to keep the temperature of the deep fat at 375° throughout frying. If it drops much lower, the breads will be greasy, if it rises above 375°, the breads will brown before they cook through to the center.

Indian Fry Bread

MAKES 16 PIECES

2 cups sifted all-purpose flour
3 teaspoons baking powder
1 teaspoon salt
1 cup milk or water
Vegetable oil for deep fat frying (you will need about 2 quarts)

Place the flour, baking powder, and salt in a medium-size mixing bowl, make a well in the center, and pour in the milk or water. Stir briskly just until dry ingredients are uniformly moistened. Turn dough out on a well-floured board or pastry cloth and pat into an 8-inch square measuring about ½ inch thick. With a sharp knife, dipped in flour, cut dough into 2-inch squares, then make a slit in the center of each, cutting clear through the dough. Fry the squares, 4 or 5 at a time, in deep hot fat (375° on a deep fat thermometer), allowing 3 to 4 minutes on each side and turning often so that the squares brown evenly and breads cook through to the center (the slits in the breads help them cook uniformly). Drain on paper toweling and serve hot.

Ancient Cherokee Village at Tsa-La-Gi
Park Hill, Oklahoma

*D*uring the fall and winter of 1838–39, sixteen thousand Cherokee were driven from their homes in the Southern highlands into the Indian territory of eastern Oklahoma. As they made their way along this infamous "Trail of Tears," four thousand Cherokee died from illness, exposure, and starvation. But the twelve thousand survivors rose from despair to found a new Cherokee Nation near Tahlequah, Oklahoma.

"The old ways," the Cherokee say, "are swift birds. They fly away or die and leave no sign." Lest their heritage be lost in modern America, the Cherokee National Historical Society has re-created, just south of Tahlequah, an ancient Cherokee Village to show how the Cherokee lived some hundred and fifty years before the U.S. Government forced them west.

This federal eviction of the Cherokee from their native lands is surely one of the shabbier pages of American history, for it was lust—for gold and for land—that drove white men to banish the Cherokee to the wilderness of the Ozark foothills. It is a dreary chapter in Cherokee history, too, for it split the Cherokee Nation into two warring factions, one of which yielded to the pressures of Andrew Jackson and signed over to the government hundreds of thousands of acres.

The Cherokee, one of the "five civilized Indian tribes," had evolved a high level of culture before white men penetrated their lands, and it is this culture that is being preserved at the Ancient Cherokee Village at Tsa-La-Gi (that word, incidentally, is the original name of the tribe; Cherokee is an Anglicization).

Descendants of the survivors of the "Trail of Tears" serve as guides at the re-created village, explaining in detail the arts and crafts being demonstrated. The Indian artisans speak only Cherokee, not because they cannot speak English, but because their ancestors, who would have lived in a village such as this, would not have known the white man's tongue.

A stockade encloses the village, in both time and space. The focal point is the circular Council House, illuminated only by the eternal sacred fire. In the woodlands surrounding it cluster thatch-roofed log lean-tos and igloo-like earthen dwellings. It's eerily quiet here as women shape pots of native clay, weave cloth and baskets, smoke fish over open fires, and prepare ancient Cherokee recipes. There are men about, too, dressed, as are the women, in period costume, feathering arrows, tanning hides, making bows and blowguns, burning out the soft centers of logs to form dugout canoes. Streams trickle through the village (the Cherokee venerated water and prided themselves on their cleanliness); birds sing in branches overhead, for this is a wildlife refuge.

The re-created village (open only in summer) is merely one of the attractions at Tsa-La-gi, which is in fact, a Cherokee Cultural Center set up by the Cherokee National Historical Society. There's a huge new outdoor amphitheater where in summer the "Trail of Tears" is staged, a historical drama written by Kermit Hunter that chronicles the story of the Cherokee from 1838 at the outset of their removal from the Southern highlands to 1907, when Oklahoma achieved statehood. The newest addition to the Cultural Center is the Cherokee National Museum, and soon to be added are the Cherokee National Archives and Library, an Herbarium-Arboretum, and yet another re-created village, this one circa 1850–90.

Tsa-La-Gi is an impressive complex, showing as it does that out of the "Trail of Tears" has come triumph at last.

Grapes grow wild over most of North America and Indian women learned early how to prepare them in a variety of ways. Here is a Cherokee recipe for grape juice, which was drunk as a beverage and, on occasion, boiled down into a thicker juice in which dumplings were cooked. Fruit dumplings were a popular Cherokee dessert, and you will find, on the pages that follow, an early recipe for Blackberry Dumplings. Indians, of course, did not have refined sugars, so this grape juice, originally, would have contained no sweetener other than the natural grape sugar, or perhaps, a bit of honey or sweet tree sap. This version calls for sugar, but you can, if you like, substitute honey. It gives the grape juice a mellower flavor.

Homemade Grape Juice

MAKES 3½ TO 4 QUARTS

5 pounds grapes (scuppernong, muscadine, or Concord),
    washed well and stemmed
2 quarts water
1 cup sugar (more, if needed, to suit your taste)

Place grapes and water in a large, heavy kettle, bring to a boil over moderate heat, then boil, uncovered, about 1 hour or until grapes are very soft. Line a large colander with several thicknesses of cheesecloth, set over large kettle or heatproof bowl, then pour in the grapes and their juice. When most of the juice has drained through, mash the grapes with the back of a wooden spoon, extracting as much additional juice as possible. Add sugar to the grape juice and stir until dissolved. Pour into quart-size jars and store in the refrigerator.

A basic bread, a heavy bread, and one not everyone will like. It is nourishing fare, however, because of the high-protein pinto beans baked into the bread, and it is a staple among the Cherokee of Oklahoma. Although the original recipe calls for no shortening, you may want to add a tablespoon of melted bacon drippings or vegetable shortening for a slightly more tender bread. You will notice as you spoon the batter into the pan that the milk seems to separate out, leaving pools on top of the mixture. Don't worry. It will all come together during the baking.

Cherokee Bean Bread

MAKES A 9 x 9 x 2-INCH LOAF

2 cups corn meal
1½ teaspoons salt
1 teaspoon baking powder
2 eggs, lightly beaten
1½ cups milk
1 tablespoon melted bacon drippings or vegetable shortening (optional)
2 cups cooked, well-drained pinto beans

Stir together the corn meal, salt, and baking powder in a medium-size mixing bowl. Combine the eggs, milk, and, if you like, the melted drippings or shortening. Pour all at once into dry ingredients and stir just enough to mix. Stir in the pinto beans. Spoon into a very well-greased 9 x 9 x 2-inch baking pan and bake in a very hot oven (450°) about 20 minutes or until bread begins to pull from sides of pan and is lightly browned on top. Cool the bread in its pan 10 minutes, then cut into squares and serve.

American Indian desserts were, for the most part, fruit desserts, sometimes raw, sometimes cooked. These blackberry Dumplings are a Cherokee favorite, but the dumplings are not light and fluffy as we tend to think dumplings must be. They are firm—rather like home-made pasta. The blackberries give out considerable juice as they cook, which the Indians no doubt drank from the bowl after they had eaten the dumplings. Huckleberries, by the way, are prepared the same way, and sometimes the dumplings are simply cooked in grape juice ("blue dumplings," the Cherokee call them). For best results, you will need a large, shallow, heavy kettle for making the dumplings. One measuring at least 10 inches across and 3 to 3½ inches deep should be about right. But it must have a close-fitting cover.

Blackberry Dumplings

MAKES ABOUT 8 SERVINGS

2 quarts fresh, ripe blackberries, washed and sorted
2 cups sugar
1½ cups water
2 cups sifted all-purpose flour (about)
1 teaspoon baking powder
2 tablespoons melted vegetable shortening or vegetable oil

Place the blackberries, sugar, and ½ cup of the water in a large, heavy kettle and bring to a boil over moderate heat. Meanwhile, stir together the flour and baking powder in a medium-size mixing bowl, then pour in the oil and remaining 1 cup of water. Stir just to mix. If dough seems too soft to roll, work in a bit more flour. Turn dough out on a well-floured board of pastry cloth and roll into a large square or rectangle about ⅛ inch thick. Cut into strips about 1½ inches long and ½ inch wide—no need to make the margins exact because the dumplings will lose their shape as they cook. When the blackberries have come to a full rolling boil, drop in the dumplings, one at a time, distributing them as evenly as possible over the surface of the berries and dropping them in with some force so that they will sink. Boil gently, uncovered, for 5 minutes, then cover tight, reduce heat slightly, and simmer 10 minutes. Turn off the heat and let the dumplings stand 5 minutes before lifting the cover. Ladle into large dessert bowls and serve. Add a drizzling of heavy cream, if you like (today's Cherokee often do), or, if you prefer, whip the cream and top each serving with a large drift of it.

Included here, more for interest than for use, are two early Cherokee recipes provided by the Indian Village at Tsa-La-Gi. If, however, you have access to fresh crawdads (crayfish) or to sassafras roots, by all means try them.

CRAWDADS

Salt the cleaned crawdads. Drop into about ⅓ of a skillet of hot grease and fry about 6 to 8 minutes, stirring occasionally, so that they will cook on all sides. Drain off grease and serve.

SASSAFRAS TEA

Place about 6 2-inch sassafras roots in a pan. Pour 6 cups of water over the roots and bring to a boil slowly. Remove from heat, cover, and let steep until tea is the right strength. Strain and serve as is, with sugar, or with sugar and cream.

Historic Front Street
Dodge City, Kansas

*I*t was once the wildest, wickedest city in the West. And who, thanks to television's *Gunsmoke*, has not heard of Dodge City, Kansas, of Wyatt Earp, Bat Masterson, Belle Starr, Doc Holliday? Dodge City today is no longer the wildest, wickedest stop on the Western cattle trail. But a little of its Old West woolliness still exists. It's called Historic Front Street.

Named for General Granville Dodge, a civil engineer who helped bring railroads to the Southwest, Dodge City was founded in 1872 along both the Arkansas River and the route of the Santa Fe Trail. It was a town like no other. It boomed first when the buffalo hunters came, and when the great herds had been wiped out, it boomed again as a cattle town. Longhorns were driven to Dodge City by the thousands from the Indian Territory (now Oklahoma), from New Mexico, Colorado, and western Kansas, to be sold on the hoof and shipped out via the new Santa Fe railroad. Then came the massive cattle drives from Texas, which, Texas style, overshadowed all the others.

Dodge City for a time was the "Cattle Capital of the World" with some three hundred thousand head clomping through its streets in a single year. Cowboys long on the trail hit Dodge hell bent for fun. And they found it.

They drank, they brawled, they shot it out on the streets so that gunfights became as much a part of the local scene as the Long Branch Salon (those men who died were buried at Boot Hill, a rise of land overlooking Front Street).

Much of Dodge and most of Front Street were leveled in 1885 by fire, and a chapter in the history of the West was closed.

But Front Street lives once again, in the heart of modern Dodge City, a faithful re-creation of the hell-for-leather cattle town. In 1958 six old Front Street buildings were rebuilt, and in 1964 another six were added. There's Rath and Wright's General Store, a theater, a "tonsorial palace" (haircut twenty-five cents, shave fifteen, bath twenty-five), an ice cream parlor (with seventeen old-fashioned flavors to try), and for those who want to sit down to a robust, early Dodge meal, there's Beatty and Kelly Restaurant (plenty of soups and stews that are representative of those served a hundred years ago. The recipes included here, provided by the Boot Hill Museum, which also administers Historic Front Street, are authentically old Dodge specialties).

And, of course, there is the Long Branch Saloon, where nightly during the summer months (June through August) "Miss Kitty" entertains, and tourists shout and clap for more. There's no "redeye" served at the Long Branch as in days past (sarsaparilla and soft drinks only), but the rinky-tink piano thumps out the old tunes that once bounced off the walls of the original saloon.

Historic Front Street, or "The Replica," as Dodge City citizens call it, is one square block of authentic Western lore. Boot Hill is still there, though its bodies have been disinterred and moved elsewhere, and the "hanging tree" stands stark against the buttermilk Kansas sky. There are still shoot-outs on dusty Front Street, only today's cowpokes are college students (employed by Dodge as guides) and the bullets are blanks.

It's the Old West all right, and the tourists who visit Dodge each year by the thousands love it.

Dried peas and beans have always been used to stretch meat. Now comes this old Dodge recipe in which the beans, themselves, are stretched—with stale bread crumbs. This, surely, is the ultimate lesson in economy, for each hearty bowl of soup costs about ten cents. It is an utterly unpretentious soup—no herbs or spices to season—but its richness of flavor will surprise you.

White Bean, Parsnip, Potato, and Turnip Soup

MAKES 8 HEARTY SERVINGS

1 small soupbone (beef, pork, ham, lamb, or mutton,
    weighing about 1 to 1½ pounds)
2 quarts cold water
1 cup dried navy or pea beans, washed and sorted
2 cups boiling water
3 medium-size potatoes, peeled and sliced thin
2 medium-size white turnips, peeled and sliced thin
1 large parsnip, peeled and sliced thin
2 to 3 teaspoons salt
¼ teaspoon pepper (preferably freshly ground)
1½ cups fairly fine, stale-but-not-dry bread crumbs
1 medium-size yellow onion, peeled and sliced tissue thin
    (optional topping)

Boil the soupbone in the 2 quarts water in a large, heavy, covered kettle about 2 hours until the meat falls from the bones; discard bones, first removing all clinging bits of meat and adding to the broth. While the soupbone boils, soak the dried beans in the boiling water in a small, covered saucepan. Add beans and their soaking liquid to the soup kettle, cover and simmer 1 hour. Add potatoes, turnips, parsnip, 2 teaspoons of the salt, and the pepper. Cover and simmer about 1½ hours, then uncover and simmer ½ hour longer. Taste for salt and add the remaining teaspoon if needed. Stir in the bread crumbs, ladle soup into large bowls, and top each portion, if you like, with a slice or two of onion.

There's an old saying: "Only a fool argues with a mule, a skunk, or a chuck wagon cook." Chuck wagon cooks, who accompanied the long cattle drives to Dodge City, Kansas City, Omaha, or other "beef capitals" of the Plains, were notoriously crotchety. And understandably so. Their job was to dish up three hefty meals a day for a dozen or more ravenous cowhands and to do so on the hot dusty prairielands. All of which meant rising long before sunup, usually about 3 A.M., and working straight through the day until well after dark. Chuck wagon cooks were, of necessity, efficiency experts, using as few utensils and implements as possible because their wagons held little. So the big pot of beans was the standby. It traveled well and could be watered down as needed or plumped up with extra dried beans, onions, and leftover bits of meat.

Chuck Wagon Beans

MAKES 8 SERVINGS

1 pound dried kidney beans
6 cups water
½ pound lean bacon, diced
2 large onions, peeled and chopped
2 cloves garlic, peeled and crushed
4 large tomatoes, peeled, cored, and chopped
2 teaspoons salt
¼ teaspoon black pepper
¼ teaspoon crushed dried red chili peppers
1 bay leaf
½ teaspoon coriander

Place the beans in a large, heavy kettle, add water, bring to the boil, and boil, uncovered, 5 minutes. Cover, turn heat off, and let stand 1 hour. Meanwhile, fry the bacon in a large skillet until crisp and brown; lift out with a slotted spoon to paper toweling to drain. Pour off all but 2 tablespoons drippings from skillet. Sauté onions and garlic in the drippings until lightly browned, 8 to 10 minutes. Set aside. When beans have stood 1 hour, bring again to the boil, add onions and garlic, bacon crumbles, and all remaining ingredients. Cover, adjust heat so mixture bubbles gently, and simmer 1 hour. Uncover and simmer very slowly 1 hour longer. Ladle into deep soup bowls and serve. Delicious with oven-hot biscuits or corn bread.

The original "western omelet," this quick scramble of eggs, onions, and tomatoes. It was popular among cowhands running fences along boundary lines to keep cattle from wandering all over the prairie and popular, too, with crewmen of the old Santa Fe railroad that swept through Dodge City.

Line Camp Skillet Supper

MAKES 4 SERVINGS

6 slices bacon, diced
6 green onions, sliced thin (include some tops)
2 medium-size ripe tomatoes, peeled, cored, and chopped
6 eggs
¾ teaspoon salt
Pinch of pepper
6 soda crackers, crumbled

Fry the bacon in a heavy skillet until crisp and brown; drain bacon on paper toweling and pour all but 2 tablespoons of drippings from the skillet. Add onions to skillet and sauté, stirring now and then, about 5 minutes until soft; add tomatoes and simmer about 15 minutes until juices cook down into a fairly thick sauce. Meanwhile, beat eggs with salt and pepper until frothy. Pour eggs into skillet and begin scrambling. When beginning to set, scatter in cracker crumbs and bacon and continue scrambling until eggs are cooked the way you like them.

This is actually a sort of omelet, the sort a chuck wagon cook might have stirred up using pungent wild prairie onions. Even with scallions, the onion flavor is pronounced, so reduce the quantity, if you like, to 2 or 3 cups. If you're fond of onions, however, prepare the recipe with the full amount. Allow yourself about half an hour to chop them. And expect a good cry.

Fried Green Onion Tops

MAKES 4 SERVINGS

2 tablespoons bacon drippings, lard, or butter
4 cups coarsely chopped scallions, including all of the green tops (for 4 cups you will need about 14 to 16 medium-size scallions)
6 large eggs, beaten until frothy
¼ to ½ teaspoon salt (depending upon saltiness of bacon drippings, lard, or butter)
⅛ teaspoon pepper

Melt the bacon drippings, lard, or butter in a very large, heavy skillet over moderate heat. Add the chopped scallions and fry, stirring now and then, 10 to 12 minutes until limp but not browned. Add the eggs, salt, and pepper and cook, drawing cooked portions of eggs around the edge of the skillet in toward the center with a wooden spoon and letting the uncooked eggs run underneath. When the eggs are uniformly and softly set—after about 3 to 4 minutes—dish up and serve.

The Harold Warp Pioneer Village
Minden, Nebraska

*T*his is a replica village rather than a restoration, but it shows nonetheless man's progress on the Nebraska prairies from the pioneer days of 1830 to the mid-twentieth century. It is a town built by one man and, to be more specific, one man's love for the countryside where he grew up.

That man is Harold Warp, son of a Norwegian immigrant, who left Minden at the age of twenty, made a fortune in plastics in Chicago, but never once forgot the Nebraska of his boyhood. When Warp heard that the one-room schoolhouse he had attended as a child was being put up for auction, he bought it. And that schoolhouse was the beginning of Pioneer Village, which now sprawls over twenty acres of plains near Minden, includes twenty-three re-created and restored historic buildings and contains some thirty thousand historical objects of heartland America: toys and trinkets, telephones and tractors, musical instruments and clocks, horse-drawn rigs and streetcars, early automobiles and airplanes, bicycles, boats, and bathtubs—a bewildering array.

Pioneer Village begins behind a cavernous main exhibit building, and it is neatly laid out in a circle so that you can walk chronologically through more than a century of Nebraska history. The starting point is the two-story log fort and stockade, built in 1869 as a defense against Indians in Webster County, Nebraska. As you proceed from it around the village circle, you visit the People's Store (a replica stocked with authentic early merchandise), the Bloomington Land Office (the restored Franklin County government building where homesteaders once filed their claims), the Fire House (a replica filled with early fire-fighting equipment), the Lowell Depot (a restoration of the last-stop station on the Burlington Railroad of the 1870s), the Grom School, which Harold Warp attended as a child, the Sod House (a replica depicting the early shanty days of the pioneers), the China Shop (another old schoolhouse, this one overflowing with antique china), the Lutheran Church (Minden's first, built in 1884), one of the oldest steam merry-go-rounds in the U.S. (it still operates much to the delight of children), the Original Pony Express Station (moved to Pioneer Village from Bridgeport, Nebraska, two hundred miles away), the Agricultural Building (filled with early plows, reapers, and threshers), the Antique Auto Building (more than one hundred old-timers here), the Old Livery Stable. And so it goes, all around the village circle. En route you will see five period kitchens, dating from 1830 to 1930 and showing the evolution of cooking as the barren Plains become America's Breadbasket. You can sample some of this hefty prairie fare at the Pioneer Restaurant, and, so that you can try it out in your own kitchen, the Pioneer Village staff has published *Pioneer Cook Book*, a small paperback of early Nebraska favorites (the recipes that follow are adapted from that book).

The Pioneer Village at Minden, then, is a memorial to the pioneer men and women who came to the prairie, conquered it, and put down roots.

As Fred A. Seaton, former U.S. senator from Nebraska and former Secretary of the Interior, said in paying tribute to Pioneer Village:

"Future generations, instead of asking, 'Why didn't

someone think to save and preserve the things our forefathers used in winning the West?' can go to the Pioneer Village and build for themselves an accurate mental picture of what their ancestors were able to accomplish with their hands and inadequate tools. It will help them gain an insight into the real history of their nation much more adequately than would thousands of printed words."

And so it does.

Corn chowder is so much an American favorite today we tend to forget that it originally was American Indian. What happened with corn chowder, as with such other Indian recipes as succotash, Brunswick stew, and "Boston" baked beans, is that early colonists, and later pioneer families moving west with the wagon trains, took the Indian foods and added their own fillips. Indian corn chowder, for example, was simply parched corn stewed in water with perhaps a dab of bear grease and, when available, a handful of wild onions. Frontier women of the Plains who had milk cows and hogs began preparing the chowder with top milk and salt pork. And thus emerged the corn chowder we relish today.

Nebraska Corn Chowder

MAKES 6 SERVINGS

8 medium-size ears sweet corn, husked
¼ pound salt pork, cut in fine dice
2 medium-size yellow onions, peeled and chopped
2 small potatoes, peeled and cubed
1 tablespoon sugar
½ teaspoon paprika
1 teaspoon salt
⅛ teaspoon freshly ground pepper
½ cup water
2 cups milk
2 cups light cream

Cut the kernels of corn from the cobs cream-style (to do so, make a deep cut down the center of each row of kernels with a sharp knife, then, using the knife, scrape the corn pulp and milk into a large bowl). Fry the salt pork in a large, heavy skillet until most of the drippings have cooked out and only crispy brown bits remain; lift the salt pork from the skillet with a slotted spoon to paper toweling to drain. Pour all but 3 tablespoons drippings from skillet; add onions and potatoes and sauté slowly until lightly browned, about 10 minutes. Add sugar, paprika, salt, pepper, and water, cover and simmer 10 minutes. Add corn, milk, cream, and browned salt pork, adjust heat so mixture bubbles gently, cover, and simmer 20 minutes—do not allow to boil. Taste for salt and pepper and add more if needed. Ladle into soup plates and serve with crisp crackers.

This rich and filling main dish frugally uses up stale bread but does not stint on butter. It was popular among the Germans and Scandinavians who made their way to Nebraska during the mid- and late nineteenth century to coax a living from the land. Not unlike the Pennsylvania Dutch egg bread, it is nothing more than butter-browned bread cubes in a softly set omelet.

Hootsla (Egg Skillet Bread)

MAKES 6 SERVINGS

⅔ cup butter
10 slices stale white bread, cut in ½-inch cubes (leave the
    crusts on)
4 large eggs
¾ cup milk
½ teaspoon salt
⅛ teaspoon pepper

Melt the butter in a large, heavy skillet over moderate heat but do not let it brown. Add the bread cubes, turn heat up slightly, and fry, tossing gently with a spoon, about 5 to 8 minutes until delicately browned. Quickly beat the eggs with the milk, salt, and pepper until frothy. Pour into skillet, tilting so that eggs run underneath the bread cubes and to the edges of the skillet. Reduce heat to moderate and cook eggs, without stirring, 5 to 8 minutes until lightly browned on the bottom and softly set on top. Spoon onto heated plates and serve at once.

Salads in the sod-house days of Nebraska were apt to be slaws (cabbage was one of the few green vegetables that kept reasonably well) or, more often, a bowl of wild greens dressed with meat drippings and vinegar. Dandelions and wild onions were abundant, and if the leaves were gathered young—before the plants blossomed—they could be made into a pungent but not bitter salad. Today many specialty food shops sell dandelion greens, but you can, if you prefer, gather them in your own yard —just be sure to pick them before they flower. As for wild onions, we find their flavor "grassy" and have substituted scallions.

Wilted Dandelions and Wild Onions

MAKES 4 SERVINGS

4 tablespoons bacon drippings
2 pounds (about 3 quarts) young and tender dandelion leaves, trimmed of coarse stems, rinsed well in cool water, and drained in a colander
3 scallions, trimmed and sliced thin (include green tops)
¼ cup cider vinegar
¼ teaspoon salt
⅛ teaspoon pepper

Melt bacon drippings in a large, heavy kettle over moderate heat, add dandelion leaves and scallions, and sauté, turning in the drippings, 2 to 3 minutes until lightly glazed. Add vinegar, salt, and pepper, toss to mix, cover, and simmer over low heat 10 to 15 minutes just until dandelion leaves are tender. Toss again and serve as a hot salad.

&

Few covered wagons traveled without a supply of vinegar, for to pioneer women it was as important as firewood and water. They used it to scrub metal pots, to shine mirrors and glass, to treat sore throats (as a gargle), to tenderize sinewy meats (either by marinating or simmering them in water acidulated with vinegar), to pickle fruits and vegetables, to minimize the strong cooking odors of cabbage and onions. They even used it to make a mock lemon pie, lemons being as scarce and valuable on the prairies as gold. Vinegar Pie is today a Nebraska classic, and it does taste surprisingly like lemon pie.

Vinegar Pie

MAKES AN 8-INCH PIE

1 cup sugar
3 tablespoons flour
¼ teaspoon ground mace
¾ cup water
2 tablespoons cider vinegar
⅓ cup melted butter
2 large eggs, lightly beaten
1 unbaked 8-inch pie shell

In a medium-size mixing bowl, blend together sugar, flour, and mace until no lumps of flour remain. Stir in water, vinegar, melted butter, and eggs and beat just enough to mix. Pour into unbaked pie shell and bake in a moderate oven (350°) 50 to 55 minutes until filling is puffed and lightly browned. Remove from oven and cool to room temperature before cutting (the filling will fall slightly and thicken to the consistency of custard).

Stuhr Museum of the Prairie Pioneer
Grand Island, Nebraska

W*hen* you approach the Stuhr Museum, you wonder if you are at the right place. This, certainly, is no pioneer prairie village. It is a modern white marble temple, designed by architect Edward Durell Stone, that seems to float in a man-made lake in the middle of the Nebraska prairie.

But this is merely the museum building. The recreated Prairie Pioneer Village is here, too, hidden from view, some fifty-seven buildings, grouped according to plans once set forth by the Union Pacific Railroad, into a turn-of-the-century town. All of the buildings are historic and have simply been relocated at the village site from elsewhere about Nebraska. The more interesting include the Danish Lutheran Church (1880), a Union Pacific Railroad Depot (1880), the Kenesaw Bank Building (1886), and the Milisen House (1879).

There is more to see here, however, than restored small-town buildings filled with museum pieces. Workshops are conducted here in summer, covering almost every phase of Plains pioneer life, which includes, of course, cooking (the recipes included here are those demonstrated at the village).

You will see here, too, an impressive collection of historic farm machinery, the sort that turned the parched

Nebraska plains into golden seas of grain. And if you should visit the Stuhr Museum during the year of America's Bicentennial, you will also see re-created an 1876 living history farm where the daily chores are done just as they were one hundred years ago in central Nebraska.

On the Nebraska plains, this old pioneer kettle of Beans-and-Sowbelly would have been cooked on a good bed of coals in the hearth. Or perhaps suspended over a campfire. Roger L. Welsch, Centennial Fellow at the University of Nebraska, who in summer conducts workshops in pioneer cookery at the Stuhr Museum in Grand Island, says he likes to prepare the recipe in the fireplace in his study. "I enjoy a nice fire in winter," he says, "and the anticipation of these fine beans, and the occasional break provided by the necessity of stirring them, amplifies the pleasure manyfold." He sets the kettle on the coals in the morning and lets the beans cook lazily all day, checking occasionally to see that they aren't boiling too dry. You can also cook the beans on top of the stove, but be sure to keep the flame at its lowest point.

Beans-and-Sowbelly

MAKES 8 TO 10 SERVINGS

1½ pounds dried pea beans or navy beans, washed and sorted
2 quarts cold water
½ pound sowbelly, salt pork, or fatback, cut in ½-inch cubes
¾ cup molasses
¼ cup cider vinegar
Salt to taste
2 cups coarsely chopped onions

Place the beans in a large bowl, add cold water, and let soak overnight. Next day, brown the sowbelly, salt pork, or fatback in a large, heavy Dutch-oven-type kettle (cast iron if you intend to cook the beans on the hearth) until most of the drippings have cooked out, leaving crispy brown bits. This will take about 15 minutes over a moderately slow heat. Dump the beans and their soaking water on top of the browned pork and drippings, stir in the molasses and vinegar, cover, and let the beans bubble gently over very low heat 6 to 7 hours until the beans are tender and the juices have cooked down into a rich brown syrup. Taste for salt and add as needed (the amount will vary according to the saltiness of the pork). Stir in the chopped onions and serve. The Nebraska pioneer way is to serve the beans on top of fresh-baked corn bread. But you can simply ladle them into big bowls and serve as is.

🐿

Pioneer Plains recipes were vague at best. Most pioneer women cooked from memory, not from recipes, and they knew instinctively when a batter looked just right or when it needed a bit more liquid or flour. Corn meal was the great Plains staple in early days, and it was used for mush and gruel and bread. This recipe is an adaptation of an early Plains recipe, and it is specific as to measurements, baking times, and temperatures because today's women, unlike their great-great-grandmothers, do "cook by the book." If you are accustomed to the more usual corn breads made with sweet milk, you may be pleased to discover how much buttermilk improves the flavor.

Buttermilk Corn Bread

MAKES A 9×9×2- INCH LOAF

1½ cups corn meal
½ cup sifted all-purpose or unbleached flour
3 teaspoons baking powder
½ teaspoon baking soda
¾ teaspoon salt
¼ cup melted butter

1½ cups buttermilk
1 egg

Stir corn meal, flour, baking powder, baking soda, and salt together in a medium-size mixing bowl. Add melted butter, buttermilk, and egg and beat briskly for about a minute. Spoon into a greased 9×9×2-inch baking pan and bake in a hot oven (425°) 20 to 25 minutes or until golden brown. Cut into large squares and serve with plenty of butter.

Antique Town
Murdo, South Dakota

❦

*I*t all began when A. J. "Dick" Geisler parked an old
buggy and a 1913 Ford Peddler's Wagon outside his
gas station in Murdo. The year was 1950 and those two
relics fascinated and delighted Geisler's customers. They
began talking about them, and pretty soon people for
miles around began coming to see them. As public interest grew, so, too, did Geisler's. Collection fever had set
in.

Cars are what Geisler collected in the beginning: vin-
tage Cadillacs and Fords, a Spacke and a Schacht, a
Chalmers and a Fuller, a Hupmobile, an Auburn, and an
Essex, a Willys-Knight, a Mercer, and a Stutz, a Paige-
Detroit and an Overland, a Cord and a Cunningham, a
Pierce-Arrow and a Packard—most of them made by
companies crowded out by mass production.

As the collection grew (it numbers more than a
hundred and fifty today), Geisler had to find a way of
housing his antique and classic cars, a way, too, of sharing them with other car buffs. So in May of 1954, he
opened the Pioneer Auto Museum on five acres of
prairieland near Murdo. Then, as so often happens with
collectors, Geisler began adding other items to his collection. First came a cluster of old farm machinery—
threshers and tractors, including a J. I. Case

steam-driven tractor, the kind that astonished Indians when it first rumbled across prairie fields, belching smoke.

Other bits of Americana began showing up for sale or auction—china, toys, dolls, glassware, lamps, musical instruments, and Geisler, now a devout collector, began buying these, too. Clearly a way would have to be found to display them. Apart from the auto collection.

Antique Town was the answer. Its first building was the old clapboard Murdo State Bank, at which Geisler had done business for years. It was about to be demolished, so Geisler bought it, tellers' windows, safe, and all. And from that day on, Geisler was in the building business—or rather the business of buying old buildings on the brink of destruction, dismantling them, trucking them to Antique Town, setting them up again, restoring them and outfitting them with furnishings and bric-a-brac of the late nineteenth and early twentieth centuries.

Antique Town today is a whole street of buildings— Main Street, South Dakota, you might say, for it is typical of dozens of turn-of-the-century one-horse towns that were scattered across the table-top country of south-central South Dakota. Lined up here are the General Store (complete with cracker barrel, pot-bellied stove, and sacks of frontier staples), the Barber Shop, Blacksmith Shop, Homestead Claim Cabin, Jeweler's, Livery Barn, Jail, the old Ford Garage, the one-room Prairie School House (with Regulator wall clock, double desk, towering wood stove and collection of primers), an old country church, the Bank, and, standing idle on a length of siding, a 1900 Milwaukee train caboose. There's even an old-fashioned popcorn machine dispensing popcorn, lemonade, and candy. And a boxcar-size Concert Band Organ, rinky-tinking out old-time tunes.

There's plenty of history here. But it isn't a heavy sort of history. It is, as Geisler says, "Those Wonderful Days of Yesteryear."

Although Antique Town does not serve meals, the following recipes, provided by Mrs. Melvin Sanderson, one of the best cooks in this area, were too good not to include.

South Dakota is "The Pheasant Capital of the World," thus women there have long specialized in the cooking of this tender, white-meated bird. The following recipe is an old one and an excellent one.

Oven Fricassee of Pheasant

MAKES 4 SERVINGS

1 pheasant (about 3 to 3¼ pounds), disjointed for frying
1 cup unsifted all-purpose flour mixed with 1 tablespoon salt and ½ teaspoon freshly ground pepper (dredging flour)
2 tablespoons unsalted butter
2 tablespoons vegetable oil
1 cup finely chopped onion
½ pound fresh mushrooms, wiped clean and sliced thin

Sauce:
4 tablespoons unsalted butter
5 tablespoons dredging flour (leftover from dredging the pieces of pheasant)
2 cups chicken broth
1½ cups light cream

Dredge the pieces of pheasant by shaking in a heavy brown paper bag in the mixture of flour, salt, and pepper. Brown the pieces of pheasant well on all sides in a mixture of butter and vegetable oil in a large, heavy skillet over moderately high heat. As the pieces of pheasant brown, transfer them to a 3-quart casserole. Sauté the onion and mushrooms in the remaining skillet drippings over moderate heat about 10 to 12 minutes until lightly browned. Spoon mushrooms and onion over pheasant in casserole.

For the sauce: Melt the butter in a medium-size heavy saucepan over moderate heat and blend in the dredging flour to make a smooth paste. Add the chicken broth and light cream and heat, stirring briskly, until thickened and smooth, about 3 minutes. Pour sauce over the pheasant. Set casserole, uncovered, in a moderate oven (350°) and bake 1½ to 2 hours or until you can pierce a large piece of pheasant easily with a fork. Check the fricassee several times as it bakes, turning the pieces of pheasant and pushing them down under the sauce so that they remain succulent and moist throughout baking. Serve oven-hot, straight from the casserole.

The simple, husky sort of fare that women prepared in the homesteading days of South Dakota. It's an economical recipe, putting to good use leftover chicken (or turkey) and stale bread. It's a big recipe, too, but then families during the frontier days were big. And their appetites, perhaps were even bigger. Halve the recipe, if you like. Or make up the full recipe *if* your family can eat it up within a day or two. Keep any leftovers well refrigerated.

South Dakota Chicken and Dressing Bake

MAKES 8 TO 10 SERVINGS

Dressing:
12 slices dry toast
1 cup coarsely chopped onion
1 cup finely diced celery
½ pound fresh mushrooms, wiped clean and sliced thin
5 tablespoons butter
1 teaspoon rubbed sage
½ teaspoon salt
⅛ teaspoon freshly ground pepper
2½ cups chicken broth

Chicken Layer:
4 cups cooked chicken meat, cut in bite-size pieces
(substitute turkey, if you like)

Sauce:
4 tablespoons butter
6 tablespoons flour
1 teaspoon salt
½ teaspoon rubbed sage
¼ teaspoon leaf thyme, crumbled
⅛ teaspoon freshly ground pepper
2 cups chicken broth
1 cup light cream or milk

Topping:
2 cups soft, fairly fine bread crumbs tossed with 2
tablespoons melted butter

Prepare the dressing first: With your hands, crumble the
dry toast into a large mixing bowl and set aside. Sauté
the onion, celery, and mushrooms in the butter in a large,
heavy skillet over moderate heat 10 to 12 minutes until
tender and golden. Mix in the sage, salt, and pepper,
then pour over the crumbled toast. Add the chicken
broth and mix well. Let stand about 10 minutes so that
pieces of toast absorb all the moisture. Toss well again,
then spread in an even layer in a buttered 13 × 9 × 2-inch
baking pan. Arrange the pieces of chicken on top of the
stuffing in as uniform a layer as possible.

To prepare the sauce: Melt the butter in a large, heavy
saucepan over moderate heat, blend in the flour, salt,
sage, thyme, and pepper, and heat and stir 2 to 3 minutes
until bubbly and golden. Add the chicken broth and light
cream or milk and cook, stirring briskly, until thickened
and smooth, about 3 minutes. Pour evenly over chicken
in pan. Scatter the buttered bread-crumb topping uniformly on top, then bake, uncovered, in a moderate oven
(350°) 1¼ to 1½ hours until chicken mixture is bubbly
and bread crumbs are nicely browned.

More frugal frontier fare from South Dakota—cabbage wedges, ground beef, tomatoes, and rice in a one-dish meal that bakes unattended.

Cabbage and Beef Bake

MAKES 6 SERVINGS

6 large ripe tomatoes, peeled, cored, and cut in thin wedges
1 tablespoon sugar
½ teaspoon leaf thyme, crumbled
⅛ teaspoon leaf rosemary, crumbled
2 tablespoons butter or bacon drippings
1 pound lean ground beef
1 cup finely chopped onion
1½ teaspoons salt
¼ teaspoon freshly ground pepper
¼ cup uncooked long-grain rice
½ large cabbage, cored, and cut in 6 slim wedges

Place the tomatoes, sugar, thyme, and rosemary in a large, heavy saucepan and cook, uncovered, over moderate heat about 45 minutes, stirring occasionally, until tomatoes are very tender and have almost cooked down into sauce (they will still be somewhat lumpy, but this is as they should be). Meanwhile, melt the butter or bacon drippings in a very large, heavy skillet over moderately high heat, add the ground beef and onion, and brown well, stirring frequently—this will take about 10 minutes. Mix in the salt and pepper, turn heat to lowest point, and let mellow while tomatoes finish cooking. Add tomatoes to the skillet along with the rice and cook, stirring now and then, about 10 minutes. Arrange the cabbage wedges in the bottom of a lightly buttered 2½-quart casserole, pour the skillet mixture evenly on top, cover, and bake in a moderate oven (350°) for 1½ hours or until the cabbage is very tender. Serve as the main dish of the meal—you will need only bread to accompany.

The Southwest
and West

Rio Grande Indian Pueblos
New Mexico

Strung along the Rio Grande like beads on a necklace, there are between Taos and Albuquerque fifteen historic Indian Pueblos where old ways persist despite the inevitable TV antennas and telephone lines. In the more open of the Pueblos (Taos, San Ildefonso, Nambé, Santa Clara) you can watch pottery being hand shaped and painted the centuries-old way, baskets being woven, leather being tanned and tooled, copper and silver being hammered into jewelry, chunks of turquoise being cut and polished. There are seasonal ceremonial dances at the Pueblos—the Corn Dance, the Buffalo Dance, the Basket Dance, the Sundown Dance. And there are feast days for which Indian women spend days baking *buha* (adobe bread) in the beehive-shaped outdoor ovens (*hornos*) and stirring up a variety of red and green chiles, ranging in pepperiness from mild to incendiary.

In autumn the scarlet chile peppers are harvested, strung up on twine, and hung from the adobe eaves to dry. And the piñons are gathered, the buttery-sweet nuts of the scrubby piñon tree (pine), which tufts the rumpled mountain slopes, the mesas, and the flatlands of the Rio Grande country. Piñons are roasted and eaten whole (much as we eat peanuts), and they are chopped and mixed into soups and stews and breads. Corn, squash, and pumpkins predominate. Especially corn, for it is to these farming Indian tribes the "source of life." Indeed their reverence for corn may be seen today in the decorative motifs of their pottery, basketry, and weaving as well as in the ceremonial Corn Dance.

Although historians believe that corn is indigenous to South America, the Jemez Indians will show you, in the Frijoles Canyon, two wild grasses from which they claim they obtained corn. In the Pueblos, corn is not merely the familiar yellow and white varieties that we know. It is also red corn and blue corn and confetti-bright mixtures of red, yellow, blue, and white all on the same cob. Each variety is used in preparing breads and soups and stews, each lending its special color, texture, and flavor. Corn is served fresh ("green," the Indians call it), roasted in the husk in adobe ovens, or cut from the cob and teamed with squash and tomatoes in slow-simmmering skillet recipes and oven dishes. It is also steamed and parched, sun dried and pounded into meal, and it is made into hominy by treating the kernels in a mixture of wood ashes and water (lye).

These ancient Indian pueblos, some of them dating as far back as A.D. 1200, look today much as they did in the beginning (if you can overlook the cars and pickup trucks and power lines). They are mud-brown villages, clusters of one-, two- (and at Taos, three- and four-) story adobe shops and dwellings set about a central plaza and round ceremonial kiva. Although the younger Pueblo members go about in jeans and tee-shirts, the older men and women do still wear traditional dress: ankle-high suede moccasins buckled in silver, long gathered cotton skirts or straight-cut trousers, blankets about the shoulders, and garlands of turquoise jewelry. For dances, everyone wears ceremonial dress—toddlers, teen-agers, young adults, Pueblo elders—dress that varies somewhat from pueblo to pueblo and ceremony to ceremony. Certain of the dances are open to the public, and if you are lucky (have an entree), you may be invited to share a ceremonial feast in one of the Pueblo homes, a smorgasbordian spread often containing fifteen to twenty different stews, chiles, breads, and desserts. At the least, you should be able to buy one of the chewy loaves of *buha*.

The Pueblos allow (if not openheartedly welcome) visitors and they are, moving from Taos south past Santa Fe toward Albuquerque: Taos (perhaps the most famous because of its impressive three- and four-story adobe apartment-like homes), Picuris, San Juan, San Ildefonso (noted for its polychrome and black-on-black pottery), Santa Clara (incised black pottery), Nambé (cast aluminum cookware and serving pieces), Tesuque, Cochiti (hand-painted white slipware pottery), Jemez (colorful hand-woven fabrics), Zia, Santo Domingo (where perhaps the finest turquoise and silver jewelry is made), Santa Ana, San Felipe, Sandia, and Isleta.

Visiting any one of the Rio Grande pueblos today means slipping into one of the earlier chapters of American history. It also means learning to understand and appreciate something of Southwestern Indian life and ceremony, coming to share the Pueblo reverence for Nature: rain to soften the ground and sprout the seed... sun to warm the seedlings and break the earth...fresh air to nourish the crops.

Finally, it means seeing the survivors of those proud people who once occupied a vast chunk of the American Southwest.

🥄

Among Southwestern Indians, squash, peppers, beans, and tomatoes are categorized as "fruits" or "vegetables of the vines," and they, like corn, are staples at all of the Rio Grande pueblos. They are prepared singly and in colorful combinations such as this one. Pueblo families like their vegetables "well done," which requires long and slow baking in the oven. If you prefer your vegetables on the crisp side, reduce the over-all cooking time by about fifteen minutes or until the vegetables are of the texture you like.

Pueblo Baked Corn and "Vegetables of the Vines"

MAKES 6 TO 8 SERVINGS

3 slices bacon, cut crosswise in thin slivers
2 large yellow onions, peeled and coarsely chopped
2 cups fresh whole-kernel corn (you will need about 2 large
    ears for this amount; to cut whole kernels from the cob,
    simply hold the ear perpendicular to the cutting surface
    and, using a sharp paring knife, cut down along the cob,
    freeing the kernels)
2 teaspoons chili powder
1 teaspoon leaf oregano, crumbled
¼ teaspoon ground cumin
1 teaspoon salt
¼ teaspoon freshly ground black pepper
3 medium-size yellow squash, sliced ¼ to ½ inch thick
1 large sweet green pepper, cored, seeded, and cut in about
    1-inch squares
2 large firm-ripe tomatoes, peeled, cored, and cut in slim
    wedges
1 cup coarsely shredded sharp Cheddar cheese

Brown the bacon in a large, heavy skillet over moderately high heat, then with a slotted spoon scoop out the
crisp brown bacon bits, drain on paper toweling, and reserve. Stir-fry the onions in the bacon drippings 10 to 12
minutes over moderate heat until lightly browned; add
the corn, chili powder, oregano, cumin, salt, and pepper,
turn heat to low, and let cook, uncovered, about 10 minutes. Meanwhile, pile the squash, green pepper, and tomatoes in an ungreased 13 × 9 ×2-inch baking pan—no
need to make orderly layers. Add the skillet mixture and
toss with the vegetables to mix. Cover snugly with foil
and bake in a moderate oven (350°) about 45 minutes or
until squash is no longer raw but still quite crisp. Uncover, stir the vegetables well, then bake, uncovered,
about 30 minutes, stirring now and then, or until squash
is done the way you like it. Scatter the shredded cheese
over the top of the vegetables and bake, uncovered, 10

to 15 minutes longer or until cheese is melted and touched here and there with brown.

Northeastern New Mexico is dry, harsh land, and only where the Rio Grande (known to the Indians as the "Great River of Life") winds its way thorugh the mountain valleys do crops seem to prosper. Elsewhere the stony ground is left to sagebrush, cactus, and the piñon tree, stunted, gnarled, and leaning with the prevailing wind. The piñon is one of the Southwest's most cherished trees, for it provides the soft, sweetish piñon nut, which Pueblo women sprinkle into soups, stews, and breads. "The trees are ready," the Indians say, along about mid-September. And if you should visit the Santa Fe area then, you will see cars lined up along the highways and Indians, Spaniards and Anglos shaking the nuts out of the cones on the trees down upon blankets spread on the ground. Before piñon nuts can be eaten or used in cooking, they must be shelled, a pesky business at best. Fortunately, shelled piñon nuts (also known as *pignoli* and pine nuts) are available throughout most of the United States. They are delicious raw or oven roasted, which is the way the Pueblo Indians prefer them.

Roasted Piñon Nuts

MAKES 1 POUND

1 pound shelled piñon nuts
Salt (optional)

Spread the piñon nuts out in a large, shallow, ungreased roasting pan and roast, uncovered, in a very slow oven (300°) 35 to 40 minutes, stirring now and then, until a uniform golden tan. Remove nuts from the oven, sprinkle lightly with salt, if you like, cool to room temperature, and serve as a snack or use in cooking.

Pumpkins are one of the "vegetables of the vines" for which we are indebted to the American Indian. They were unknown to Europeans before the discovery of America and seem to have grown well throughout much of the New World, for they were mentioned in the diaries of colonists in New England, Virginia, and the Carolinas as well as in the Southwest. Pueblo women bake pumpkin much as we bake acorn or butternut squash (two other Indian gifts to the world table). And they stir pumpkin purée into bread. In years past they would have made their own pumpkin purée, but modern Pueblo women are as apt to short-cut that tedious method as we are by substituting canned puréed pumpkin. Here, then, is an old Pueblo recipe, set down in contemporary terms. This, by the way, is a sweet bread—much like cake—so you needn't butter the slices.

Piñon-Pumpkin Bread

MAKES A 9 × 5 × 3- INCH LOAF

2¾ cups sifted all-purpose flour
2 teaspoons baking powder
1 teaspoon ground cinnamon
½ teaspoon ground cloves
½ teaspoon ground mace or nutmeg
½ teaspoon salt
1 cup roasted, unsalted, coarsely chopped piñon nuts (see
    preceding recipe for directions on roasting piñon nuts)
1⅔ cups canned, sweetened pumpkin purée
½ cup melted butter
⅔ cup firmly packed light brown sugar
3 eggs, lightly beaten

In a large bowl, stir together the flour, baking powder, cinnamon, cloves, mace or nutmeg, salt and nuts; set aside. In a second large bowl, blend together the pumpkin purée, melted butter, sugar, and eggs. Mix in the flour mixture, a little at a time, beating well after each addition, to make a stiff dough. Spoon dough into a well-greased and floured 9 × 5 × 3-inch loaf pan, spreading well to the corners and smoothing the top as level as possible with a rubber spatula. Bake, uncovered, in a moderate oven (350°) 50 to 55 minutes or until loaf pulls from sides of pan and is lightly browned. Cool bread upright in its pan on a wire rack for 5 minutes, then loosen bread around the edges with a thin-bladed spatula, turn out onto rack, and cool upright for about 20 minutes before serving. To serve, cut in slices about ½ inch thick.

Sage grows wild in Pueblo country and it is an herb popular among the Indians. One of their best recipes—this spongy yeast and soda bread—uses as flavorings wild sage and a curd cheese, similar to cottage cheese, which is available in and around Santa Fe. This version substitutes the garden variety of sage and commercial cottage cheese but is nevertheless very much like the original Indian recipe.

Pueblo Sage Bread

MAKES A TALL ROUND LOAF (6 TO 7 INCHES IN DIAMETER)

2¼ cups sifted all-purpose flour
2 teaspoons sugar
2½ teaspoons dried sage, finely crumbled
½ teaspoon salt
½ teaspoon baking soda
4 teaspoons active dry yeast
¼ cup lukewarm water
4 teaspoons melted lard or vegetable shortening
1 cup cream-style cottage cheese, at room temperature
1 egg, at room temperature

Sift together onto a piece of wax paper the flour, sugar, sage, salt, and baking soda and set aside. Soften the yeast in the lukewarm water. In a large bowl, beat the melted lard or vegetable shortening with the cottage cheese and egg until well blended. Stir in the softened yeast mixture. Add the sifted dry ingredients, about ½ cup at a time, beating well after each addition. You may have to work in the last bit of flour with your hands if the dough is too stiff to beat with a spoon. Shape the dough into a smooth round ball, place in a warm, greased large bowl, and turn ball of dough in the bowl so that it is lightly greased on all sides. Cover with a clean dry cloth and let rise in a warm, dry spot until doubled in bulk— about 1½ hours. Punch dough down, turn onto a floured board, and knead 2 to 3 minutes, just until springy to the touch. Shape dough into a flat round loaf, place in a greased 2-quart, straight-side baking dish (a soufflé dish is perfect), again cover with cloth and let rise until dough about half fills the dish—30 to 40 minutes. Bake the loaf, uncovered, in a moderately hot oven (375°) about 30 to 35 minutes or until nicely browned on top and the loaf sounds hollow when thumped. Remove loaf from oven, loosen around edges of baking dish, turn loaf out on a wire rack, and cool upright to room temperature before cutting. To serve, cut into wedges with a sharp serrated knife. And accompany with plenty of butter.

Buha is what the Pueblo Indians call this chewy, hard-crusted yeast bread. It is a feast-day specialty, and at such times Pueblo women will make up batches using as much as a hundred pounds of flour. In the Pueblos, it is baked in the hardwood-fired, outdoor *hornos* (adobe ovens). It can also be baked in modern ovens, although it lacks the woodsy flavor of the horno-baked loaves.

Buha (Adobe Bread)

MAKES 2 ROUND LOAVES (EACH 6 TO 8 INCHES IN
DIAMETER)

1 tablespoon active dry yeast
⅓ cup lukewarm water
3 tablespoons melted lard or vegetable shortening
1¼ teaspoons salt
3½ cups sifted all-purpose flour (about)
¾ cup water

Soften the yeast in the lukewarm water. Stir in the
melted lard or vegetable shortening and the salt. Beat in
the flour, adding alternately with the water, to make a
fairly stiff dough. Place in a warm, greased bowl, turn
dough in bowl so that it is greased on all sides, cover
with a clean dry cloth, and set in a warm spot, away
from drafts, to rise until double in bulk—about 1 hour.
Punch dough down, turn onto a floured board, and knead
hard for 5 minutes, working in more flour as needed to
keep the dough from sticking to your hands or to the
board. Divide dough in half, shape each half into a
smooth round loaf, then place each in a lightly greased
8-inch layer cake pan. Brush loaves lightly with melted
lard or vegetable shortening, cover with clean dry cloth,
and let rise again until double in bulk, about 1½ hours.
Bake loaves, uncovered, in a hot oven (400°) 45 to 50
minutes until nicely browned and loaves sound hollow
when thumped with your fingers. Transfer loaves to wire
racks and cool to room temperature before cutting. To
serve, tear into chunks (the Indian way) or cut into
wedges with a sharp, serrated knife.

Utah Pioneer Village
Salt Lake City, Utah

To drive through the Rockies today is to wonder how the covered wagons ever crossed them, scaled the heights, and hurdled the canyons as they made their painstaking way west. But cross them the pioneer wagons did, in fair weather and in foul when sudden downpours turned dusty creek beds into raging streams and parched flats into quagmires. Many of the wagon trains were headed for California and Oregon, but one group of pioneers, headed by the Mormon leader Brigham Young, found their "promised land" in the valley of the Great Salt Lake. The year was 1847 and Young's one hundred and fifty Mormon followers were the first to settle around what is now Salt Lake City. As he stood on the heights, gazing out across the green valley beyond the shimmering lake, Young announced, "This is the place." Then named all the land before him "Deseret," a word from the Mormon scripture, the Book of Mormon, meaning "honey bee," the symbol of industry.

The Mormons were an industrious lot and within a few decades of their arrival had made the desert "blossom as a rose." They thrived in the land of the Great Salt Lake, and this corner of America is known yet as Mormon Country. You can see here reminders of Utah's pioneer past: at Brigham Young's house (the Beehive House), at Temple Square (home of the high-spired Mormon Tabernacle), and at Utah Pioneer Village, a re-created nineteenth-century settlement that is filled with mementos of the early Mormon days. History comes alive as you walk down the carefully landscaped village paths and boardwalks (curbed in part by redwood ties from the first transcontinental railroad bed), as you tour through the old homes and buildings, now restored and refurnished. You see what life was like for the farmer, the village tradesman, and for their wives and families, too.

Originally, the site of Pioneer Village was the pasture and show ring for a string of American saddle-bred horses. The main museum building was once the stable, and the Round House (a replica of Utah's first State House) was the winter training ring.

While the horse shows were in full swing, a furniture dealer named Horace A. Sorensen, together with his wife, was busily acquiring a collection of old covered wagons, coaches, and early vehicles, along with some outstanding pieces of antique furniture and pioneer household implements.

When World War II made it impractical, if not impossible, to stage horse shows, Mr. and Mrs. Sorensen dreamed up the idea of a pioneer village. The Round House was converted into a small museum for the National Society of the Sons of the Utah Pioneers. It opened in the fall of 1948 and from there the project grew.

At about this same time, it became clear that with the building of the Wanship Dam in the mountains east of Salt Lake City, the little pioneer village of Rockport would be inundated, ruining many fine old buildings. A request was made to preserve some of these, and they were moved into the pasture near the big barn.

As Utah Pioneer Village grew, other old buildings were brought in, restored, and furnished according to the period. Two old country stores were acquired, complete with counters, fixtures, and original stock. Today in Pioneer Village you will see virtually every variety of shop and public building that existed in Utah's pioneer days. And you will see, too, a map of the old Mormon Trail, a pony express station, and a number of early pioneer homes on the Utah frontier. (There are no cooking demonstrations at Utah Pioneer Village, but you will find locally a number of restaurants serving forth sturdy pioneer fare, and you will also find an excellent booklet, *Famous Mormon Recipes*, written by Winnifred Jardine, food editor of the *Deseret News* and a great-granddaughter of Brigham Young.)

Utah Pioneer Village now belongs to the National Society of the Sons of the Utah Pioneers (in 1956, the Sorensens deeded their entire collection, together with the property, to that organization). Still, the Sorensens keep an active hand in the continuing restoration and an eye on the village activities.

The village *is* active, not merely a series of museums. Daily, Ben and Lars, a team of oxen, take hundreds of school children and other visitors for a covered wagon ride around the village, and the animals end their trip by kneeling to "pray" for their passengers. A small herd of buffalo roams on part of the land, and teams of horses are occasionally hitched to wagons or old coaches. "Pioneer Day," on July 24 each year, brings wagons, buggies, handcarts, and coaches from all parts of Utah for a big parade, and several times during the season when the village is open—April through October—bands of Indians swoop down into town to dance and to demonstrate their arts and crafts.

Meanwhile, a blacksmith shop is open for all to see, a buggy shed, the Gay Nineties House, a print shop, a drugstore, a meeting house and school, a post office, a barbershop, with its collection of individual shaving mugs just as they were used a hundred years ago. There is a loom room, a millinery and dress shop, even jail cells from the ghost town of Kimberly.

Utah Pioneer Village recaptures and preserves the Mormon and pioneer spirit that opened up Utah. And a visit here leaves a lasting impression of the obstacles overcome as well as the day-to-day life of those courageous settlers.

Thick soups, especially those made with dried peas and beans, sustained many a pioneer family on the westward push. This Mormon split pea soup traveled well and, when fortified and flavored with sausage balls, made a satisfying meal. It was served forth with fresh-baked biscuits or steamy chunks of sour-dough bread and, whenever available, fresh fruit for dessert.

Green Split Pea Soup with Sausage Balls

MAKES 10 TO 12 SERVINGS

3 quarts water
1 tablespoon salt
½ teaspoon pepper
½ teaspoon marjoram
1 pound green split peas, washed and sorted
1 pound sausage meat
½ cup flour
1 large yellow onion, peeled and chopped
1 large potato, peeled and diced
3 celery ribs, diced

Bring water, salt, pepper, and marjoram to a boil in a very large, heavy kettle. Stir in split peas and let return to the boil. Roll sausage meat into balls about the size of walnuts (1 inch in diameter), roll in flour, then drop into soup. Cover and simmer 1 hour; uncover and simmer 1 hour longer, stirring occasionally. Add onion, potato, and celery, cover, and simmer 1 hour longer. Ladle into soup bowls and serve.

This recipe, says Winnifred Jardine, a great-granddaughter of Brigham Young, food editor of the *Deseret News* in Salt Lake City and author of the booklet *Famous Mormon Recipes*, has been handed down from generation to generation in the family of Benjamin Morgan Roberts, a member of the famous Mormon Battalion. "He and his sons used it often when they were 'batching' out on their ranch in Southern Utah," she says. And it proves how frugal pioneers could simmer odds and ends into surprisingly good fare.

St. Jacob's Soup

MAKES 4 TO 6 SERVINGS

¼ pound salt pork, cut in small dice
2 large potatoes, peeled and cubed
2 large yellow onions, peeled and sliced thin
2 cups water
4 large ripe tomatoes, peeled, cored, and cut in thin wedges
2 teaspoons salt
⅛ teaspoon pepper
2 tablespoons salt pork drippings
2 to 3 teaspoons sugar (if needed to mellow "tartness" of
    tomatoes)

Fry the salt pork slowly in a large, heavy skillet until all the fat cooks out and only crispy brown bits of salt pork remain; set aside. Boil the potatoes and onions in the water in a covered large saucepan about 15 minutes until almost tender. Add the tomatoes, salt, pepper, crispy salt pork bits, and salt pork drippings and simmer uncovered, stirring now and then and breaking up tomatoes, about 45 minutes or until all flavors have gotten together. Taste and, if too tart, add sugar to mellow the flavor. Spoon into soup plates and serve.

Meat, among the pioneers, was more apt to be lamb than beef because lambs were carried west with the wagon trains. They were small, undemanding animals that could be turned loose to forage among the skimpiest desert grasses. This pie, nothing more than a robust stew baked underneath a biscuit crust, was made with lamb and, as a special treat, when that meat was available, with beef. The addition of grated cheese to the biscuit crust was a later fillip, added when the pioneers had successfully settled in to ranching and farming the Utah valleys.

Wagon Train Lamb (or Beef) and Vegetable Pie with Cheese-Biscuit Crust

MAKES 6 SERVINGS

2 pounds boned lamb stew meat or beef chuck, cut in 1-inch cubes
½ cup flour
2½ teaspoons salt
¼ teaspoon pepper
¼ cup bacon drippings
3 cups water
1 teaspoon cider vinegar
½ teaspoon sugar
Pinch of ground cloves
1 bay leaf
3 carrots, peeled and sliced
3 potatoes, peeled and diced
1 yellow onion, peeled and cut in thin wedges
2 tablespoons flour blended with 3 tablespoons cold water

Cheese-Biscuit Crust:
2 cups sifted all-purpose flour
4 teaspoons baking powder
¼ teaspoon salt
¼ cup lard or vegetable shortening
1¼ cups grated sharp Cheddar cheese
⅔ cup milk

Dredge lamb or beef in a mixture of flour, salt, and pepper. Brown well on all sides in the drippings in a large, heavy kettle. Add water, vinegar, sugar, cloves, and bay leaf, adjust heat so liquid simmers gently, cover, and simmer about 1½ hours until meat is tender enough to cut with a fork. Add carrots, potatoes, and onion, cover, and simmer 20 to 25 minutes longer until vegetables are tender. With a slotted spoon, lift meat and vegetables into a 2-quart casserole. Blend flour-water paste into liquid in kettle and heat and stir until thickened and smooth. Taste and add more salt and pepper if needed. Pour over meat and vegetables in casserole.

To make the crust: Place flour, baking powder, and salt in a large bowl, cut in lard or shortening with a pastry blender or two knives until mixture is the texture of uncooked oatmeal, then stir in cheese. Make a well in the center, pour in milk and mix quickly and lightly with a fork until dough holds together. Turn onto a floured board and knead three or four times. Roll dough into a circle slightly larger than the rim of the casserole. Fit on top of casserole, trim off ragged edges, then turn edge under even with casserole rim and crimp, making a decorative border. Cut several deep slashes in the crust with a sharp knife, then bake in a hot oven (400°) 20 to 25 minutes until lightly browned. Serve at once.

A hundred years ago in Utah's pioneer days, Mormon "Sisters" would move from one homestead to another to help stitch quilts or hook rugs out of rag-bag scraps. They were fed for their efforts, of course, and though they might not get meat, it being scarce, they could usually count on hefty, filling servings of this egg-and-potato salad.

Quilter's Potato Salad

MAKES 6 TO 8 SERVINGS

4 large potatoes, boiled, peeled, and cubed
4 hard-cooked eggs, peeled and diced

⅓ cup finely minced onion
½ teaspoon salt
⅛ teaspoon pepper

Dressing:
1 teaspoon dry mustard
1 teaspoon salt
3 tablespoons sugar
2 eggs
3 tablespoons melted butter
½ cup hot cider vinegar
1 cup heavy cream, whipped

Place potatoes, hard-cooked eggs, onion, salt, and pepper in a large bowl and toss well to mix. For the dressing, blend together dry mustard, salt, and sugar in the top of a double boiler; add eggs and beat well to mix. Stir in melted butter and vinegar, set over simmering water, and cook and stir until thickened. Cool to room temperature and fold in whipped cream. Pour over potato mixture and stir well to mix. Chill several hours before serving.

🍂

The recipe for these delicate, fine-textured, not very sweet doughnuts comes from Winnifred Jardine, who says of the recipe in her booklet *Famous Mormon Recipes*: "This recipe belonged to Emily Dow Partridge Young, wife of Brigham Young and my great-grandmother. You'll find the doughnuts as tender and crisp and delicious as anything made out of a modern cookbook." Nutmeg, Mrs. Jardine explains, was a chief spice in early days and was grated tediously by hand over tiny metal nutmeg graters. The original recipe was four times this size, but in America's growing-up years, both families and appetites were larger than they are today.

Brigham Young's Buttermilk Doughnuts

MAKES ABOUT 1½ DOZEN

1 cup buttermilk
1 large egg, beaten until frothy
⅔ cup sugar
3 cups sifted all-purpose flour
1 teaspoon baking soda
¾ teaspoon baking powder
½ teaspoon salt
½ teaspoon nutmeg
2 tablespoons melted butter
Oil or shortening for deep fat frying
Confectioners' or granulated sugar to sprinkle over doughnuts

Combine the buttermilk, egg, and sugar in a large mixing bowl. Sift together the flour, soda, baking powder, salt, and nutmeg, then mix in. Stir in the melted butter. Turn dough out on a floured pastry cloth, pat into a ball, and roll around on cloth so dough is lightly floured all over. Roll out with a floured rolling pin to a thickness of ¼ inch. Cut with a floured 2½-inch doughnut cutter, then fry doughnuts and "holes" in deep hot fat (375°) about 3 minutes until golden brown on both sides. Reroll scraps, cut, and fry. Drain doughnuts on heavy paper and, while still hot, sprinkle with sugar.

Tressl's Frontier Town
Blackfoot, Idaho

Twenty years ago, Frontier Town was visible only to a farmer named Addie Tressl. As he plowed his fields in southeastern Idaho, gazing out now and then toward a lavender backdrop of mountains, scenes flashed through his mind like an old two-reeler Western: scenes from the days of Lewis and Clark, who first penetrated Idaho's northern wilderness...scenes of later explorers who tried to run "the Accursed Mad River's" white-water rapids only to die amid the debris of their splintered boats...scenes of the frozen winters of the 1820s and '30s, when American and British trappers, trying to corner the market in beaver pelts, fought it out with themselves as well as with the Blackfoot, Crow, and Snake Indians...scenes of the sun-baked summers, when pioneers, headed for the green paradises of Oregon and California, cursed the dead Idaho earth that barred their way...scenes of the 1860s gold rush...and scenes of more recent years when settlers channeled the waters of the Snake River onto the parched plains and made farming possible for men like Addie Tressl.

Tressl did well at farming, growing potatoes, wheat, peas, and beans. But it was the Old West that filled his thoughts, sent him scouring the Idaho countryside for ghost towns, turned him into a collector of early Idaho memorabilia.

As Tressl's collection grew, so, too, did his dreams. Why not build a replica Old West village and fill it with the antiques and artifacts that he had collected?

And this, as it turns out, is precisely what Tressl did do—right on his own farm. First he laid out a typical Old West Main Street and a village square. Then, one by one, he hammered together the Palace Saloon, complete with swinging doors; the trading post, whose stock includes a ninety-year-old jar of mincemeat; a hat and dress shop, where a milliner sits hunched over an antiquated sewing machine; a barbershop-cum dentist's office-cum-court of law; an assay office festooned with beaver pelts and filled with ore samples; a butcher's shop (posting the rock-bottom meat prices of a century ago).

Once Addie Tressl got started, there seemed to be no stopping him. Frontier Town grew and grew and grew. Today, in addition to those buildings described earlier, it has its own cobbler's shop, schoolhouse, town hall, Chinese laundry, hotel, blacksmith shop, chapel, and at the north end of Main Street a replica of Fort Apache. Beyond it lie replicas of Boot Hill, Alder Gulch, and an Indian camp.

Although Frontier Town encompasses a wider span of time and space than an authentic Snake River village would have encompassed, Addie Tressl makes no pretension. He built Tressl's Frontier Town out of a love for Western pioneer history; he takes pride in placing authentic antiques in their proper settings. He takes pride, too, in touring visitors through the village personally and, when asked, will tell them where in the area they can find the sort of pioneer food that sustained Idaho's early settlers (two recipes are included here).

Not many tourists come to Blackfoot in winter, so Tressl closes the village gates—except to the family of skunks who have made Frontier Town their winter home.

Idaho is both beef and sheep country, but enough of the old "sheep war" animosity exists that, if you ask a cattle rancher whether he likes lamb, he will answer "Is that an animal?" Northern and central Idaho are, for the most part, beef country. But in southern Idaho there are sheep, too. This stew, then, can be made with either beef or lamb, as it is in different parts of Idaho, depending upon whether one is a "beef man" or a "sheep man."

Frontier Lamb (or Beef) and Dumplings

MAKES 6 SERVINGS

2 pounds boned lean lamb shoulder or beef chuck, cut in 1-inch cubes
4 teaspoons bacon drippings
2 large yellow onions, peeled and chopped
½ teaspoon rubbed sage
½ teaspoon leaf thyme, crumbled
¼ teaspoon pepper
2 teaspoons chili powder
2 teaspoons salt (about)
2 large tomatoes, peeled, cored, and chopped (reserve juice)
1 quart beef stock or water

Dumplings:
1 cup sifted all-purpose flour
1½ teaspoons baking powder
½ teaspoon salt
2 tablespoons vegetable shortening or lard
½ cup milk

Brown the lamb or beef well on all sides in the bacon drippings in a large, heavy kettle over fairly high heat; remove from kettle and drain on paper toweling. Add onions to kettle and sauté in remaining drippings about 10 minutes until lightly browned and limp. Return meat to kettle, add sage, thyme, pepper, chili powder, salt, tomatoes together with their juice, and beef stock or water. Cover and simmer slowly 1½ to 2 hours until meat is very tender. Taste for salt and add a bit more if needed.

To prepare the dumplings: Sift flour with baking powder and salt into a small mixing bowl; cut in the vegetable shortening or lard until crumbly and the texture of uncooked oatmeal. Add milk all at once and mix briskly with a fork just until mixture holds together. Uncover kettle, bring liquid to a fast boil, and drop in the dumplings by rounded teaspoonfuls, spacing evenly over the surface of the stew so that they don't touch one another. Reduce heat and simmer dumplings, uncovered, 10 minutes, then cover kettle and simmer 10 minutes longer so that dumplings will fluff up. To serve, spoon dumplings into soup bowls and top with the stew.

These ham-and-potato dumplings are an old Idaho favorite, a recipe brought to the frontier by Norwegian immigrants some hundred years ago. *Pult* is delicious served hot with fat chunks of butter. And it is even better for breakfast, sliced cold, then browned in butter. The trick in making pult is to grind the potatoes fine, to drain them of as much excess water as possible, then to mix in only enough flour to make the dumpling balls hold together.

Pult (Ham-Stuffed Grated Potato Dumplings)

MAKES 4 TO 6 SERVINGS

8 medium-size potatoes (Idaho potatoes are particularly
    suitable)
¾ teaspoon salt
½ cup milk
8 to 10 tablespoons all-purpose flour (about)
¼ pound ground cooked ham
5 quarts boiling salted water (1 tablespoon salt is about right)

Peel the potatoes and cut in 1-inch cubes, then grind in a meat grinder fitted with a fine blade. Bundle the ground potatoes up in a double thickness of cheesecloth and squeeze out as much potato water as possible. Place the drained potatoes in a large mixing bowl, add the salt, then, using your hands, alternately, work in the milk and the flour, adding only what flour is needed to make the mixture hold together. To test it, scoop up a handful and shape into a ball. It should hold together firmly but it should not be gluey or dry. To shape the pult, take up level tablespoonfuls of the ground ham and roll into small balls. Then, scooping up handfuls of the potato mixture, shape it around the ham, enclosing it and forming balls about 2½ inches in diameter—roughly the size of tennis balls. Pat each ball firmly as you shape it so that it will hold together during cooking. This amount of potato mixture and ham should yield 8 balls of pult. When all have been shaped, drop gently into a very large kettle of boiling salted water, spacing evenly so that the balls do not touch one another. Reduce heat under kettle so that water simmers gently and cook the pult, uncovered, 45 minutes. Never let the water boil hard or the pult may disintegrate. Lift out with a slotted spoon, drain quickly on paper toweling, then serve with pats of butter. Refrigerate whatever pult is left over, then next day for breakfast slice each ball ¼ to ½ inch thick and brown quickly on both sides in butter. Delicious!

Old Town San Diego
San Diego, California

Modern San Diego engulfs Old Town today, an elevated expressway zooms by above it, and the unsuspecting motorist may be startled to gaze down—fleetingly—upon this historic place.

But to absorb its atmosphere fully, to return to the San Diego of a century and a half ago, you must prowl the streets of Old Town, moving from the deep shade of the restored buildings through fountain-splashed courtyards into glarily sunny streets.

The streets are designed for walking—no cars allowed—and the six blocks of Old Town can be covered in a leisurely half day even if you pause to browse in the shops and boutiques of Bazaar del Mundo and take time for lunch at one of Old Town's dozen indoor and outdoor restaurants (the food they serve has both a Mexican and an early California flavor as do the recipes included here, which were Old San Diego favorites).

This is an adobe town, today as in the mid-1830s, when it was described as "forty dark brown looking huts . . . and three or four larger ones, whitewashed, which belong to the *gente de razon*" (upper class). One of the finest of these homes was—and is yet—La Casa de Estudillo, a grand hacienda built around a lushly landscaped courtyard by a wealthy tax collector-mayor named José Antonio Estudillo, who also happened to be the son of Captain José María Estudillo, who once commanded the Presidio.

The Presidio, together with the mission founded by Fray Junípero Serra in 1769, was San Diego's first settlement, although San Diego Bay had been discovered two hundred and twenty-seven years earlier by Juan Cabrillo.

Early visitors to San Diego found it dull (George Vancouver described it in 1793 as "dreary and lonesome, in the midst of barren, uncultivated country"), but the Presidio soldiers seemed to have found it otherwise. Many married local Indian girls, moved outside the Presidio confines, built haciendas in the countryside, and began to till the land. About 1820 a new town was laid out around a central plaza in the Spanish fashion, and this "new town" is today Old Town.

Drought, an ill-planned location, and fire eventually brought decline to Old Town, and gradually a new city catering to traders, trappers, and gold seekers grew up around the waterfront. Even Estudillo's marvelous *casa* was left, after his death, to decay, a process hastened along by a caretaker who sold every item he could, even the roof and the floor tiles.

In 1905, the remains of the old house were bought by millionaire John D. Spreckles, son of "Sugar King" Claus Spreckles. The younger Spreckles saw that the casa was faithfully restored, and it stands today at both the geographic and spiritual heart of Old Town San Diego State Historic Park. It is as true to the original as painstaking research and rebuilding could make it. Even the old adobe that had washed from the walls over the years was recently reclaimed and recycled to make new adobe bricks (the house has been further restored since the original Spreckles renovation). Period furnishings— most of them the massive, intricately carved Spanish and Mexican pieces popular in early San Diego—fill its thirteen rooms, which include a chapel and a completely outfitted early California kitchen. The house has become popularly known as "Ramona's Marriage Place," the fictitious Ramona made famous by novelist Helen Hunt Jackson. And although the house was not the setting described for the marriage, romanticists have chosen to believe that it is, and continue to toss coins into the Wishing Well in the courtyard outside.

Other Old Town highlights include the haunted Whaley House (you may even hear the agonized pacing of Yankee Jim Robinson, who was hanged in 1852 on the site of the house for trying to hijack a pilot boat in San Diego Harbor); the Machado-Stewart Adobe (a humble, dirt-floored house where author Richard Henry Dana once visited); the little frame building (circa 1850) where the first issue of *The San Diego Union* came off the press in 1868 (it is today a sort of newspaper museum complete with old Washington Press, trays of type, kerosene lamps, a cookstove, and a calendar wall clock).

There are other historic houses about Old Town, notably the two-story, balcony-hung adobe Casa de Bandini at one corner of the plaza, and the Machado-Silvas Adobe, where the Mexican flag was once hidden from American troops.

The area's shops and restaurants, clustered at the Bazaar del Mundo and at Squibob Square, are new, although they have been built in the old adobe style so that they fit unobtrusively into Old Town. There are palm-shaded patios everywhere about Old Town, fountains and flowers, birds chirping overhead. And there are also artists busy at their easels, capturing on canvas the grace and style of San Diego of a hundred and fifty years ago.

Early California was Spanish, for it was Fray Junípero Serra, first father-president of the California missions, who, in working his way north up the coast from San Diego, opened "the golden gate." In 1769 he founded the Mission San Diego de Alcalá, the Mother Mission of California, which is operated today as a church. When Fray Junípero Serra died in 1784, there were in California nine missions, four presidios, and two pueblos. The cuisine of early California, consequently, was Spanish, and it remains so today, particularly in Southern California and in Old Town San Diego. The soup that follows typifies the kinds of recipes that were brought into California by the Spaniards.

Sopa de Cebolla (Onion Soup)

MAKES 4 SERVINGS

2 large Spanish onions, peeled and chopped fine
2 tablespoons olive oil
1 quart beef stock or broth
½ teaspoon salt (about)
⅛ teaspoon pepper
2 egg yolks, lightly beaten with 1 tablespoon cider vinegar
8 small rounds or triangles of toast

Sauté the onions in the olive oil in a large, heavy saucepan over moderate heat 15 to 20 minutes, stirring often, until soft and richly golden—but not brown. Add the beef stock, salt, and pepper and simmer, uncovered, 10 minutes. Place the egg yolk-vinegar mixture in a small tureen and stir in the onion soup. Taste for salt and add more if needed. Float the toast rounds on top and serve.

As happened with English colonists on the East Coast, the Spaniards in California began experimenting with New World foods, in this case chili peppers and tomatoes, which they combined with green beans and onions, olive oil and vinegar. The result is this peppery bean "salad," delicious hot or cold.

Ejotes (Green Beans)*

MAKES 6 SERVINGS

2 pounds fresh young green beans, washed, tipped, and
    "snapped" in half
2 tablespoons olive oil
1 medium-size Spanish onion, peeled and chopped
1 clove garlic, peeled and minced
2 small green chili peppers, minced
2 medium-size ripe tomatoes, peeled, cored, and cut in thin
    wedges
1 teaspoon cider vinegar
1 teaspoon salt
Pinch of black pepper

Sauté the beans in the olive oil in a large, heavy kettle over moderately high heat, stirring constantly, about 2 minutes—just until their green color heightens. Add onion, garlic, and chili peppers, then fry and stir 4 to 5 minutes until onion is no longer crisp. Add tomatoes, vinegar, salt, and pepper. Mix well, cover, turn heat to moderately low, and simmer 20 to 25 minutes until beans are tender but still a bit crisp. Serve hot or chill well and serve cold.

This much-loved Old San Diego dessert is again a combination of Old and New World foods: pumpkin, oranges, apples, and raisins. It is a dark, bittersweet fruit compote, good hot or cold with thick sweet cream. Acorn squash, by the way, can be substituted for the pumpkin when pumpkins are out of season.

*Ejotes reprinted by permission of the publishers, The Arthur H. Clark Company, from Early California Hospitality, by Ana Bégué de Packman, Copyright © 1938.

Dulce de Calabaza (Pumpkin Sweet)

MAKES ABOUT 8 SERVINGS

1 medium-small pumpkin or 2 large acorn squash, halved,
   seeded, cut in 1½-inch chunks, and peeled
3 cups dark molasses or, for a less strong molasses flavor, 2
   cups dark corn syrup and 1 cup dark molasses
2 cups water
2 thin-skinned oranges, sliced thin and seeded (you want the
   rind and all for the proper bittersweet flavor)
3 tart apples, cored and cut in 1-inch wedges but not peeled
½ cup seedless raisins

Place pumpkin or squash, molasses, water, and oranges
in a very large, heavy kettle, cover, and simmer 1½ to 2
hours until pumpkin is tender but still firm enough to
hold its shape; uncover and simmer slowly, stirring frequently, until liquid cooks down and thickens a bit—
about 30 minutes. Add apples and raisins, pushing well
down into mixture, and simmer, uncovered, ¾ to 1 hour
longer. You'll have to stir mixture frequently and perhaps add a bit more water to keep it from sticking. Serve
hot or cold, topped with heavy sweet cream.

An old Southern California specialty, these crispy fritters are made from a *choux* (cream puff) paste, fried in
deep hot fat, then dried out in a slow oven. They may be
flavored with vanilla, rum, lemon, or orange flower
water, and they may be made thick or thin—it depends
upon whether you squirt them through a pastry tube fitted with a wide- or small-mouthed tip.

Churos (Spanish Fritters)

MAKES ABOUT 1 DOZEN THICK FRITTERS, 2 DOZEN THIN
FRITTERS

1 cup water
¼ cup butter, cut in small pieces
2 tablespoons granulated sugar
Pinch of salt
1¼ cups sifted all-purpose flour
3 large eggs
1 tablespoon orange flower water (obtainable in specialty
    food shops) OR 1 teaspoon vanilla, lemon, or rum
    extract
Vegetable oil for deep fat frying (you will need about 3
    quarts)
¾ cup confectioners' sugar (about)

Place the water, butter, sugar, and salt in a small, heavy
saucepan and bring to the boil over high heat. Remove
from heat and mix in flour all at once, beating until
smooth and glossy with a wire whisk. Add the eggs, one
at a time, beating well after each addition. You will notice that as you add each egg the mixture will separate
into clumps. This is perfectly normal. Just keep beating
vigorously until it is smooth again. When all eggs have
been added, continue beating until paste comes together
in a ball, leaving the sides of the pan clean. Mix in the
flavorings of your choice. (Orange flower water is the old
California favorite.) Spoon mixture into a pastry tube or
bag fitted with a plain tip with a ¼-inch or ½-inch opening. Pour oil into a large deep fat fryer and heat over high
heat to 375° or 380° on a deep fat thermometer. Carefully
press the paste through the tube or pastry bag into the

Note: Once the oil in which you fried the fritters has cooled to room temperature, you can strain it through cheesecloth, pour it back into its original
bottles (a funnel makes the pouring easier), and store on a cool dry shelf to
use again for deep fat frying.

hot fat, making fritters about 5 to 6 inches long and curling them round as you press them into the hot fat. Don't try to fry more than four fritters at one time, as they will stick together. Deep-fry the fritters, turning with a fork, until puffed and golden brown on all sides—about 5 minutes. Lift with a slotted spoon to baking sheets lined with several thicknesses of paper toweling or with clean dry dish towels. When all fritters have been fried, set them, uncovered, in a very slow oven (about 200°) and let them dry out for 25 to 30 minutes. As soon as the fritters come from the oven, sift the confectioners' sugar over them, turning the fritters so that all sides are liberally dusted with sugar.

Appendix

A Cross-Reference of Recipes by Category

Beverages

Homemade Grape Juice
Mulled Cider

Soups

Arkansas Chicken and Autumn Vegetable Soup
Dried Corn Soup
Green Split Pea Soup with Sausage Balls
Mixed Bean Soup
Nebraska Corn Chowder
Okra Soup
St. Jacob's Soup
Shaker Vegetable Batter Soup
Sopa de Cebolla (Onion Soup)
Un Caldo Gallegos Bueno (A Good Gallegos Soup)
White Bean, Parsnip, Potato, and Turnip Soup

Beef

Abe's Butter-Browned Steak with Coffee-Mustard Sauce
Cabbage and Beef Bake

Country Meat Loaf
German Breslauer Steaks
Grandma Jagger's Beef Stew
Indian Corn Stew
Miner's Spiced Kettle of Beef and Vegetables
Mulligan Stew
Salem Tavern Sauerbraten
Texas Border Hot Pot

Veal and Lamb

A White Fancy of Veal
Breast of Lamb Carbonnade with Caper, Bread Crumb,
    and Butter Gravy
Frontier Lamb (or Beef) and Dumplings
Wagon Train Lamb (or Beef) and Vegetable Pie with
    Cheese-Biscuit Crust

Pork and Ham

Arroz Amarillo con Chorizos (Yellow Rice with Sau-
    sages)
Baked Ham, Wild Rice, and Mushrooms North Woods
    Style
Beans-and-Sowbelly
Pork Loin and Cream Gravy
Powell House Apple-Smothered Pork Chops
Pult (Ham-Stuffed Grated Potato Dumplings)
Sausage Loaf
Williamsburg Ham

Game and Game Birds

Long Island Roast Duckling with Sage-Bread Stuffing
    and Giblet Gravy

Mills House Roast Venison with Juniper-Red Currant
  Sauce
Oven Fricassee of Pheasant
Plimoth Roast Goose with Corn Bread and Currant
  Stuffing

Chicken and Turkey

A Fricassee of Chicken
Chicken Pie with Rose Water, Currants, Prunes, and
  Raisins
Potpie
Roast Turkey with Lemon and Ham Stuffing Balls
South Dakota Chicken and Dressing Bake

Seafood

Clam Pie
Cod Fish Hash
Cod Steaks and Oysters in Lemon Sauce
Conklin House Scallop Chowder
Haddock Chowder
Jamestown Scalloped Oysters
Pickled Shrimp
Sailor Ben's Oyster Stew
Zarzuelas de Pescado (Fish Fillets in Spicy Tomato
  Sauce)

Eggs

Arkansas Boiled Egg Pie
Fried Green Onion Tops (a sort of omelet)
Hootsla (Egg Skillet Bread)
Line Camp Skillet Supper
Pickled Eggs

Gravies, Sauces, and Syrups

Brown Sugar Cranberry Sauce
Corn Cob Syrup
Foamy Egg Sauce
Giblet Gravy
Juniper-Red Currant Sauce
Plum Sauce
Thin Chocolate Sauce

Vegetables

Corn Oysters
Chuck Wagon Beans
Creamy Baked Shredded Cabbage
Ejotes (Green Beans)
Fresh Corn and Mushrooms in Cream
Fried Cymling Squash
Fried Grated Potatoes
Gelbe Rüben (Carrots with Mashed Potatoes)
Hoppin' John
How to Dry Corn
Leather Britches Beans
Mills House Sautéed Mushrooms, Bacon, and Onions
Parnsips Stewed in Dark Beer or Stout
Potato Filling
Pueblo Baked Corn and "Vegetables of the Vines"
S-Que-Wi (Cherokee Cabbage)
Scalloped Tomatoes the Maine Way
Sturbridge-Style Creamed Hashed Onions
Sweet Taters and Apples

Salads and Salad Dressings

Celery Salad
Country Dressing

Guacamole (Avocado Salad)
Hot Sweet-Sour Kraut and Cabbage Salad
Kings' Arms Cabbage and Pepper Slaw
Quilter's Potato Salad
Shakertown Coleslaw
Wilted Dandelions and Wild Onions

Breads

Brethren Cheddar Bread
Brigham Young's Buttermilk Doughnuts
Buha (Adobe Bread)
Buttermilk Corn Bread
Cherokee Bean Bread
Corn Pones and Ash Cakes
Hoosier Biscuit
Hush Puppies
Indian Fry Bread
Jonathan Apple Bread
Middleton Place Gardens Cheese Biscuits
Miss Emma Lou's Sally Lunn Bread
Moravian Sugar Cake
Mulberry Muffins
Old Virginia Spoon Bread
Piñon-Pumpkin Bread
Pueblo Sage Bread
St. Augustine Sponge Bread
Shaker Raised Squash Biscuits

Desserts

Apple Frazes
Apple Pandowdy
Blackberry Dumplings
Blodklub (Blood Pudding)
Churos (Spanish Fritters)
Desperation Pudding

Dulce de Calabaza (Pumpkin Sweet)
1820s Water Ice Lemon
Gooseberry Fool
How to Dry Apples
Kiss Pudding
"Little Fellows"
Marlborough Pudding
Meringue-Topped Tart Lemon Custard Pie
Original Peanut Butter Pie
Pleasant Hill Pecan Pie
Potato Pudding
Rose Water Ice Cream
Salem Suet Pudding
Schnitz Pie (Dried Sour Apple Pie)
Steamed Brown Sugar Chocolate Pudding with Foamy
      Egg Sauce
Steamed Carrot and Potato Pudding
Syllabub
Vinegar Pie

Cakes

Brown Sugar Pound Cake
Caraway Gingerbread
Mary Todd Lincoln's White Almond Cake
New Hampshire Blueberry Cake
Nothing Crumb Cake
Shoo-Fly Cake
Washington Cake

Cookies

Brick-Oven Ginger Cookies
Lumberjack Cookies
Moravian Christmas Cookies
Old-Fashioned Sour Cream White Cookies
Soft Sugar Cookies

Candies and Nuts

Roasted Piñon Nuts
Texas Pralines

Pickles and Relishes

Good Room Zucchini Pickles
Green Tomato Mincemeat
Old-Fashioned Apple Butter
Sweet-Sour Pickles
Williamsburg Lodge Watermelon Rind Pickle

Indexes

General Index

Recipe Index

About the Author

Jean Anderson, a native of North Carolina, holds a B.S. in Food and Nutrition from Cornell University and a M.S. in Journalism from Columbia University. She has been a newspaper women's editor, managing editor of *The Ladies' Home Journal*, and senior editor of *Venture Magazine*. She is the author of THE FAMILY CIRCLE COOKBOOK, THE DOUBLEDAY COOKBOOK, THE FOOD OF PORTUGAL, JEAN ANDERSON COOKS: *Her Kitchen Reference & Recipe Collection*, and JEAN ANDERSON'S NEW PROCESSOR COOKING. She is the co-author of THE NEW DOUBLEDAY COOKBOOK and THE ART OF AMERICAN INDIAN COOKING.

The Best Recipes from America's Favorite Farm Magazine...